The Kidnapping

Tommy Conlon is a sportswriter with the *Sunday Independent*. He has co-authored books with some of Ireland's most successful sportsmen, including Ronnie Whelan, John 'Bull' Hayes, and Keith Earls, whose autobiography *Fight or Flight* won the Sports Book of the Year at the 2021 An Post Irish Book Awards. He is a native of Ballinamore, County Leitrim.

Ronan McGreevy is an *Irish Times* news reporter and videographer. He is the author of *Wherever the Firing Line Extends: Ireland and the Western Front* and editor of *Centenary: Ireland Remembers 1916*. His latest book, *Great Hatred: The Assassination of Field Marshal Sir Henry Wilson MP*, was the *Business Post* history book of the year. In 2018, for his work on remembrance and the First World War, he was named a Chevalier de l'Ordre des Arts et des Lettres by the French government. He is a native of Carrick-on-Shannon, County Leitrim.

The Kidnapping

*A hostage, a desperate manhunt
and a bloody rescue that shocked Ireland*

TOMMY CONLON AND
RONAN McGREEVY

SANDYCOVE

an imprint of

PENGUIN BOOKS

SANDYCOVE

UK | USA | Canada | Ireland | Australia
India | New Zealand | South Africa

Sandycove is part of the Penguin Random House group of companies
whose addresses can be found at global.penguinrandomhouse.com.

First published 2023
001

Copyright © Tommy Conlon and Ronan McGreevy, 2023

The moral right of the copyright holders has been asserted

Set in 13.5/16pt Garamond MT Std
Typeset by Jouve (UK), Milton Keynes
Printed and bound in Great Britain by Clays Ltd, Elcograf S.p.A.

The authorized representative in the EEA is Penguin Random House Ireland,
Morrison Chambers, 32 Nassau Street, Dublin D02 YH68

A CIP catalogue record for this book is available from the British Library

ISBN: 978–1–844–88663–0

www.greenpenguin.co.uk

Penguin Random House is committed to a
sustainable future for our business, our readers
and our planet. This book is made from Forest
Stewardship Council® certified paper.

Contents

CONTENTS

PART ONE
Taken

1. 'I'm Don Tidey; I'm the hostage'

Through the clump of pine trees, Recruit Garda Tom Barrett could see the silhouettes of two men crouched down with guns. They appeared to be wearing military-style clothing. Recruit Garda Francis Smith could see them too. One of the men was cleaning a rifle with a white cloth.

Smith took in the scene for a second before breaking the silence. 'Soldier! Answer my call,' he shouted.[1] There was no reply.

Another garda recruit, Gary Sheehan, was standing a few yards away from Smith. 'Is that you, Frank?' he asked him. 'Yes,' replied Smith, who then checked if there was a soldier with him. There was.

Sheehan then addressed one of the gunmen in the clearing. 'Can you answer, Soldier?' Again, no reply. He turned to his supervisor, Sergeant Liam Wall, who was watching from a raised embankment some yards behind him. 'Sergeant, there's a man here and he won't speak to us,' he told Wall.[2]

It was 2.30 p.m. on Friday, 16 December 1983, and the light was fading fast. The sky was grey with rain clouds. As far as the eye could see, uniformed men were beating at the sodden earth with metal probes and swatting aside thick undergrowth in the search for a man who had been missing for twenty-three days. Occasionally an Irish army Alouette helicopter appeared overhead.

Ten search teams comprising soldiers and gardaí were scouring the forested uplands some five miles north of

Ballinamore, Co. Leitrim, close to the Cavan border. In the distance was Sliabh an Iarainn, the Iron Mountain, the highest point in south Leitrim. Its iron deposits were long gone, and so were most of the people. Further north were the dark hills of the Cuilcagh Mountains.

This was rough, poor land, deemed fit for little other than sheep and trees. Those who stayed were engaged in an attritional battle against the thin topsoil and the heavy rains which turned the land to a gluey daub every spring.[3] Yet this part of Leitrim could grow Sitka spruce like few places in Europe. But in the long hiatus between planting and harvesting, the people left and the trees grew unhampered.

The fields between the patchwork of forests and the unkempt woods were small, wet and full of rushes. Barely passable lanes linked the planted forests, which were typically between twenty and thirty acres in size. The trees were grown for the commercial timber industry and intended to yield a supplementary income for hard-pressed local farmers.

The search teams combed the area, one for every mile radius from the centre of Ballinamore, which had become the headquarters for what was the largest operation of its kind in the history of the state. What had started out as a wide-sweeping search had now funnelled down to a patch of terrain that was microscopic on maps, and so remote it would rarely have been visited even by locals. To get there, the security forces had to take the minor road out of Ballinamore, then turn onto a side road barely wide enough for cars to pass each other, and veer off that side road onto hillside passes no wider than country lanes.

Finally, there was no road at all, just forests and fields and rural silence. A few farmhouse dwellings were nestled here and there in the landscape, peopled by families well used to the elements and to hardship.

The search was unofficially named Operation Santa Claus, a festive title that belied its seriousness. A man's life was at stake, and so too was the reputation of the Irish state when it came to dealing with its greatest national security threat – the Provisional IRA. The media were diligently tracking every twist and turn of a drama that had already been running for over three weeks.

The search parties were each allocated the name 'Rudolph', and a number from 1 to 10. The man they had come to rescue was Don Tidey, a British-born supermarket executive who had been kidnapped from his car while bringing his daughter to school in south Co. Dublin on the morning of 24 November. The businessman was being held hostage in a small hillside wood about two and a half acres in size that comprised young pines some fifteen feet high with multiple protruding branches, making for a densely camouflaged location. It was known locally as Drumcroman Wood but would quickly become familiar nationwide as Derrada Wood after the local post office address. Access was hindered by high tangles of briars. Even in broad daylight it was a dark and gloomy place. On a dank December afternoon, the winter light was weaker still. The searchers were moving around in semi-darkness. They could not use torches in case they alerted the kidnappers, if indeed the kidnappers were in there.

Rudolph 5 had twenty-four men in its group that day. They were operating at a considerable distance from the other search parties. Occasionally its members drifted apart from each other, losing touch with the people left and right, becoming disorientated by the forest darkness or separated

1. Soldiers and gardaí search the remote rushy fields near Ballinamore in south Leitrim.

2. Security forces and media among the throngs in Ballinamore, the headquarters for what was the largest operation of its kind in the history of the state. The search was unofficially named Operation Santa Claus.

3. An army convoy rolling through Ballinamore to join in the search.

4. What had started as a wide-sweeping search became concentrated on a small patch of terrain so remote it would rarely have been visited, even by locals. To get there, the security forces had to take the minor road out of Ballinamore.

by the uneven ground and protruding branches.[4] They continued their arduous progress, not knowing they were about to walk straight into the gang's lair.

It was a lair that had been prepared well in advance of the abduction. The chosen hide was a hollow in the ground at the base of some trees.[5] Its surface was covered by black polythene, lined with straw, while overhead it was sheltered by sheets of black plastic tethered to tree trunks and blanketed in leaves and twigs.[6] This was where the IRA gang and their captive ate, slept and washed. They toileted nearby.

After several days of relative tranquillity in their bolthole, a crisis was looming. The kidnappers could also hear the search parties closing in. They would have to make a decision: fight or flight? They'd been hearing the gardaí and soldiers roaming through the hinterland for a number of days; the engines of cars and army trucks, the rotors of the helicopter hovering in the sky. The gang knew they were being surrounded; their refuge was mutating into a trap. And now the voices were getting closer. It was time to leave.

Their hostage was forced at gunpoint to his feet. The kidnappers removed his hood and replaced it with a balaclava. They took his shackles off and told him to follow them once they gave the order.[7]

Meanwhile, the Rudolph 5 search party was closing in a V shape on Derrada Wood. It consisted of a garda inspector, a sergeant, four detectives, two uniformed gardaí, ten recruit gardaí and six soldiers. The soldiers had standard-issue FN rifles, and five of the policemen were armed with Uzi machine guns; the rest were unarmed. The men at either end of the formation had radios to call back to the centre of the operation – Echo Base in Ballinamore.

The search team entered the wood, eyes adjusting to the darkness as they pushed through the branches, droplets of water falling on them from the heights of the trees. Then Recruit Garda Barrett stopped in his tracks, frozen by the tableau he saw ahead: a black plastic covering, stretched and knotted between tree trunks; camping equipment, food litter and other detritus. There was human activity here. He drew back immediately to inform the others.[8]

The realization brought a chilling frisson to the members of Rudolph 5: this was the place. The epicentre of the manhunt was in front of them; the needle in the haystack had been found. Sergeant Wall, who was in charge of the Rudolph 5 garda recruits, was now lying flat on a raised bank. He turned his body to address the recruit gardaí waiting to advance. 'Be careful,' he murmured, 'there are men with guns in there.'[9]

Some members of Rudolph 5 then spotted the two armed men in flak jackets and balaclavas. But were they friend or foe? Army Rangers personnel involved in the search were also wearing military fatigues and had blackened faces. One gunman was holding a rifle pointed upwards, the other was kneeling with his weapon pointing down.

The air was suddenly dense with tension and fear. Then Smith and Sheehan broke the silence, before the latter turned to Wall: 'Sergeant, there's a man here and he won't speak to us.'[10] Instantaneously, a shattering burst of semi-automatic machine-gun fire rang out. The situation had transformed in an instant.

Recruit Garda Gary Sheehan fell immediately. Another burst of fire felled a soldier, Private Patrick Kelly, just as he was getting into a crouched position to fire back. Neither man had a chance; both had been raked with bullets.

Many years later Garda Sergeant Joe O'Connor, a trainee on the day, would recount the fateful moment in court. 'I heard a groan or grunt where Garda Sheehan had been,' he said, recalling that the young recruit's feet went from under him as blood poured from multiple bullet wounds; his cranium was shattered and his brain exposed. The twenty-three-year-old, who had begun garda training only three months earlier, died instantly. His garda cap, fastened by its chinstrap, remained on his head.

Patrick Kelly, thirty-six and a father of four, was shot with a line of bullets from ankle to head and fell backwards. Kelly did not die instantly; he slowly bled to death. His comrades heard him plead: 'Please don't leave me, I'm not going to make it.'[11] Private Paddy Shine, who was just a yard or two away, would later tell an inquest he saw his comrade fall back against the trees with blood on his neck. He dived for cover as he heard Kelly calling, 'Paddy'.[12]

The kidnappers followed up their gun attack by detonating a stun grenade, designed to cause confusion and terror. It made such a noise that gardaí and soldiers thought a bomb had exploded. Taking advantage of the reaction, the gang moved in on three soldiers at gunpoint and ordered them to disarm. One of them was Shine. 'I thought [these] people were desperate enough to get out that they would have shot me as well,' he would recall.[13]

One gunman put his rifle to the back of Shine's head and ordered him to instruct his fellow soldiers not to shoot. Shine put his hands in the air and shouted, 'Don't shoot, don't shoot.' He was pushed forward and told to run.

The gang now took the soldiers' weapons. Members of the Irish army, officially known in the Irish language as Óglaigh na hÉireann, were now being held at gunpoint by

men who believed themselves to be the true and rightful
Óglaigh na hÉireann.

Next the gang seized Denis Breen, a Ballinamore-based
garda, and a number of garda recruits and made them walk
in front of them, along with the captured soldiers, as human
shields.

One of the recruits was Francis Morgan, who had dropped
to the ground in the mayhem. He saw eight or nine people
coming out of the trees, three of them wearing combat gear
and carrying rifles and sub-machine guns. A garda and two
soldiers were lying beside him. A gunman ordered them to
stand up. 'Dead heroes no good,' he warned them.[14]

Paul Gillen was nineteen, a garda recruit from Dublin's
inner city. He could feel the muzzle of an assault rifle in the
small of his back. 'Don't be a dead hero. We shot one of you,
we'll shoot again,' a gunman told him in a northern accent.[15]

Next the gardaí and soldiers were ordered to start running
across a field with their hands held high. Behind the captive
gardaí and soldiers the kidnappers kept their weapons
cocked. As they came to a fence, one pointed a gun in Shine's
face and ordered him to provide help crossing it. Shine pulled
him over the fence. At one stage Morgan became aware of
an armed detective to his right and one of the gunmen firing
a volley of shots in the detective's direction.

Meanwhile, in the kidnappers' panic to get away, they'd abandoned the man who was at the centre of the entire drama
and provided him with an opportunity. 'There was a burst of
gunfire,' Don Tidey would recall later. 'Then more gunfire
and, frankly, from that moment on, it became a battleground.
Once firing had broken out, everybody made their own
arrangements.'

'My arrangement under fire was to hit the ground, which I did. I rolled down an incline into bracken and took in my circumstances. There was gunfire. There was to the best of my recollection an explosion, which I judged was a grenade. When I looked up I was looking into the muzzle of a weapon just a short distance from my forehead. The situation froze. I looked along the length of the barrel and saw a soldier.'[16]

This was Private Patrick McLaughlin, and behind him was at least one garda, Francis Smith. All of them were wary about the person confronting them. Smith recalled that this unkempt man 'looked like one of the criminals that started the gunfire in the wood'. Tidey, after twenty-three days of wondering about his fate at the hands of his kidnappers, was equally unsure now about his fate at the hands of his rescuers.

'I am the hostage!' he cried out, gesturing to his chest. The sudden hand movement seemed to agitate the soldier, who perhaps feared this fellow might be reaching for a weapon. But Private McLaughlin held his discipline and assured himself the man was not, in fact, armed. 'By the grace of God, he didn't pull the trigger,' Tidey said.[17]

Smith crawled up to them. 'Who are you?' he demanded. 'I'm Don Tidey,' came the reply. 'I'm the hostage. There are vicious men up there. They have grenades. Follow me.'[18] Still not sure about this stranger, the security forces weren't inclined to do so.

'No, we'll go our way,' Smith responded. He and another recruit garda, Joseph O'Connor, along with McLaughlin and Tidey, crawled across a path and hurried out of the wood. Not knowing who the man was, they forced Tidey to remove his wellingtons to ensure he did not run away.

Despite Tidey's protestations, his English accent and the absence of any weapon, his handlers still did not fully believe he was the man they'd been looking for. Tidey had scratches on his face from being dragged through brambles, plus a thick beard, adding to the confusion.

The group followed the line of a drain. 'I was led for two or three hundred yards across the field,' Tidey remembered. His trousers were nearly dragged off him by the weight of the muck and water.

Watching from the adjacent road, Detective Sergeant Walter 'Nacie' Rice could see garda recruits running from the wood. One lost his hat in the confusion, a disciplinary offence, and returned to retrieve it. 'For f***'s sake, leave that f***ing hat behind you!' Rice exclaimed.[19] Next thing he saw the party that included Tidey clambering up to a ditch that bordered the road.

Tidey was handed over to him and other detectives from An Garda Síochána's Security Task Force, including Detective Inspector William 'Bill' Somers, who helped him over a gate and onto the road. But there was no great welcome for this wild-looking creature here either. Somers also needed clarity. He 'held a gun to my head to ascertain who I was', Tidey later recalled.[20]

In the Special Criminal Court almost twenty-five years later, Somers gave his account of the incident: 'The first thing I saw was a person in green combat gear and I thought it was one of the terrorists making a break.'[21] Then, on second glance, he thought it might be Tidey, but he wasn't taking any chances. Somers pointed his gun at the man, and once again Tidey declared his name and his innocence. Finally, his rescuers were satisfied they had the hostage.

Once they reached the edge of Derrada Wood, the kidnappers split up. Two made their way to a nearby farmhouse, owned by local man Charlie McTague. A blue Opel Kadett

5. Derrada Wood today. It is now a lot smaller than it was in 1983. This view shows the side from which Don Tidey made his escape and the road where Detective Garda Donal Kelleher was shot in the legs.

6. Derrada Post Office, which gives its name to the wood where Don Tidey was kidnapped. It has been closed since 1985.

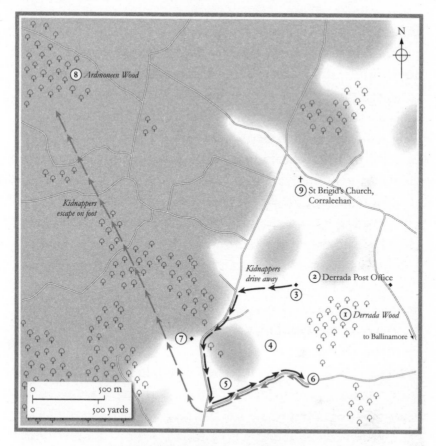

Derrada area – key locations

1. *Derrada Wood:* Location of the hide where Don Tidey is held for twenty-three days.
2. *Derrada Post Office:* Gardaí and soldiers whom the kidnappers take hostage and walk across fields emerge to freedom at Derrada Post Office.
3. *Charlie McTague's house:* The kidnap gang picks up a car at this house.
4. After the shoot-out between kidnappers and security forces, Don Tidey makes his escape here.
5. One of the kidnap gang, in the car they have picked up at the McTague house, leans through the car window and shoots towards the gardaí with a machine gun. Garda Donal Kelleher, escorting Don Tidey to safety, is wounded in both legs.
6. Still in the car they have picked up at the McTague house, the kidnappers run into a garda roadblock and a shoot-out ensues. The kidnappers abandon the car.
7. *John Curnan's house:* Curnan owns Derrada Wood, described by one local woman as 'an IRA hill'. He is later convicted for his role in assisting the Tidey kidnappers.
8. *Ardmoneen Wood:* After the shoot-out at the garda roadblock the kidnappers use a fire-and-manoeuvre drill to escape across the fields – the last one covering the retreat of the others with bursts of gunfire. They head north-west in the direction of Ardmoneen Wood, a huge plantation on the Cavan–Leitrim border.
9. *St Brigid's Church, Corraleehan:* In his sermon at Sunday Mass two days after Don Tidey's rescue, Fr Con Dolan criticizes parishioners who supported the gang while they were holding Tidey hostage and then helped them escape. Weeks later, *Today Tonight* does a vox pop outside the church and finds local people unwilling to condemn the actions of the IRA.

with the keys in the ignition was there in the yard. The others continued to shepherd their hostages across a number of fields until finally abandoning them with dire warnings to keep walking and not to turn around. They then hightailed it back to the farmhouse where they joined the rest of the gang. As their hostages emerged on to the road beside Derrada Post Office the kidnappers were attempting to make their escape in the Kadett.

Meanwhile, the group that had just taken custody of Tidey were making their way along the road. Suddenly the Kadett came roaring round the bend towards them. Tidey assumed it was an unmarked garda car. Somers tried to flag it down. One of the kidnappers leaned out through a window and fired a burst from his machine gun. Gunfire also came from the boot of the car. Tidey dived to the ground, injuring the tip of his elbow.

Detective Garda Donal Kelleher was hit in both legs and felt a burning pain in his left thigh. 'I thought we were all dead, and expected to be hit again,' he remembered.[22] The gunfire almost hit Tidey, who ended up lying in a low ditch beside him.

Rice, who had a revolver, fired some shots at the car but it was already speeding out of range. He picked up an Uzi machine gun and ran after them. Somers later recalled dragging Tidey through a gap in the ditch and then into a deep drain out of sight of the car.

The Kadett powered on. At the next crossroads a roadblock had been set up by uniformed gardaí and detectives. Just a matter of seconds earlier they had heard the unmistakable rat-a-tat-tat of gunfire as the kidnappers opened up on Somers and his party. Detective Garda Eugene O'Sullivan, then twenty-nine, was one of the personnel at the crossroads roadblock. 'There's a burst of gunfire,' he recalled later, 'and [then] there's a shout on the radio: "Do not shoot at the blue car, a guard has been taken hostage."'[23] But the gardaí who'd been taken hostage were not in the Kadett, of course; they were making their way back to the action after their forced march at gunpoint.

O'Sullivan picks up the story. 'So next thing a blue car comes around the corner at high speed, screeches to a halt. We hesitate.' They have parked an unmarked garda car, a Ford Granada, to act as a blocker. 'The Granada is parked in the middle of the crossroads. There's some of us to the right of the Granada, some of us to the left. I'm on the driver's side of it because I was driving. We hesitate because of the call "Don't shoot". A guy gets out in full paramilitary dress, as in green khaki combat-type gear, wearing a balaclava, with what looks like an Armalite, and fires a burst in our direction. I can still feel the whizz of the bullets going by my head. We were that close to oblivion.

'We hit the ground, return fire. He has taken cover behind the Kadett very quickly. They have abandoned the car and taken to the field, shooting as they go. They retreat in military fashion: fire, retreat, another guy fires, they retreat. We fire. And then they disappear from sight into the fields.

'I'm lying across a ditch at that stage. The man next to me was [Detective] Noel McMahon and he was tremendous under fire. Absolutely fearless. He had an Uzi sub-machine gun; I had my Smith & Wesson revolver. I fired two shots initially and then four. And then I remember reloading, but by the time I reloaded the shooting had stopped and they have just disappeared into the undergrowth.'

The kidnappers used a fire-and-manoeuvre drill to escape across the fields – the last one covering the retreat of the others with bursts of gunfire. They headed north-west, in the direction of Ardmoneen Wood, a huge plantation on the Cavan–Leitrim border.

Shortly afterwards their radios are crackling again with another message: Detective Garda Kelleher has been wounded in the previous incident. O'Sullivan and his colleagues are summoned to that scene. It is there they finally set eyes on Don Tidey. Somers and Rice want to get the former hostage out of there pronto. 'So, they put him into my car and they say, "Go go go! Get him out of here,"' O'Sullivan remembers.

Somers, a garda and another detective, Tom Conroy, pile into the car too. O'Sullivan recalls putting his foot down for the first mile or so. 'And I remember Inspector Somers saying to me, "Slow down, slow down, take it easy now, we're clear." Then he said, "This is Mr Tidey, this is Don Tidey." And he said there had been casualties up in the woods, but at that time we didn't know who or what.'[24]

Donal Kelleher was taken to Ballinamore garda station and from there to Cavan hospital, where medics found a bullet lodged in his right thigh that had passed through his left thigh. Bill Somers would later find five separate bullet tears in his clothing. His wristwatch had been broken.

The rescue of Tidey did not immediately ease the tensions. In fact, a chaotic, panic-stricken situation was about to get more complicated still. A second blue car entered the equation on the other side of the hill.

Derrada Wood was owned by a local farming family, the Curnans. A neighbour of theirs, Hugh Prior, had just driven away from their house in a blue Ford Cortina. He was stopped at a checkpoint outside Derrada Post Office and questioned by two detectives. They believed they had sufficient reason to arrest him. But not having a car at their disposal, they commandeered Prior's.

About a minute later they approached an intersection that had another checkpoint, this one manned by army and garda personnel. Word had just gone out on the radios about a blue car being driven by terrorists who were shooting on sight. That was the Opel Kadett, but its make and model hadn't been conveyed over the radio. A few jumpy members of the security forces thought Prior's Cortina was the car in question and opened fire, smashing its windscreen and narrowly missing the two detectives sitting in the back. Prior was grazed in the neck by a bullet, leaving him with burn marks.[25]

Another search party was about a mile away. 'We were on the side of a hill,' recalls Joe Feely, then a garda based in Ballinamore.[26] 'And coming out on the radio was the message that the kidnappers were up a hill and there were shots being fired in a wood at the top. Now, we happened to be actually going up a hill, and there was a wood at the top of our hill too, so everyone got very nervous and we were kind of down to a crawl.

'No one at the scene was able to give the exact location where this was taking place because [Garda] Denis Breen was the local man [in the search party at Derrada] and he'd been taken hostage and they took his radio off him. So there was no one able to pinpoint it at that particular time. "It's a wooded area on a hill" – that was basically the description coming out over the radio.'

Eventually they got word that the shooting had happened in Derrada Wood. 'So we came back towards the scene,' said Feely. 'I remember seeing young recruits lying up against the ditch with tunics on them but no shirts. And I remember [Inspector] Seamus O'Hanlon talking to an army officer, saying: "There's bodies up there, I know there's bodies up there, we have to go up and search." And I remember seeing himself and the army officer go back up to the woods and the army officer had a handgun and he discharges it – nerves or whatever – and everyone hits the deck.'

Back in the wood, Inspector Seamus O'Hanlon had seen men with hands in the air and assumed the kidnappers had been captured. As he looked again, he noticed the man with his hands in the air was in fact a garda. He heard a voice shout: 'Garda dead over here.'[27] As the action moved towards the outside of the wood, a sudden quiet descended on where the shooting had taken place.

O'Hanlon hurried over and recognized the slain young man immediately. Gary Sheehan was a neighbour's child; O'Hanlon had served with Detective Garda Jim Sheehan, Gary's father, in Carrickmacross. O'Hanlon would later recall in court: 'He had a large wound in his head and he was dead. I said an Act of Contrition in his ear.' He asked another garda to say an Act of Contrition in the ear of Private Kelly.[28]

The bodies needed due care and consideration. Gardaí radioed back to Echo Base requesting a doctor and a priest. Local GP Dr Sean Bourke was summoned from Ballinamore and taken to the scene. He saw Private Kelly in a sitting position up against a tree, and with the aid of a torch examined him before certifying he was dead. Close by, he saw the body of Garda Sheehan lying face down; his cap was tilted sideways on his head. One side of his face was badly lacerated.[29]

Classes were just finishing up at St Felim's College, the town's secondary school, when the principal, Fr Thomas Keogan, was approached by uniformed personnel. 'The guards asked me to go out to give the last rites to the two men that were killed. They brought me out in the squad car, as far as I can remember. They brought me into the road leading into Derrada Wood and lent me a pair of wellingtons for going up through the fields.'

The area was now flooded with security forces, all emotionally charged. 'I went up through the fields and there went off a shot and we were told to lie on the ground – "Lie down!" They thought the gunmen were still there. We were lying on the ground for twenty minutes, half an hour, on a freezing winter's evening. What happened, I think, was that the gardaí and army were high with excitement, so it was one of them let off the shot. Anyway, we went up through the field and in through the undergrowth and the two men were there. They were fairly close to each other.'[30]

Fr Keogan administered the last rites. 'You anoint them with the oil of the sick or the dying. You say a prayer that they will be received into the Lord's home, and you say the Act of Contrition, where you're sorry for all the sins of your life. And then you pray for them.'

His duties performed, Fr Keogan was escorted out of the woods and back to the roadside. After Christmas, he visited the grieving families and told them he had administered the last rites to Gary and Patrick. 'I think they took a small bit of consolation from knowing that,' he remembers.

Night-time came and the countryside was lit up with fires from tar barrels burning at crossroads to keep gardaí and soldiers warm. Ballinamore resembled a war zone with garda cars and armoured personnel carriers on the streets, and soldiers at every corner. Senior garda officers briefed the media on events so far, and they reassured everyone they were closing in on the fugitives. In fact, they were doing nothing of the sort.

2. Getting Away with Murder

Profound relief that Tidey had been found unharmed was mixed with profound sorrow that his liberation had led to the deaths of two servants of the state. The bodies of Sheehan and Kelly lay overnight where they had fallen, as their comrades feared the hideout might have been booby-trapped.

Detective Inspector Edwin Hancock, from the garda technical bureau, arrived at Derrada Wood the following morning.[1] He found the bodies of the two men lying approximately twelve feet from each other. Private Kelly's flak jacket was open and his beret was on the ground beside him. Recruit Garda Sheehan was wearing a raincoat.

Forensics officers began their work on the scene. The camp had been well stocked. The kidnappers left behind a gas stove, saucepans, a pressure cooker, twelve toilet rolls, sugar, tea, milk, marmalade, soup packets, curry powder, apples, onions, tomatoes, a large amount of Calvita cheese, five brown sleeping bags and paramilitary uniforms. All of it would be subjected to forensic analysis.

Some distance away the forensics team recovered a transistor radio which was tuned to Echo Base, the garda communications hub in Ballinamore. The gang had been eavesdropping on the official search channel.[2]

With Tidey now safe, the garda operation became a manhunt. The mood among the search parties was grim and determined. There was now no doubt about the ruthlessness of the gang they were facing and all involved were resolved to meet fire with fire. Soldiers were told to use 'maximum aggression'. One told the *Irish Times*: 'Those guys don't want to be taken alive and we are not interested in taking them alive.'[3]

With nerves shredded among the security forces, another accidental shooting in the early hours of the morning of 17 December also came perilously close to a fatality. John Gerard Wrynne, a twenty-seven-year-old local man, was driving just outside the security cordon when he came upon a checkpoint in Gorvagh. He stopped the car and it was searched. Wrynne knew one of the local gardaí and after a brief conversation thought he was being waved on. As he accelerated away, a soldier assumed he was trying to escape and fired four shots at his car. One hit Wrynne in the head; he crashed his car into a ditch. His wife Mary, in the passenger seat, escaped uninjured. The couple had been married only the previous September. Wrynne underwent emergency surgery in a Dublin hospital and eventually recovered.

The bodies were taken out of the woods around noon on Saturday after the state pathologist, Professor John Harbison, had conducted a post-mortem.

Corporal P. J. Higgins and Private Patrick Kelly had been great pals as well as comrades-in-arms for many years. By coincidence, Higgins had, on that Saturday morning, been detailed to take a section of eight soldiers and provide security around the forensics personnel and others who were working at the hideout. 'I only saw it from a distance. It wasn't a dugout. Plastic [was] strung from one tree to another. It wasn't a big hole in the ground, it was a plastic-covered shelter. There was this small enclave just for them to settle into but there was no big hole five or six feet down.'[4]

7. The bodies of Private Patrick Kelly and Garda Gary Sheehan being removed from Derrada Wood.

8. Local man John Gerard Wrynne's crashed car at Gorvagh. The morning after Tidey's rescue Wrynne, an innocent man, was shot by a soldier in the mistaken belief that he was trying to speed away from a security checkpoint.

Around midday, as he remembers it, the ambulances arrived for the bodies. He was less than fifty yards away. 'The saddest thing I ever saw, to see Paddy Kelly's body being taken from Derrada Wood under a plastic bag, a polythene bag,' he says. 'I saw Corporal John Ruane bringing out Paddy Kelly's body. There was about six men carrying the stretcher and John Ruane was at the front on the left-hand side. And when he came out of the woods he turned left and headed towards the ambulance.

'Paddy Kelly, I think his knee was bent, I'm only judging by the bag. It wasn't an actual body bag, it was like a lump of polythene, white polythene. And they come out of the woods and they turn to the left and the ambulance is facing out and they put him into it. The two bodies came out together. It's enshrined in my memory. Never forget it as long as I live.'

The previous evening there had been a few pit stops along the way before Don Tidey was returned to the bosom of his family. With Eugene O'Sullivan driving the car out of Derrada, Inspector Somers decided their VIP should be brought straight to Ballyconnell garda station, some twelve miles away in Co. Cavan. They would drive into Ballinamore and keep going.

'Ballyconnell was the local garda headquarters,' O'Sullivan explains. 'Now, the world's press were in Ballinamore, on the street, and I drove up the street nice and gently, Don Tidey in the back. A camera crew walked across in front of me. I stopped to let them go by and they walked by and we just went nice and easy through the town and on [for] Ballyconnell without anybody noticing that Don Tidey was in the back of the car.'[5]

From Ballyconnell a call was made to garda headquarters

in Dublin that Tidey had been rescued. The message was conveyed through garda channels to the minister for justice, who made a statement in the Dáil saying the hostage had been freed but that there had been casualties.

Some time later Tidey was escorted away, to be taken to Cavan garda station. But by then the press posse had descended on Ballyconnell station. As O'Sullivan, Tom Conroy and Bill Somers ushered their ward to the waiting car, photographer Peter Thursfield captured the image that would make the front page of the *Irish Times* the next day. It became the iconic photo of the saga. Tidey was examined by a doctor at Cavan station. Later that evening O'Sullivan and his colleagues drove the businessman back to his home in Woodtown, where he was reunited with his children.

Back in Ballinamore, the search for the kidnappers continued. The terrain that needed to be covered was expanding with every minute that they remained at large. From funnelling down to Derrada Wood on Friday morning, the gardaí and army were now looking at an expanse of mountain and bog and field and forest all around them. The fugitives could have scattered in any direction; there were so many places for them to hide.

The 60,000-acre Ardmoneen Wood was one possibility. Army Rangers personnel with night-sight rifles were dropped in, but the forest was big enough for the kidnappers to go undetected, if they were there at all. Other Rangers waited on top of a concrete tower to cut off the retreat if the gang was spotted.[6]

Soon the weather turned against the searchers. Fog and mist lingered in the following days; visibility was down to thirty yards in places and the army helicopter could not be

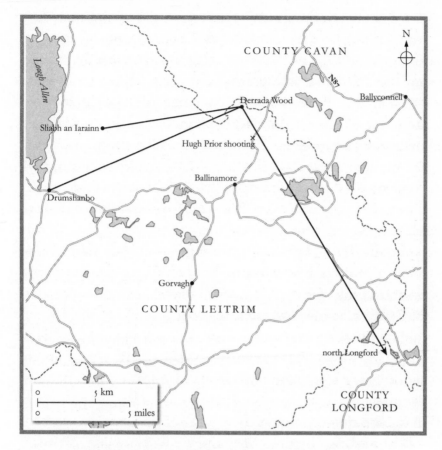

Aftermath of Don Tidey's rescue – key locations

Derrada Wood: Don Tidey is rescued here on 16 December.

Ballinamore: Following his rescue, gardaí discreetly take Tidey through Ballinamore, away from the awaiting press.

Ballyconnell: Tidey is driven to the local garda headquarters in Ballyconnell, Co. Cavan, twelve miles from Ballinamore.

Drumshanbo: Following their stand-off with security forces at Derrada Wood two of the kidnappers escape west in the direction of Drumshanbo.

Sliabh an Iarainn: The remaining kidnappers escape towards Sliabh an Iarainn, which links Drumshanbo to Ballinamore via a winding network of narrow roads.

Hugh Prior shooting: Shortly after the Derrada shoot-out security forces open fire on a car driven by local man, Hugh Prior. They believe it contains the kidnappers and are unaware it has been commandeered by two gardaí. The three occupants narrowly escape serious injury.

Gorvagh: The morning after the Derrada shoot-out a local man, John Gerard Wrynne, is shot by a soldier while going through a checkpoint.

North Longford: Five days after Tidey's release two kidnappers make their way to north Longford where local republicans help them to reach a safe house.

flown. Publicly, the gardaí were telling the media that they were confident their quarry was within a 'ring of steel', a phrase concocted by the press at the time and one that Chief Superintendent J. J. McNally was also happy to deploy. McNally was the leader and public face of the search operation. He did not demur when a figure of 2,000 gardaí and soldiers was quoted by the press. In reality, at any one time, the number on the ground was a lot smaller. A grim, sardonic mood descended on the searchers, many wondering if they would get home for Christmas. One Task Force detective mentioned with gallows humour 'Lovely Leitrim', the sentimental song by the country and western star Larry Cunningham that had been a smash hit in the 1960s. The lyrics portrayed the county as a sort of bucolic paradise. But this particular searcher, and many more of his fellow toilers, were finding the place far from 'lovely' during those arduous days and nights. 'When all this is over,' he drawled, 'I'm going to shoot Larry Cunningham. Lovely Leitrim my eye. This is definitely the last place on earth – God what I'd give right now for a chance to put my feet up before a fire.'

The security cordon, said the RTÉ journalist Brendan O'Brien, was more like a 'rubber band' than a ring of steel, and rubber bands are inclined to snap.[7] Privately, gardaí feared their manhunt was already in vain. Support for the Provisional IRA locally was sporadic and mainly confined to patches of the rural hinterland. But it was sufficient to enable the kidnappers to hide out from the authorities if they needed food and shelter or perhaps a guide through the local terrain.

The last putative sighting of the gang was three days after the release of Don Tidey. A detective spotted two men entering one of the many woods after nightfall. An army infantry company was summoned, this one from Galway, bringing to six the number of companies operating in the area. Search parties had to wait until the following morning before beginning. By then the two gang members, if they were in the wood, had disappeared.

There were certainly four kidnappers, possibly five. Early in the escape they had split up and headed off in different directions. One pair headed west in the direction of Drumshanbo towards Sliabh an Iarainn, which links Drumshanbo to Ballinamore via a winding network of narrow roads through the mountain parish of Aughnasheelin.[8] Another individual may have availed himself of his local knowledge by making his own escape towards Sliabh an Iarainn.

Gardaí let it be known they were looking for four IRA members in connection with the kidnapping. Three of the suspects – Brendan 'Bik' McFarlane, Gerard McDonnell and Tony McAllister – had escaped during the mass breakout from the Maze prison in Belfast the previous September.[9] A fourth man, Oliver McKiernan, had escaped from Portlaoise prison in 1974 and had been living under an assumed name in a mobile home near Aughnasheelin for a number of years.

Subsequently, Seamus McElwaine, a notorious multiple murderer from Monaghan who was shot dead by the SAS in 1986, was named as a fifth suspect in the abduction and killings at Derrada Wood.

According to one account of the manhunt, two of the kidnappers called to the house of a republican sympathizer looking for John Joe McGirl. A native of Aughnasheelin, McGirl was by far the most prominent and senior Sinn Féin/ IRA activist in the region. A vice-president of Sinn Féin, he was a long-time member of Leitrim County Council and ran a pub and undertakers on Main Street, Ballinamore.

Active in the IRA border campaign of the late 1950s, McGirl was elected to the Dáil in 1957 while serving time in prison for membership of the organization. After the Maze breakout, McGirl busied himself finding safe houses for escapees who fled across the border into the Republic. At one stage gardaí suspected that twelve of the fugitives were living locally. This was a concentration of experienced manpower that the IRA could call on for operations in the South. The kidnapping of Don Tidey was one such operation.

It was surveillance of McGirl's movements by the security forces that ultimately brought the national search for Tidey to the Cavan–Leitrim border, and thence to Derrada Wood. McGirl had been tracked in his car for a number of days driving to and from this remote location; it was believed he was bringing supplies of food and other materials to the kidnappers.[10]

He wasn't available to meet the two IRA kidnappers when they called to the safe house that Friday night/Saturday morning. McGirl had been arrested on Friday morning along with three other known republicans who lived locally. A phone call he'd made to a prominent Sinn Féin member in Northern Ireland, possibly on the night of the fifteenth, had been recorded by intelligence officers in the RUC because the callee's phone had been tapped; a transcript of the conversation was swiftly passed on to their police counterparts in the South.[11] It was this development that led to his arrest on the morning of the murders at Derrada. The four republicans were held for forty-eight hours.

Instead, at the safe house, the runaways were introduced to Francis McGirl, a nephew of John Joe. Three years previously, Francis McGirl had been acquitted on a legal technicality of the 1979 bombing at Mullaghmore, Sligo, that killed Lord Louis Mountbatten, two boys and an eighty-three-year-old woman. Francis McGirl had grown up in Aughnasheelin and knew the terrain well. He took the two men on foot to a wood between Aghacashel and Drumshanbo. They spent the night of 16 December hiding out in the woods. In the early hours of the following morning, two men from Drumshanbo teamed up with the fugitives and guided them into Arigna, a neighbouring mountain where coal had been mined for decades. They were now well beyond the 'ring of steel'. From there they were taken by car to Sligo and on to Mayo.[12]

The second opportunity to catch the kidnappers came just three days later. On Tuesday night, 20 December, Francis McGirl and his two accomplices were stopped at a checkpoint in Ballycroy, Co. Mayo. Sergeant Des O'Rourke and gardaí Anthony Dempsey and Martin Lavelle were looking for Christmas bootleggers of poitín.

O'Rourke turned his flashlight into the back seat and noticed a firearm on the lap of one of these strangers. Immediately a man got out of the car and pointed a machine gun at him.[13] The three gardaí were tied up with their own belts and made to lie face down on the road. Sergeant O'Rourke's car was commandeered.

A local republican, Mary McGing, then a member of Sinn Féin's ard comhairle and the party's candidate for Connacht-Ulster in the following year's European elections, had arranged for the three to stay in a house in Claremorris. She had asked a schoolteacher, Colman O'Reilly, who was an officer in the local Fianna Fáil cumann and not a supporter of the Provisional IRA, if he could loan her the keys of his new and unoccupied bungalow for a purported meeting of

Sinn Féin members. O'Reilly agreed, unaware of the real purpose of the meeting. At the bungalow, McGing provided sleeping bags and food for the three men.

The Ballycroy incident sparked an immediate garda reaction. Known republican activists were arrested and questioned, and gardaí gleaned enough information to hone in on the house in Claremorris. The local chief superintendent, Patrick O'Connor, informed garda headquarters that they intended to surround the house and capture those inside. Having botched the Ballinamore operation, and with a nation stunned by the two murders, there was a great deal at stake with this new attempt.

Members of the Security Task Force, established by garda management in the wake of the Tiede Herrema kidnapping in 1975, set off from Claremorris garda station. There were supposed to be twelve gardaí in total in three cars but some didn't turn up, apparently deciding it would be better to wait until morning to raid the house. Nevertheless the rest of the garda party continued with the plan.

Sergeant Patrick Tuohy knocked on the door and called for those inside to drop their weapons and come out. What followed was an embarrassing farce. The third car, which had left Claremorris garda station and was supposed to cover the front of the house, did not arrive on time. An armed detective at the back accidentally discharged his weapon and the gardaí at the front rushed to join him, believing the kidnappers were trying to escape that way.[14]

As they did so, three men emerged through the front door and ran up the long driveway into the darkness. An armed detective waiting at the side of the property fired a shot over their heads but didn't attempt to shoot them, despite explicit instructions to do so if necessary. The three men ran across a field into the darkness and were not seen again.

The ineptitude of the police raid was compounded by the absence of a cordon near the house. It took between four and five hours for the area to be sealed off, by which time the kidnappers and their helper had long gone.

Back in Leitrim, the other kidnappers were making their own arrangements. Two of them were spirited into a safe house within the cordon around Ballinamore. They were subsequently moved under the cover of darkness to other safe houses.

After five days, contact was made with republicans in north Longford. The two kidnappers were brought by back roads and had narrow escapes en route. At Greagh Cross, on the Ballinamore to Cloone road, gardaí were about to set up a checkpoint, but the men got through just in time. A similar incident happened at Gulladoo on the Leitrim–Longford border. They also got caught up in the traffic one morning going to Carrigallen mart, but it provided cover for them. After several close shaves, they finally reached a safe house outside the danger zone and remained there for a couple of months.

The killers of Private Kelly and Recruit Garda Sheehan had gotten away with murder. They continue to get away with murder to this day.

3. Enemies of the State

The fatal confrontation at Derrada Wood involved two Irish 'armies', both styling themselves Óglaigh na hÉireann, and both laying claim to be the legitimate defence forces of Ireland. It was not the first time they had come into conflict.

The two polities on the island which emerged out of the Government of Ireland Act 1920 (Northern Ireland) and the Anglo-Irish Treaty (the Irish Free State) were not legitimate, according to the many purists who wanted a thirty-two-county sovereign republic and nothing less. The partition of Ireland was imposed by the British, they reasoned, so therefore the Irish Free State and Northern Ireland were soiled offspring from the moment of conception. They were the misshapen twins of an ill-begotten union between duplicitous British imperialists and servile Irish politicians. The new constitutional arrangement could not be allowed to stand.

The members of the Provisional IRA gang that abducted Don Tidey and murdered a soldier and garda were similarly indoctrinated. They believed the IRA was the one true Irish army. The actual defence forces of the Republic were, according to the PIRA's guiding bible, the Green Book, 'illegal armies and illegal forces whose main tasks are treasonable and as such morally wrong, politically unacceptable and ethically inexcusable'.[1] It was therefore right and proper that the Provisional IRA should arrogate to itself the name officially designated to the Irish defence forces, Óglaigh na hÉireann. By that logic, Private Patrick Kelly of 6 Infantry

Battalion transport company, Custume Barracks, was merely an impersonator in uniform.

With the state over sixty years old at this stage, the question of who had the right to bear arms was settled conclusively in the minds of the overwhelming majority of people in the south. The Irish defence forces had that right, as did An Garda Síochána. But, in the pivotal years between 1912 and 1923, multiple political organisms on the island, unionist and nationalist, had claimed it. The question was particularly pertinent for nationalism in 1913 with the founding of the Irish Volunteers, the progenitor of the IRA.

Between the Easter Rising of 1916 and the truce of July 1921 which ended the War of Independence, Irish nationalism was possessed by what Éamon de Valera described as a 'magnificent discipline'.[2] Militant and constitutional nationalists were united in a single goal, to end British rule in Ireland.

The Easter Rising was initially unpopular and wrought terrible destruction on Dublin. Approximately 1,500 rebels staged the attempted coup. They were, as the historian Roy Foster put it, a 'minority of a minority', but one that changed the course of Irish history. On Easter Monday morning 1916, Patrick Pearse stood outside the General Post Office and proclaimed Ireland to be a republic, and a 'sovereign independent state'. The rebels were then comprehensively defeated, as they knew they would be, and no republic emerged from the ruins of the GPO. Pearse's proclamation was no more than a rhetorical aspiration, but for generations of republicans thereafter it was a living document and the source of legitimate justification for their various enterprises, irrespective of the absence of a popular mandate. 'Republicans' would become the catch-all descriptor of those who opposed the Free State and supported violent opposition to the six Ulster counties remaining in the Union.

The general election of December 1918, in which Sinn Féin won 73 of the 105 seats in Ireland and two-thirds of the nationalist vote, was embraced by the independence movement as an electoral mandate for the war with Britain that followed. Sinn Féin had stood on a policy of abstentionism from the Westminster parliament, and duly set up a counter state with its own parliament (Dáil Éireann) in Dublin.

The goals of the IRA during the War of Independence, which lasted from January 1919 to July 1921, were shared by the nationalist population at large. The Dáil took official responsibility for the IRA in April 1921 and those involved in the War of Independence were given state pensions afterwards.

Prior to the truce, the British prime minister David Lloyd George labelled the IRA a 'murder gang' and promised to crush Irish resistance in the same way that the Union had crushed the Confederacy in the American Civil War. But he came to realize that taking on the IRA was also taking on the will of the Irish people. The invitation to Éamon de Valera and Michael Collins to talks in Downing Street in July 1921 was an implicit acknowledgement that the 'murder gang' represented the will of nationalist Ireland.

De Valera, for reasons he never convincingly explained, was not part of the negotiating team that signed the Anglo-Irish Treaty on 6 December 1921 in Downing Street. He had exhorted the five-member Irish delegation to report back to him before signing anything. Yet the delegation, led by Collins and Arthur Griffith, had plenipotentiary powers to sign the document on behalf of Sinn Féin and, therefore, on behalf of the Irish people. Under threat from Lloyd George of renewed British military action in Ireland – 'immediate and terrible war' – they signed the treaty.[3]

An independent Irish state was now established for the first time. The Irish Free State had full control over all domestic and foreign policy and its own army. Yet it remained within the British Empire, and members of Dáil Éireann would have to swear an oath of allegiance to the king.

On 7 January 1922, the treaty was passed in the Dáil by 64 votes to 57, after a protracted debate characterized by personal attacks and untrammelled bitterness. The treaty would lead to an irrevocable split in nationalist Ireland, which endured for the whole of the twentieth century.

Four days after it was signed, the IRA convened a meeting. The mood was angry. Some IRA commanders who had risked their lives in the War of Independence were not prepared to compromise on their demands for complete separation from Britain. The centrality of the 1916 Proclamation in their doctrine was encapsulated by the anti-treaty chief of staff Liam Lynch during the ensuing Civil War: 'We have declared for an Irish Republic. We will live by no other law.'[4]

There were now two governments and two armies in the South – each disputing the other's right to exist. The shadow government was led by Sinn Féin in its various iterations and the IRA; the other one was democratically elected. During the Civil War the anti-treaty side argued that the views of the democratically elected government, and those who supported it, were irrelevant. In March 1922 de Valera declared that the 'people never had a right to do wrong' and he notoriously warned that the IRA 'would have to wade through Irish blood, through the blood of the soldiers of the Irish government, and through, perhaps, the blood of some of the members of the government in order to get Irish freedom'.[5]

The Civil War that broke out in June 1922 lasted eleven months and caused approximately 1,300 deaths. By the standards of other European civil wars at the time, the Finnish and Russian ones most notably, the death toll was slight, but the physical damage done to the country was enormous, with much of its infrastructure destroyed. Railways, the arteries of the island, were particularly badly affected. The cost of the war, £30 million, exceeded the total annual tax take for the infant state.

The two sides, erstwhile brothers and sisters in arms, brought out the worst in each other. Some of the most egregious atrocities were carried out by government forces. Eighty-one anti-treaty prisoners were executed, some shot without even the pretence of a trial. In March 1923 nine republican prisoners were tied to a landmine in Ballyseedy, Co. Kerry, and blown up. Eight died instantly. These deeds would motivate many republicans never to accept the new state.

The anti-treaty forces adopted the same guerrilla tactics used by the IRA during the War of Independence but, critically, the pre-treaty version of the IRA had had the support of the people. The first general election of the new independent state was held in June 1922. It became a de facto referendum on the Anglo-Irish Treaty. The Irish public voted by 78 per cent to 22 per cent in favour of pro- or treaty-neutral candidates. The people had spoken: they supported the treaty and the constitutional arrangement that flowed from it. The Free State was legitimate; it was mandated by over three-quarters of the population that had voted.

The anti-treaty side carried on regardless. The Civil War

was deeply unpopular with a population already weary from eight years of continuous conflict, going back to the outbreak of the First World War in 1914. The IRA was blamed by the mainstream press, the political classes and the Catholic Church for the destruction wrought by what was clearly a futile insurrection against the will of the people.

The Civil War ended, inevitably, in comprehensive defeat for the IRA. Its chief of staff, Frank Aiken, who would go on to become a minister of long standing in successive Fianna Fáil governments, issued a 'dump arms' declaration on 14 May 1923, with the bitter rejoinder that the 'foreign and domestic enemies of the Republic have for the moment prevailed'.

There was no peace treaty. Old grudges were preserved and would fester across subsequent generations. In effect the Civil War never ended, it just morphed into a smaller-scale and more sporadic conflict.

The Provisional IRA would continue to see itself as the successor to the anti-treaty IRA. When one Provisional IRA commander was asked by *Magill* magazine in 1980 what they had achieved in the first ten years of conflict in Northern Ireland, he responded: 'First of all the IRA is not ten years old, it's over sixty years old.' The Sinn Féin TD Maurice Quinlivan once observed that, in some places, an aversion to the state was passed on through the generations. 'A certain section of the people never bought into the state. To them it was always a republic, not a free state, and they would have seen the outbreak of hostilities in 1969 as just a continuation of the struggle for independence.'[6]

Many descendants of those first irredentists felt the need to carry on the fight against the Free State government and its successors. 'Naturally the atmosphere of my home was not only republican but also anti-Free State and generally derogatory of politics and politicians,' remembered Seán Ó Broin, whose father Seán Sr had been killed during the Civil War. 'I learned that the Free State was a British dominion created by an English Act of Parliament.'[7]

Even the language of Irish republicanism denigrated the Republic and its inhabitants: 'Free State', 'Free Stater', 'shoneen', 'west Brit', 'collaborationist' were just some of the pejorative expressions used to convey their scorn.

The Civil War had been about many things, but the status of Northern Ireland was not one of them. Collins had hoped mutual animosity towards the new northern state would unite southern nationalists and stave off civil war. An IRA campaign in the North in May and June 1922, which Collins fomented, ended in disarray, however.

The forces aligned against them included 27,563 members of the Ulster Special Constabulary, the equivalent in the North of the Black and Tans in the South. The latter force had been set up in 1920 as an auxiliary to the Royal Irish Constabulary and would become notorious for their excesses during the War of Independence. The Ulster Special Constabulary was backed up by 5,000 British soldiers, who had artillery and naval support. The IRA could muster about 8,500 in opposition.[8]

The odds were simply too great. Though bitterly divided on the treaty itself, pro- and anti-treaty forces were united in their opposition to partition. When in June 1922 pro- and anti-treaty IRA forces invaded the border villages of Belleek in Fermanagh and, twelve miles away, Pettigo in Donegal, Winston Churchill, then secretary of state for the colonies, ordered the use of artillery to shell them, killing eight of their number.

The IRA in the 1920s was the first generation of that organization to discover it could not eliminate the British presence by military means in Northern Ireland.

Both pro- and anti-treaty sides were of the view that partition would be short-lived anyway. It was anticipated that the Boundary Commission, set up as part of the treaty to examine the allegiances of residents in border areas, would transfer the Catholic-majority counties of Fermanagh and Tyrone, plus Derry city and south Armagh, to the Free State, thus rendering the remaining rump too weak to be viable.

So, when the Boundary Commission reported back in 1925, its recommendations came as a shock to nationalist Ireland. It envisaged only a minor change in boundaries and even recommended the transfer of territory from the South to the North. The Free State government was in no place militarily to challenge the commission's recommendations and accepted the outcome in return for the state's share of the imperial debt being written off. A belief among six-county nationalists that the southern establishment had sold out and abandoned its own people became an article of faith, one that persists to this day. Generations of northern republicans have perpetuated this grievance against the southern state.

Over time, it would be the status of the North that would supplant the treaty as the issue dividing militant republicans from constitutional parties. The goal of ending partition united all strands of nationalist opinion, but only a small minority wanted to pursue this aim by violent means.

At the end of the Civil War, the anti-treaty Sinn Féin TDs had attended a Dáil of their own making, in effect a parallel parliament with a parallel government. The charade could not long endure. The founding of Fianna Fáil in March 1926 by de Valera and his followers was the result of frustration with Sinn Féin's policy of abstentionism from the legitimate parliament.

The launch of what would become Ireland's most successful political party marked the end of anti-treaty Sinn Féin as a serious electoral force. The success of Fianna Fáil in the 1932 Irish general election, and the peaceful handover of power from its bitter foes in Cumann na nGaedheal, ensured the survival of Irish democracy.

Once he was in government, one of de Valera's first acts was to abolish the oath of allegiance to the British Crown. Another was to lift the ban on the IRA imposed by the previous government. The paramilitary organization was allowed to parade in public and to hold rallies; its prisoners were released from jail.

Many in the IRA saw de Valera as one of their own. He, too, had participated in the Easter Rising and opposed the treaty, but circumstances had changed and they hadn't. He hoped to persuade them to leave the gun behind, as he had done. De Valera would be irritated, then exasperated and finally contemptuous of the IRA. 'We have put up with things which no other government in the world would tolerate,' he declared in 1935. 'We have hoped all along that common sense and patriotic instincts would at last assert themselves. Our hopes have, apparently, been disappointed.'[9]

The IRA continued to carry out violent attacks on gardaí. They intimidated jury members and broke up public meetings of their opponents, most notably those of the crypto-fascist Blueshirts. 'We will not allow free speech to traitors,' the prominent socialist and republican Frank Ryan warned.[10] In 1936 they killed retired Rear Admiral Henry Somerville because he was attempting to recruit young Irishmen in Cork to serve in the Royal Navy.

It was one of a number of killings that prompted de Valera finally to break with the organization. The IRA was banned from June 1936. Gerry Boland, the then minister for justice, said the ban would 'smash the IRA just as effectively as we have smashed the Blueshirts'.[11]

It marked the final alienation of the IRA from the Irish state. There would be no equivocation thereafter on the part of Fianna Fáil or any other party in government. There was only one state and one army.

Still the IRA did not disappear. As far as they and their dwindling number of supporters were concerned, the only true government was the self-styled 'Government of the Republic of Ireland'. This consisted of seven members who had been elected to the second Dáil in 1921. They included the extremist Mary MacSwiney, sister of Terence MacSwiney who had died on hunger strike in Brixton jail in 1920, and George Plunkett, father of the Proclamation signatory Joseph Mary Plunkett, who had been executed in 1916.

They had both lost their Dáil seats in the 1927 general election. Plunkett twice lost his deposit in subsequent elections.

In December 1938 this supposed 'government' handed over all authority to the IRA's Army Council. With this leap of logic, and an almost comical level of delusion, the self-appointed 'Government of the Republic of Ireland' was now run by a coterie of unelected fantasists and violent zealots.

A month later the IRA declared war on Britain on behalf of the Irish people, who were never consulted about the decision and would never have agreed to it. The IRA statement demanded the withdrawal of Britain from all of Ireland and gave a four-day deadline.

Though its declaration was met with universal derision, the IRA was in deadly earnest. Operation Sabotage involved more than 300 attacks in Britain in 1939. Power plants, Tube tunnels and railway stations were targeted, culminating in the deaths of five people on 25 August 1939, when bombs went off in Coventry, just over a week before the start of the Second World War.

The Irish government's response was to deploy the full panoply of anti-terrorism legislation it had inherited from the British. The passage of an Emergency Powers Act and a Treason Act, both in 1939, approved the death penalty for offences carried out by the IRA in Britain or Ireland. The Offences Against the State Act allowed for non-jury courts and would be used against generations of republicans to come.

During this period de Valera displayed what the author and former Special Branch detective Gerard Lovett described as 'breath-taking ruthlessness'. In March 1940 six IRA prisoners went on hunger strike seeking political status for their comrades. Despite multiple entreaties from erstwhile IRA comrades, de Valera would not back down. Two hunger strikers, Tony D'Arcy and Seán McNeela, died in quick succession.

The IRA responded by detonating a large landmine at Special Branch headquarters in the lower yard of Dublin Castle. In August 1940 detectives Patrick McKeown and Richard Hyland were shot dead at 98a Rathgar Road in south Dublin during a raid on a suspected IRA safe house. Two IRA members captured at the scene, Paddy McGrath and

Tom Harte, were executed by firing squad three weeks later. The IRA killed five gardaí during the Second World War and six IRA men were executed, five by firing squad.

De Valera's government feared the IRA's activities would drag Éire, as it was known since 1937, into the Second World War, either by attacking the North, thus provoking the British, or by co-operating with Nazi Germany in an invasion of Ireland. In November 1940 the IRA's publication *War News* declared that 'England's enemy is Ireland's ally' – by which it meant Germany and Mussolini's Italy.

The IRA had begun collaborating with the Nazis in 1934 when Seán Russell, its chief of staff, met a German agent named Oskar Pfaus in Ireland. In April 1939 Russell went on a fundraising campaign to the United States. In early 1940 he travelled secretly to Germany with a view to getting Nazi support for IRA activities. He was given full diplomatic privileges, including a villa in a Berlin suburb, a fully stocked library, war maps and a radio.

In May 1940, while the Wehrmacht was invading the Low Countries and France, Russell was being trained by German secret service agents in sabotage. He even met with the German foreign minister, Joachim von Ribbentrop. Russell requested that Frank Ryan, his IRA comrade who had fought in the Spanish Civil War against Franco's nationalists, be released from prison in Spain. This was granted. In August 1940 Russell and Ryan were sent back to Ireland on a U-boat, but without any military commitment from Germany.

One hundred miles off the coast of Galway, Russell became mortally ill, most likely with a stomach ulcer, though there was no doctor on board the submarine to certify the cause of death. His body was buried at sea, wrapped in a Nazi flag. Ryan returned to Germany, where he died in 1944.

The full horrors of the Holocaust had not unfolded when Russell died. Those activists who in 1951 unveiled a statue to him in Dublin's Fairview Park were better informed. In 2003 Mary Lou McDonald, now Sinn Féin president, delivered a speech at the Russell memorial.

Defenders of Russell argue that he was never a true believer in Nazi ideology; he merely subscribed to the old adage that England's difficulty was Ireland's opportunity. Nonetheless it is an incontrovertible fact that Russell was a willing collaborator with the most evil regime in human history.

The decade between 1935 and the end of the Second World War saw the most serious stretch of violence between the Irish State and the IRA until the advent of the Troubles. Nine IRA men in total died. In turn, the IRA killed six Special Branch officers and four civilians. They carried out twenty-two attacks on gardaí and sixteen on the defence forces. The Irish government jailed 463 republicans and interned nearly 1,200 without trial.

The IRA that emerged after the war was a demoralized rabble. On Easter Monday 1949 the Irish state officially became a republic. But it was not recognized by those who called themselves Irish republicans. Belatedly, however, the IRA realized it could not take on the British, Northern Irish and southern authorities at the same time. Making enemies of the Irish security forces was therefore now deemed to be a counterproductive strategy.

It was Tony Magan, as chief of staff, who formulated Standing Order No. 8 of the IRA code. 'Volunteers are strictly forbidden to take any military action against twenty-six county forces under any circumstances whatsoever,' it said. This was an overdue acknowledgement of the reality that the vast majority of people living in the Republic of Ireland supported the security forces and were repulsed by IRA attacks on them.

Standing Order No. 8 did not extend to civilians in the Republic, however. During the Troubles they would be targeted for extortion, robbery and kidnapping.

4. A Disastrous Campaign

Three decades after partition, Sinn Féin still had substantial support north of the border. In the 1955 British general election it won 152,310 votes, albeit that the Nationalist Party, the forerunner of the Social Democratic and Labour Party (SDLP), chose not to participate in that contest. Taking its cue from that result, the IRA decided it had enough popular support in Ulster to carry out a new military operation. It was to prove a fatal mistake.

The IRA's border campaign, also known as Operation Harvest, began in December 1956 and ended in 1962. Exclusively concentrated along the North–South border, its purpose was to destabilize the North to the extent that the British government would opt for withdrawal, leading to the creation of 'an independent, united, democratic Irish Republic'.[1]

The campaign was ill conceived and poorly planned, with predictable results. More IRA members ended up dying – eight in total – than RUC officers. The worst single loss of life was self-inflicted. Four IRA men blew themselves up in a farmhouse at Edentubber, Co. Louth, on 11 November 1957.

Seán South, a pious Catholic from Limerick, and twenty-year-old Fergal O'Hanlon from Monaghan died following a calamitous raid on an RUC barracks in Brookeborough, Co. Fermanagh, on New Year's Day 1957. Fourteen IRA men led by Seán Garland decided to attack the barracks, believing it would be lightly guarded. They laid two mines at the door of the barracks, but both failed to explode. RUC sergeant

Kenneth Cordner ran to the top floor, from where he fired on the IRA party below, killing South and O'Hanlon and wounding another man, Paddy O'Regan. The IRA unit retreated in chaos. The dying South and O'Hanlon were deposited in an isolated barn; their comrades fled across the border.

The two deceased were accorded martyrdom status and their deaths prompted a wave of sympathy across the country, even among those not inclined to support the IRA. Their funerals were huge affairs. Subsequent generations would learn of South and O'Hanlon through the well-known ballads 'Seán South of Garryowen' and 'The Patriot Game', Dominic Behan's acidic take on republican pieties. The military catastrophe which led to their deaths is hardly known at all to the general public.

In March 1957 Sinn Féin, still standing on an abstentionist ticket, had its best result in an Irish general election since 1927, winning four seats and 5.3 per cent of the vote. It proved to be an electoral chimera. As Operation Harvest dragged on, what public support there was for the republican cause ebbed away.

Éamon de Valera and his successor Seán Lemass dealt ruthlessly with the IRA, once again introducing internment without trial, as did the Stormont government. Within a few months of the campaign launch, 125 republicans were incarcerated in southern jails. Lemass, who wanted better relations with the North, was particularly critical, stating: 'Far from contributing to the reunification of the country, it is obvious they are having the very opposite effect and are, indeed, a main impediment to the development of a more constructive approach.'[2]

Sinn Féin lost all its TDs and more than half its vote in

the 1961 general election; the border campaign ended in failure in February 1962.

Seven years later, in August 1969, the Troubles began with the Battle of the Bogside, in which Catholic residents of Derry fought running skirmishes with the RUC and the Ulster Special Constabulary (the B Specials) for three days. Both government and people in the South were shocked by the treatment of Northern Irish civil-rights campaigners who had been beaten off the streets in 1968 and 1969. The demands for the implementation of 'one man, one vote' in local elections, and for an end both to the gerrymandering of electoral boundaries and to discrimination against Catholics in public employment and social housing, seemed eminently fair and reasonable to outsiders. So the sight of protesters being assaulted by the RUC and loyalist mobs was profoundly shocking to a southern audience watching these scenes on the nightly news.

While there was overwhelming sympathy in the South for beleaguered nationalists in the North, there was also a fear that the violence would spill over the border. On the night of 13 August 1969 taoiseach Jack Lynch addressed the nation and said the 'Irish government can no longer stand by and see innocent people injured and perhaps worse'. This created expectations in Catholic areas around the border that the Irish army would invade, but Lynch meant no such thing. Any military intervention by the South would have ended in quick and complete failure. A report commissioned by Lynch in 1970 found the Irish army could deploy a maximum of 2,500 troops for an incursion. They would have faced almost ten times that number of men on the British side.[3]

The end of the border campaign had led to a period of introspection within the republican movement. In the 1960s it embraced fashionable left-wing ideologies, and broadened its horizons from the sole aspiration of a united Ireland. Meanwhile the IRA had not kept its weapons inventory up to date. In August 1969, according to some sources, there were just 120 members in Belfast and twenty-four weapons. 'The meagre armaments at our disposal were hopelessly inadequate to meet the requirements of the situation,' Belfast Brigade O/C Billy McMillen admitted.[4]

The organization was entirely unprepared for the violence that broke out in the summer of 1969 across the North. Thousands of Catholic families were burnt out of their homes by loyalist mobs. The IRA was perceived to have failed in its duty to protect the Catholic community, giving rise to the mortifying popular joke that IRA stood for 'I Ran Away'.

The beginning of the Troubles provoked an irrevocable split in Irish republicanism. In December 1969 the IRA, influenced by the old southern guard, some of whom had embraced socialist politics, voted by more than two to one to end the policy of abstentionism and to sit in the Westminster, Stormont and Dáil parliaments if elected. This amounted to a de facto recognition of partition and the separate jurisdictions on the island of Ireland. It was too much to stomach for doctrinaire republicans. They split from the organization and called their new entity the Provisional IRA.

The founders included an Englishman who grew up in London as John Stephenson and renamed himself as Seán Mac Stíofáin; the veteran republican and schoolteacher from Longford, Ruairí Ó Brádaigh; former IRA chief of staff Séamus Twomey; and John Joe McGirl, the republican from Aughnasheelin. According to multiple reports, the concept of the Provisional IRA was agreed at a meeting upstairs in McGirl's pub in Ballinamore on 17 August 1969.[5]

Sinn Féin split along similar lines in January 1970. One wing abandoned abstentionism and became Official Sinn Féin. The remainder established Provisional Sinn Féin. The Provisional IRA and Provisional Sinn Féin were two sides of the same coin, with many activists moving seamlessly between the terrorism of the former and the politics of the latter.

Though the PIRA and Provisional Sinn Féin were initially a minority within the republican movement, they would quickly become dominant. Provisional Sinn Féin declared its goal to be the 're-assembly of the 32-County Dáil, which will then legislate for and rule all Ireland'.[6] The Provisionals, abbreviated in popular parlance to 'the Provos', sought the end of both administrations on the island of Ireland. Prominent republicans such as the Sinn Féin vice-president Máire Drumm made bellicose noises about the southern state. 'We have fought the British Army, we have brought down Stormont and we'll bring down Leinster House,' she declared in 1972.[7]

Ó Brádaigh declared in December 1971: 'The fight in the North was in grave danger of leaving the twenty-six counties far behind. We must show them that we want to disestablish both states, north and south.'[8] This comment was used by the Irish government at a High Court hearing in 1982 to justify the continuation of Section 31 of the Broadcasting Act, the ban on Sinn Féin spokespeople from the airwaves.[9]

'Leinster House must go too,' Joe Cahill, the chief of staff of the IRA, said at the same time, but Leinster House was not a rigged parliament like Stormont, with its permanent Ulster Unionist Party majority. The Dáil commanded the allegiance of the population at large in a way Stormont never did.

The Provisionals used the Republic as a base for operations in the North; members could carry out attacks and then flee to relative safety south of the border. There they operated training camps, stored weapons and built up a network of safe houses. The need for funds prompted them to engage in criminal activities such as armed robbery, smuggling and kidnapping.

In 1970 an arms crisis almost brought down the Fianna Fáil government. Jack Lynch denied authorizing two cabinet ministers, Neil Blaney and Charles Haughey, to smuggle guns into the state for the defence of the nationalist population in the North. The rights and wrongs of what happened have been debated ever since, but a clear and unambiguous message did emerge from the affair: no Irish government would ever arm republican paramilitaries in the North. They were on their own.

Soon after the eruption of the Troubles, the Irish state once again deployed its full panoply of legislative powers to deal with paramilitary republicans, beginning with the Special Criminal Court, re-established by the Lynch government in 1972. The court operated without a jury, owing to fears that republican sympathizers would intimidate jurors in IRA-related cases.[10]

In 1971 Section 31 was first introduced. This was extended in 1976 to include anybody representing Sinn Féin, even if they were not speaking on issues related to the Troubles.[11]

Thousands of republicans were jailed and there were persistent complaints of ill-treatment in prisons and allegations of a 'heavy gang' within An Garda Síochána using excessive force on republican suspects. A mutual loathing between paramilitaries and the Irish security forces persisted throughout the Troubles and would find its apotheosis in Derrada Wood.

5. Dispensing Death and Destruction

Northern Ireland during the Troubles became one of the most militarized zones on the planet. The IRA was up against the British army, one of the best resourced in western Europe. Even moving about could be difficult. The South was a much easier locale, but eventually the scale of republican activity there made conflict with gardaí inevitable.

IRA terrorists raided quarries for explosives and stole weapons from barracks. Gelignite was moved to central stores and guarded by the Irish army following a spate of thefts. Most urgently, however, the IRA needed cash to pay for weaponry and logistical support; its members staged hundreds of robberies on banks, post offices and businesses. In the Republic, the number of armed robberies vaulted from seventeen in 1970 to 132 in 1972. In a country that had been almost untouched by serious crime, this provoked widespread unease and hostility to the republican movement.[1]

At one point Ruairí Ó Brádaigh felt obliged to claim innocence on behalf of Provisional Sinn Féin, suggesting their members were not involved. Robberies, he declared, were 'completely contrary to the national interest'. But senior gardaí in receipt of reliable intelligence had no doubt about who was responsible.

Armed robberies inevitably led to casualties. The Provos shot dead British Leyland employee James Farrell during a wages robbery in Dublin in August 1973. Bernard Browne, a Catholic from Tyrone, was shot and killed when he tried to prevent a PIRA gang from robbing a supermarket in Killygordon, Co. Donegal, in January 1978. A year later civil servant Eamon Ryan was in the wrong place at the wrong time when a PIRA gang entered the AIB bank in Tramore, Co. Waterford. He was shot dead in front of his son.

One of the largest robberies was the theft of IR£200,000 from a mail train at Sallins in Co. Kildare in March 1976. The Sallins Train Robbery is best known now for the miscarriage of justice that ensued. Nicky Kelly, one of the men convicted, became a cause célèbre and eventually received a presidential pardon and compensation of over €1 million. Less well known is that the robbery was carried out by the Provisional IRA, one of several raids in the South that netted the organization millions of pounds.[2]

In April 1974 a rogue IRA gang led by Eddie Gallagher and his pregnant partner, English heiress turned militant republican Rose Dugdale, carried out the largest art heist in world history up to that date. They stole nineteen paintings from the Beit collection in Russborough House, Co. Wicklow, and assaulted the owners, Sir Alfred Beit and his wife Clementine, Lady Beit. The paintings, which included works by Goya, Rubens and Vermeer, were worth the equivalent of €100 million today. The IRA demanded ST£500,000 and the release of the Price sisters, Dolours and Marian, from jail. But Dugdale was caught with the paintings at a rented house in Glandore, Co. Cork, two weeks later. She eventually received a nine-year prison sentence. Gallagher remained at large.[3]

According to a British army assessment of Provisional IRA finances in 1978, more than half of the ST£950,000 that it raised came from robberies in Ireland.[4] In an assessment of the organization's finances published in *Magill* magazine in 1980, journalist Ed Moloney estimated that the Provos had stolen one third of the IR£5 million taken in armed robberies between 1977 and 1980 in the Republic.[5]

Republicans also resorted to kidnapping – first to bargain for prisoners, then to raise funds. The first significant kidnapping was that of German industrialist Thomas Niedermayer, managing director of the Grundig factory in Belfast. He was abducted from his home two days after Christmas in 1973 by republican terrorists.

The IRA briefly attempted to negotiate his release with the British government in return for the release of republican prisoners from English jails, including the Price sisters, who had been jailed for the Old Bailey bombing of March 1973. It turned out that Niedermayer was killed soon after he was abducted; his body was found in 1980 on a rubbish tip a couple of miles from his Belfast home. His hands had been tied and his mouth gagged. Ten years later his grieving wife Ingeborg drowned herself in the Irish Sea off Bray and the couple's daughters, Gabrielle and Renate, subsequently died by suicide too, as did Gabrielle's husband Robert, all between 1990 and 1999.[6]

On 4 June 1974 the IRA carried out its first kidnapping in the Republic. Lord and Lady Donoughmore were abducted from their stately home at Knocklofty House, Co. Tipperary. Four IRA members attacked the couple as they returned from a dinner party. The pair put up a brave resistance, Lady Donoughmore biting the hand of one of her assailants.

The Donoughmores were not as well connected as the kidnap gang thought they were. The gang travelled with a copy of *The Stately Homes of Ireland*, trying to find wealthy targets to kidnap. This time their aim was to secure the transfer of the Price sisters back to a jail in Northern Ireland. The Donoughmores were held for four days before being released in the Phoenix Park after the amenable British home secretary, Roy Jenkins, agreed to allow the Prices to be repatriated.[7]

One year later another rogue IRA outfit led by Gallagher and Marion Coyle kidnapped Tiede Herrema. The Dutch industrialist was managing director of the Limerick-based factory Ferenka, the largest employer in the city. He was abducted on his way to work on the morning of 3 October 1975. A cabinet meeting in Dublin was informed of the kidnapping later that day and agreed not to give in to the demands of the kidnappers in any circumstances.

Herrema was driven first to a house in Kinnitty, Co. Offaly, and then to another safe house in Mountmellick, Co. Laois. The kidnappers demanded the release of three prisoners: Dugdale, who was now the mother of a child with Eddie Gallagher; Coyle's partner, Kevin Mallon; and Laois republican James Hyland. The kidnappers later increased their demands to include a IR£2 million ransom and flights to the Middle East.

For the first two weeks of his incarceration, Herrema was kept in a position of sensory deprivation similar to that which Don Tidey would later endure. Blindfolded and with wads of cotton wool jammed into his ears, the industrialist did not know where he was being held or by whom.

The kidnap party spent almost four weeks at No. 1410 St Evin's Park in Monasterevin, Co. Kildare. The security forces eventually discovered the location and a siege of the house ensued, lasting eighteen days. The government refused to yield despite the kidnappers threatening to kill their hostage. Herrema's wife Elisabeth told RTÉ the ransom should not be paid.

The stand-off was reported worldwide and brought unwanted international attention to the Republic. The kidnapping of industrialists threatened the viability of the country's business model, much of which was predicated on attracting foreign direct investment. It could not be allowed to succeed. Gallagher and Coyle eventually surrendered after Gallagher complained of severe headaches.[8]

In Tiede Herrema, the IRA had kidnapped a former Dutch resistance fighter and concentration camp survivor from the Second World War. There was an overwhelming sense of public sympathy for this blameless man. His release was hailed as a resounding success for the Irish security forces. The Herrema kidnapping led to much recrimination within the Provisional IRA, which resented the publicity and pressure that Gallagher's maverick operation had put on them. Though the leadership denied sanctioning the kidnap, few believed their protestations. The kidnapping was a major setback for the PIRA in their ongoing quest for public support.

The next significant IRA kidnapping was that of Ben Dunne Jr, the thirty-four-year-old son of the Dunnes Stores founder of the same name. Ben Jr was abducted as he crossed the border into the Republic on 17 October 1981 after visiting one of his stores in the North.

A green Opel Ascona swerved in front of the businessman and pinned his black Mercedes into the hard shoulder. He was forced at gunpoint out of the car and a hood was placed over his head. Four masked men took him to a farmyard. Judging by the smell, the hooded Dunne believed it to be a piggery.

His captors demanded the phone numbers of his father and his wife. 'What do you think you are worth?' one of them asked Dunne. 'Nothing. You'll get nothing for me,' came the reply. A gang member phoned up Dunnes Stores head office and demanded IR£500,000 for his return.

Dunne was held captive for six days at a farmhouse in south Armagh. A search for him was staged on both sides of the border. Gardaí put Dunnes Stores executives under surveillance, as they would with Quinnsworth executives during the Tidey kidnapping. The Fine Gael/Labour government, the same coalition that would be in charge during the Tidey operation, again decided that under no circumstances would it allow a ransom to be paid. That included, if necessary, allowing the hostage to die, as taoiseach Garret FitzGerald later recalled:

> It was agreed that this kind of crime could not be seen to pay and that was the reason we took the tough line we did in the Dunne case. A man's life was at stake and it's very difficult to tell a man's wife and his family that you're going to stop them from doing what they need to do in order to save his life. Balanced against that realization was the fact that ransom money could be used to buy weaponry and that weaponry could kill many more people than an individual who had been kidnapped.[9]

The Dunne kidnapping would lead, like the Tidey rescue two years later, to a confrontation between the Provisional IRA and the Republic's security forces. Two detectives from the Security Task Force and an Irish soldier were searching an area around Roche Castle in Co. Louth when they spotted masked men in the company of a well-known priest, Fr Dermod McCarthy, outside a shed where they believed Dunne was being held. McCarthy had been sent by Ben Dunne's father to negotiate with the kidnappers. A brief exchange of fire followed. The kidnappers and their quarry fled across the border. McCarthy was taken into garda custody.

'They were querying and questioning me and I could tell they didn't believe my story,' he said afterwards. 'They asked me where I was from and I said, "Originally Ballinamore". They immediately stiffened and exchanged looks, I presume because that region of south Leitrim close to the border was a well-known republican hotbed.'[10]

The priest was told by gardaí that his meddling was complicating the search and if he really wanted to help, he would go to the Dunne family and ask them to make a public appeal. McCarthy went on television that evening and, looking straight at the camera, appealed directly to the terrorists. 'I know you to be shrewd, intelligent men,' he said. 'I appeal to you, in the name of God and in the name of common sense, cut your losses now, release Ben and get out while you still have time.'

Time was not something the kidnappers had. The hunt for Dunne intensified on both sides of the border, much to the disquiet of republicans in the area, who did not appreciate this level of scrutiny on their other clandestine activities. Dunne was eventually released outside a graveyard in south Armagh. His kidnappers gave him three bullets, one from a revolver and two from an Armalite, as souvenirs.

'The first thing I did was get into a grave,' the tycoon recalled later. 'I looked up and I could see the stars in the sky. I thought, "Good God, they could shoot me and throw the earth back in," so I crawled out of that grave. I didn't really feel that I was free until I got home a few hours later.'[11]

The kidnapping ended peacefully, so was a ransom paid? A report in the *Irish Times* in December 1983 suggested that Ben Dunne Sr had paid about IR£500,000, some time after his son was freed, to ensure no reprisals would be taken against his staff or management.

Asked in 2014 by RTÉ presenter Miriam O'Callaghan if a ransom had been paid, Ben Dunne Jr responded: 'Money changed hands to the best of my knowledge. I was never troubled again.' When asked if a reported IR£1.5 million was handed over, Dunne said: 'That amount I know is wrong. I don't think I was ever worth IR£1.5 million. I was never told. I was told different stories. He [Dunne Sr] told me that what he had done was none of my business and I would never know. I think it is wrong to pay ransoms, but it is very easy for me to say that.'

He also revealed that his kidnappers told him 'if I as much as opened my mouth that they knew where my children went to school, they knew where my wife shopped. Intimidation is an extraordinary thing.'

Loyalist paramilitaries targeted the Republic and were responsible for the biggest atrocity of the Troubles, the Dublin–Monaghan bombings of 17 May 1974, which killed thirty-four people. Yet successive Irish governments regarded the Provisional IRA as the greatest threat to the state, and several high-profile murders reinforced that view.

The Fine Gael senator Billy Fox was shot dead in 1974 outside his fiancée's home in Co. Monaghan. Christopher Ewart-Biggs, the British ambassador to Ireland, and civil servant Judith Cooke were blown up by a landmine at Sandyford, Dublin, in July 1976. Infamously, Lord Louis Mountbatten, two teenage boys and an elderly woman were killed when the Provisional IRA planted a bomb on his boat at Mullaghmore, Co. Sligo, in August 1979.

Eleven gardaí were murdered by republican paramilitaries

during the Troubles. Six were killed by the Provisional IRA, four by the offshoot Irish National Liberation Army (INLA) and one by Saor Éire, a short-lived fringe republican outfit with a Marxist ideology. The Provisional IRA killed one Irish soldier and shot one prison officer, Brian Stack, also in 1983.

The killing of Stack, who died from his wounds eighteen months later, was the first time an officer of the Irish state was deliberately targeted by republicans. On the night of 25 March 1983 Stack, the chief prison officer in Portlaoise jail, was attacked outside the National Stadium in Dublin after a boxing match. The Provisional IRA confessed to the shooting thirty years later following the intervention of Gerry Adams, but claimed it was not authorized by the Army Council.[12]

The killing of officers of the Irish state had the effect of further alienating the vast majority of people from Sinn Féin/IRA. In his autobiography published in 2000, former Labour Party cabinet minister Barry Desmond wrote: 'Gerry Adams, Martin McGuinness and Gerry Kelly have a lot to answer for. I walked behind the coffins of the gardaí and army public servants who were murdered in cold blood by the Provos. As I tried to convey my sympathy on those awful occasions, I never forgave these IRA apologists for the pain and suffering I witnessed on the faces of the widows and children they maimed for life.'[13]

Richard Fallon was the first garda to be killed during the Troubles. On 3 April 1970 he was shot dead while investigating an attempted robbery at the Royal Bank of Ireland in Arran Quay, Dublin. Saor Éire claimed responsibility.

The first garda killed by the Provisional IRA was Inspector Samuel Donegan, who died when a booby-trap bomb on a country lane exploded during a patrol just across the border in Co. Fermanagh on 8 June 1972. Donegan went to inspect a crate which had the word BOMB! written on it, but it was a hoax. When he went to examine a similar container a few hundred metres further up the road, it exploded. He died that evening. In June 2023 he was posthumously awarded a gold Scott Medal, the highest honour for bravery in An Garda Síochána.

In September 1975 a husband-and-wife couple, Noel and Marie Murray, shot dead an off-duty garda, Michael Reynolds, in a park in Killester on Dublin's northside. Reynolds had shown incredible bravery when he gave chase to the pair after they robbed the Bank of Ireland branch in Killester. Marie Murray shot Reynolds in the head as he grappled with her husband.

The couple were sentenced to death on 9 June 1976, the killing of a garda being a capital offence, but their sentences were later commuted to life imprisonment. The Murrays had been members of Sinn Féin and the Official IRA. Though they had left the organizations two years previously, the murder they committed was regarded as political and they were tried at the Special Criminal Court. The Irish public regarded the murder of Garda Reynolds as another example of how republicans viewed An Garda Síochána.[14]

Their next fatal attack on gardaí would lead indirectly to the resignation of the president, Cearbhall Ó Dálaigh. On 16 October 1976 Garda Michael Clerkin and four colleagues responded to a report of suspicious activity at a derelict house in Garryhinch, Portarlington, Co. Laois. They had earlier received information that a bomb was being prepared at the house in advance of an assassination attempt on Fine Gael TD Oliver J. Flanagan, a ferocious critic of the Provisional IRA.

On arrival at the premises the policemen began a search, during which a booby-trap bomb exploded, killing Garda Clerkin and seriously wounding his colleagues. Detective Garda Tom Peters lost his sight and hearing as a result of the blast. This episode of murder and maiming generated revulsion in the Republic, being seen as a direct attack on the police force nationally. 'Garda Clerkin is a symbol of the state to which the overwhelming majority of the Irish people owe their allegiance,' *The Kerryman* newspaper declared. 'The people who killed Garda Clerkin despise that vast majority which owes an allegiance to that state.'[15]

In September the Dáil had passed the Emergency Powers Act, which had been in abeyance since the end of the Second World War. Detention without charge would be extended from two days to seven. Gardaí could detain a suspect on the basis that the suspect knew about subversive activities even if he or she was not directly involved in that activity. Gardaí would be given powers to search premises without a warrant. On 24 September President Ó Dálaigh referred this proposed legislation to the Supreme Court for consideration. The bill was judged to be constitutional and Ó Dálaigh announced he would sign it into law on the following day – 16 October.

The feeling in government was that the booby-trap murder of Garda Clerkin was a direct response by the PIRA to the president signing the bill into law. The following day Paddy Donegan, the minister for defence, incensed by the murder of Garda Clerkin, called the president a 'thundering disgrace' for referring the bill to the Supreme Court. Pointedly, he did so in front of an audience of army officers at Mullingar Barracks. Donegan's comments sparked a furore. He then offered his resignation to the taoiseach, but the taoiseach refused it, and praised his minister's contribution to the defence of the state in the face of a Fianna Fáil Dáil motion that he resign. After the taoiseach chose to take no action against the minister, President Ó Dálaigh resigned a week later.[16]

Garda Clerkin's funeral in his native Monaghan town was charged with emotion and distress. Charlie Flanagan, the former minister for justice, recalls travelling as a teenager with his father, Oliver J. 'It was the darkest day,' he recalls, 'just a chilling experience. The exposure to the atmosphere of grieving, young people crying, the silence of the funeral cortège. I still feel it.'[17]

Attacks on gardaí by republican paramilitaries escalated in the next decade. In 1980 Detective Garda Seamus Quaid was shot dead by PIRA member Peter Rogers at Cleariestown, Co. Wexford. Limerick native Quaid, a father of four, was widely known in GAA circles, having won an All-Ireland senior hurling medal with Wexford in 1960. He and a colleague had stopped Rogers, who was driving a van loaded with explosives.[18] Rogers would claim in a BBC interview in 2014 that he had been ordered to carry out a bombing in England by Gerry Adams and Martin McGuinness. Both men denied this.

Three gardaí were killed by the INLA in the early 1980s. Garda Henry Byrne and Detective John Morley were shot dead in the aftermath of an armed robbery at the Bank of Ireland in Ballaghaderreen, Co. Roscommon, on 7 July 1980. Garda Patrick Reynolds was twenty-three when he was shot and killed in Tallaght on 20 February 1982.

Incidents like these prompted John Hume, the then SDLP leader, to note how republicans believed themselves to be the ultimate arbiters of Irishness despite the absence of a popular mandate. 'They are more Irish than the rest of us, they believe. They are the pure Irish master race,' he said. 'They know better than the rest of us. They know so much better that they take unto themselves the right, without consultation, to dispense death and destruction.'[19]

As the Troubles dragged on, support for the IRA in the South dwindled to a small coterie of sympathizers and zealots. An *Irish Times* poll in November 1980, taken during the first hunger strike by republican inmates of the Maze prison, showed only 5 per cent of the Irish public approved of the PIRA and 48 per cent had no time for it whatsoever. A further 41 per cent approved of the ideals of the Provisional IRA but disagreed with the use of violence. Public opposition and mistrust would only increase following the events of December 1983.

6. Banana Republic

The 1980s was a decade of despair in the Republic. The promise of the 1960s and early 1970s, when living standards rose in tandem with the population, created expectations that the country could finally overcome centuries of poverty and emigration. Those hopes had atrophied in the 1980s, to the extent that many were once again questioning the capacity of the Irish state to provide a living for its people.

On his daily morning radio programme, and weekly on his TV chat show, *The Late Late Show*, the enormously popular and influential RTÉ broadcaster Gay Byrne would regularly lament the state of the nation. He frequently declared, half in jest and fully in earnest, that the country was 'banjaxed'.

Byrne once told *Hot Press* magazine:

> There was a man stood up in the audience on the *Late Late Show* three or four years ago, and we all laughed at him, and we were in the midst of one of these interminable economic discussions, and he said, if we had any manners we'd hand the entire island back to the Queen of England at nine o'clock tomorrow morning and apologize for its condition. And everybody got a great laugh out of that, but as every week passes, I think that guy had something.[1]

In 1980 the Boomtown Rats released the song 'Banana Republic', the lyrics of which were written by the band's lead singer and charismatic front man, Bob Geldof. 'Banana Republic' was dripping with contempt for the Irish establishment.

Dubliner Geldof and his bandmates had gotten out of Ireland four years earlier, seeing no future for themselves at home. In London they signed a record deal and in 1978 became the first Irish rock band to reach No. 1 in the UK pop charts with the single 'Rat Trap'.

Geldof's visceral frustration with the country of his birth was already familiar to Irish audiences. In 1977 he had appeared on *The Late Late Show*, and used the opportunity to get a few issues off his chest. His public role, as he saw it, was 'the denunciation of nationalism, of medieval-minded clerics and corrupt politicians'.[2] By nationalism he meant the veneration of republican violence, both at that time and in the past.

In 'Banana Republic', he was true to his word. From the very opening couplet, repeated for emphasis throughout the song, he made no secret of his scorn. The regressive forces he mentioned on *The Late Late Show* came in for some livid treatment too, especially armed republicanism. The single reached No. 3 in both the UK and Irish charts.

Though it would take another two decades to prove definitively, there were already malodorous suspicions surrounding one of the 'corrupt politicians' that Geldof had referenced. In December 1979 Charles Haughey became leader of Fianna Fáil and taoiseach. The following month he made a televised state-of-the-nation address, which, when his own lavish spending was eventually exposed, came to be seen as a high-water mark of political hypocrisy in Irish life. Haughey stared down the camera lens and told the people of Ireland they would have to wear the hair shirt of fiscal austerity, while he himself was wearing luxury shirts from the illustrious Parisian tailor Charvet. 'The figures which are now just becoming available to us show one thing very clearly. As a community we are living away beyond our means,' he famously warned the viewers.[3]

The public finances were indeed in a dire condition. So much so, the taoiseach continued, that the state would that year borrow £IR1 billion, the equivalent of one seventh of the entire national output, to keep the lights on and public-sector salaries paid. At the time people had no idea that Haughey himself was the embodiment of living beyond one's means, with debts of around IR£1 million.

The wretched state of the economy contributed to the political turbulence of the early part of the decade. Between June 1981 and November 1982 there were three general elections and three changes of government. A Fine Gael/Labour minority government took power following the election of June 1981 in which two hunger strikers, Kieran Doherty and Paddy Agnew, won seats, thereby depriving Fianna Fáil of an overall majority. That government fell in a row over the budget and a controversial tax on children's shoes.

Another election was held in February 1982 and the coalition was replaced by a scandal-hit minority Fianna Fáil administration led by Haughey. One of those scandals involved the discovery of double murderer Malcolm Mac-arthur in the Dalkey apartment of the attorney general Patrick Connolly in August 1982.

The year would come to be summed up in an acronym that entered Irish folklore: GUBU, standing for 'grotesque, unprecedented, bizarre and unbelievable'. They were the words Haughey himself had used at a press conference to describe the arrest of Macarthur at the home of the chief law officer.

That government fell when the Workers' Party, along with independent TD Tony Gregory, withdrew their support because of further budget cuts. Another election was held in November 1982. This time Fine Gael and Labour won a slim majority and would govern for the next five years.

The economic problems that assailed these administrations were of a magnitude not seen since the nadir of the 1950s. In January 1983 unemployment reached an all-time high of 179,900, amounting to one in eight of the workforce, including one in five of those under the age of twenty-five.[4]

Irish citizens were once again leaving the country in droves. During the decade, 450,000 people, predominantly young adults, emigrated from the Republic. Unlike their predecessors, many were well educated, and this 'brain drain' further hollowed out the economy.

The population of Ireland decreased between 1986 and 1991, the first decline since the 1950s.[5] The west of Ireland was particularly badly affected, and Leitrim perhaps worst of all. The county lost almost one in ten of its residents in the 1980s, reaching a historic low of just 25,301 people in 1991.

The early 1980s were also characterized by a heroin epidemic on the streets of Dublin that ruined many inner-city communities and created thousands of addicts. A referendum in September 1983, which enshrined a prohibition on abortion in the constitution, was but one battle in the divisive culture wars between conservatives and social liberals during that decade.

'It's been a lousy year for most of the people of Ireland,' concluded the *Sunday World* at the end of 1983. 'A government which promised so much has delivered so little. The factories continue to close, redundancies continue to rise, and the dole queues lengthen. It's been miserable. Even those with jobs look forward to 1984 with little joy. Savage taxation has made most take-away pay packets laughably inadequate. Except nobody's laughing.'[6]

The violence in the North compounded the sense of

hopelessness. The Provisional IRA had said in 1978 that it was committed to a 'long war'. The mid-seventies conviction that one more bomb attack, one more atrocity, one more attempt to make Northern Ireland ungovernable, would persuade the British to leave, was proven to be wishful thinking of the darkest hue. The prospect of a united Ireland remained as unrealistic as ever.

The upstart INLA, which was now becoming a serious threat to the hegemony of the Provos, carried out the deadliest attack of 1982 – the Droppin Well pub bombing in Co. Derry, which killed eleven soldiers and six civilians in December of that year. They also blew up the Mount Gabriel radar dome in Co. Cork in the mistaken belief that it was a NATO facility.

Attempts to reach a political settlement floundered. The collapse in 1974 of the power-sharing assembly set up under the Sunningdale Agreement left a political vacuum. In October 1982 the British government established another Northern Ireland assembly, an early attempt at devolution. Sinn Féin won five seats on an abstentionist ticket but the moderate nationalist SDLP stayed away because the assembly would be a majority unionist body and would have no power-sharing dimension, or input from the Republic.

In May 1983 Garret FitzGerald convened the New Ireland Forum to look for a political way out of the Troubles. The unionist parties declined to participate and Sinn Féin was excluded. The unionist-dominated assembly and the exclusively nationalist forum demonstrated how the violence had led to further polarization in an already divided society.

Sinn Féin and the Provisional IRA had gained a new momentum from the hunger strikes, which ended in October 1981. The success of Bobby Sands in the Fermanagh-South

Tyrone by-election in April 1981 was followed in August by the retention of that seat by Owen Carron, the election agent of the now dead hunger striker. These victories convinced the Sinn Féin/IRA leadership to pursue an electoral strategy in tandem with its continuing terrorism campaign. This was infamously articulated at the Sinn Féin ard fheis in October 1981 by republican spokesman Danny Morrison. 'Will anyone here object if, with a ballot paper in this hand and an Armalite in the other, we take power in Ireland?' he asked delegates.

The strategy led to a breakthrough a year later when the party polled 64,191 votes in the Northern Ireland assembly elections of 1982 – over 10 per cent of the total poll, or about 35 per cent of the nationalist vote. This was followed in the June 1983 British general election by Gerry Adams being elected MP for the West Belfast constituency. Adams was part of a new generation of northern republicans who were supplanting the southern leadership. The joint strategy was there to stay, but elections cost money and this in turn put pressure on republican finances.

By the start of 1983 the Provisional IRA was having trouble raising money through its usual sources. Increased security around cash deliveries had made bank raids a much more difficult proposition; armed escorts had become mandatory. Under pressure from the Irish government, banks had also invested in security screens, alarms and CCTV. These measures contributed to a decline in the number of armed bank robberies in the Republic, from 306 in 1981 to 158 in 1982, and just seven in 1983. The Provos were struggling for finance.[7] They were going to have to look elsewhere for cash.

7. It Was All About the Money

America was a primary source of finance, and weapons, for the IRA in the first decade of the Troubles. By the 1980s, however, the US authorities were coming under fierce pressure from the British and Irish governments to stem the flow of material across the Atlantic.

In May 1980 an FBI squad was established specifically to target the IRA in America. Over the following two years this unit set up a sting operation targeting an arms network run by George Harrison, the main gun smuggler. Harrison was a combat veteran of the Pacific theatre in the Second World War. According to some accounts he sent across 2,500 guns and large quantities of ammunition and explosives in the first decade of the Troubles.

In June 1982 the FBI broke up an operation in New Orleans and New York which included the attempted purchase of five surface-to-air missiles (SAMs) capable of bringing down British army helicopters. One of those arrested, Gabriel Megahey, told agents he had $1 million to spend on weaponry for the IRA. Megahey, who received a seven-year jail term, had been under constant FBI surveillance, and there was an informer within the ranks too.

'It was better than sex,' boasted FBI agent Lou Stephens, who was in charge of the operation. 'Three times better. We really saved a lot of lives.'[1]

Also arrested was Michael Flannery from the Irish

Northern Aid Committee (Noraid), an outfit that had raised millions of dollars for Sinn Féin/IRA but was now becoming notorious. These American reversals made the Republic an even more important source of money and arms.

The IRA's southern command had been tasked with financing the northern operations, which needed IR£2 million a year. Unknown to them, there was also an informer within their ranks. Kerry-born Seán O'Callaghan had joined the IRA at the age of seventeen, and killed a Catholic RUC officer in 1974 at the age of twenty, but then turned against the organization. At the time of the Tidey kidnapping he was acting as a double agent, informing the gardaí about planned IRA operations in the Republic. In 1998, after spending many years in jail, he published a book entitled *The Informer: The True Story of One Man's War on Terrorism.*

According to O'Callaghan, the southern command was berated at a meeting in Midleton, Co. Cork, in late 1982 for its failure to raise enough cash. 'The IRA was hovering on the brink of bankruptcy,' he said. 'It had no money to expand. [The row] arose because there was a feeling that the southern command was failing to provide the IRA with the kind of money it [expected]. It was felt they would need an extraordinary intervention if they were to raise that kind of money.'[2]

One Sinn Féin insider recalls the period:

I spent a great deal of time at 44 Parnell Square [Sinn Féin headquarters] in 1983. We were developing this money-making strategy. In 1983 the 'key' Irish government concern was our ability to produce counterfeit money. We had a Heidelberg printer – a massive machine – and had acquired plates to print Irish punts, which was not great but enough to have gardaí going crazy to find the plates. The economy and the Irish punt could have been seriously damaged. We got sterling plates in 1984 and the Brits went crazy.[3]

The plan was to flood the Republic with these notes during the Easter bank holiday weekend of April 1983. Shops, pubs, bookies and banks would take in these plausible counterfeits and give back legitimate money in change, which would go to the IRA. It would involve not only IRA activists, but hundreds of sympathizers. Such a widespread operation risked exposure and the gardaí were duly alerted in advance when they arrested a man in Shannon town, Co. Clare, with 150 fake £10 notes.

The scam went ahead, but not at anything like the level that was hoped. Several IRA sympathizers were arrested and jailed as a result.[4]

Kevin Mallon, the IRA's director of operations, who had recently been released from jail after seven years, was given the job of organizing a finance strategy. How he did it was at his own discretion.

At forty-eight, Mallon was one of the oldest active members of the IRA. Originally from Coalisland, Co. Tyrone, he was lucky to escape the hangman's rope during the border campaign, when he was tried on a charge of killing an RUC sergeant, Arthur Ovens, in a booby-trap explosion in August 1957 near Coalisland. Mallon was found not guilty of murder, but was sentenced separately to fourteen years for arms and conspiracy offences.

Released in 1963,[5] he would go on to become a long-time member of the IRA's Army Council. His escape by helicopter from Mountjoy jail in October 1973, with two other senior republicans, was a coup for the IRA and an acute embarrassment for the Irish government. He was serving a twelve-month sentence at the time for membership of the IRA.

Two months later Mallon was spotted at a dance in the Montague Hotel in Portlaoise. An off-duty garda, Dermot Doran, attempted to arrest him outside the hotel, at which point Mallon's then girlfriend, Marion Coyle, allegedly pointed a handgun at the officer, and then at another garda who arrived on the scene. Coyle pulled the trigger, but the gun jammed. The two gardaí held on to Mallon, who denounced them as 'Free State bastards'.

Mallon was jailed for a further ten years for aiding and abetting another person to discharge a firearm at a garda with intent to murder him.[6] Coyle was acquitted because the trial judge was not satisfied there had been a positive identification: nine months had elapsed between the incident and her being singled out in an ID parade by a garda who had been on the scene.[7] Coyle's acquittal left her free for the kidnapping of Tiede Herrema.

On 19 August 1974 Mallon escaped from Portlaoise prison with eighteen other republican inmates. They blew a hole in the outer wall of the perimeter and fled. The jailbreak was another acute embarrassment for the Fine Gael/Labour coalition. Inevitably, more stringent conditions were imposed on republican prisoners, leading to hunger strikes in 1975 and 1976.

Mallon's status within the republican movement was recognized when he was taken, while on the run, to talks in Feakle, Co. Clare, in December 1974.[8] The talks were with Protestant clergymen, acting as conduits for the British government, and led to a prolonged IRA ceasefire.

Mallon was eventually recaptured with a loaded pistol

under his bed at a house in Foxrock, Co. Dublin, in January 1975.[9] Republicans accused the Irish government of bad faith as the IRA was on ceasefire, but the authorities were still smarting from his double escape. He was returned to Portlaoise to serve the rest of his sentence. Finally released from jail in November 1982, he was immediately appointed as IRA director of operations.

The Dublin middle-class recruit Kieran Conway, who joined the IRA in the 1970s, described Mallon as the 'closest thing the modern IRA had to a Michael Collins ... I was completely bowled over by him. Mallon was a hard-drinking, hard-talking, seriously hard man with buckets of charisma.'[10]

Mallon's time in jail hardened his attitudes towards the 'Free State bastards' and the polity they represented. He was utterly ruthless in his methods and did not care for Sinn Féin's entry into electoral politics. He would do what was necessary to raise the money, as O'Callaghan recalled:

> After Kevin Mallon came out of jail, he turned up in Kerry a couple of times. He came out of jail with some clear ideas in his head and one of them was what the Army Council described as special operations. There was a little team in Dublin that were part of the southern command team. Suddenly we were told they were no longer part of southern command. They had become this special operations team under the control of Mallon.[11]

The IRA's chief finance officer had an alternative in mind to armed robberies and counterfeit money scams. A kidnapping could raise a huge amount of money in one fell swoop, obviating the need for smaller, riskier operations.

*

As a youngster, Mallon had been a bookie's runner and he never lost his penchant for backing horses and greyhounds. His understanding of that world informed the IRA's first kidnap attempt of 1983.

In February a gang took the racehorse Shergar from Ballymany Stud in Co. Kildare. Shergar had won the Epsom Derby by ten lengths, plus the Irish Derby and three other races in a dazzling career as a three-year-old in 1981. The public loved this distinctive horse with the white blaze on his forehead and the white socks, and whose tongue would loll from the side of his mouth as he demolished the opposition in race after race. He was retired to stud, where he was expected to generate enormous revenue, covering mares at IR£70,000 a time.

Shergar was not only one of the most exceptional thoroughbreds in racing history, he was also a prestige symbol of Ireland's world-class horse-breeding capability, at a time when the country had few such industries. His owner, the Aga Khan, had sold forty 1 per cent shares in the racehorse for IR£10 million.

In 1982 Shergar fathered thirty-seven foals and the stud book for 1983 was already full. A lot of wealthy people were expecting to make a lot of money. In theory, Mallon's kidnap plan was logical. The abduction of a racehorse, even one as well loved as Shergar, would not be comparable to the kidnapping of a human being with all the emotional pressure and appeals from that person's family and friends. It would be, he believed, a near victimless crime.[12]

Conway, an IRA intelligence officer in the early 1980s, told a BBC documentary in 2018 that the operation made sense in the context of the time. 'I didn't personally meet anybody who objected to us kidnapping a horse. He was an extremely valuable horse. The Aga Khan was known to be an extremely rich man. He would not be concerned about the political implications of giving the IRA money, unlike perhaps a southern businessman. I had no difficulty with that operation at all.'[13]

Armed and masked men entered Ballymany Stud on the evening of 9 February 1983. They broke into the home of head groom Jim Fitzpatrick and forced him at gunpoint down to the stables, from where Shergar was loaded into a waiting horsebox and taken away.

At first there was no indication who had taken the horse, but the gang left a loaded magazine behind them at the entrance to the stud. The magazine was traced to a rifle used by the Provisional IRA in south Armagh.

The kidnapping of Shergar brought more unwanted international attention to Ireland. The story acquired an element of black comedy; clairvoyants became involved and the wisecracking chief investigator, Superintendent Jim Murphy, who wore a trilby hat, nonchalantly informed the world's press he had no clue where Shergar had been taken.

The farming community, animal-welfare campaigners and the Irish equine industry regarded the abduction of Shergar as a disgrace. The Irish Farmers' Association (IFA) called on its 150,000 members to check all their sheds, fields and outhouses for the missing steed. 'There has been a terrific response from the farming community,' one IFA executive said at the time. 'We want every farmer in the Republic to be in a position to say tomorrow night that Shergar is not on his property.'[14]

The IRA demanded a ransom of IR£2 million using the codeword King Neptune, but after three days the coded phone calls stopped. The fate of Shergar remains the great unsolved mystery of Irish crime. Somebody, somewhere, knows what happened to him and where he is buried, but nobody has ever come forward.

O'Callaghan gave his version of what he thinks happened in a television documentary broadcast in 2004:

> The day I met Gerry Fitzgerald [the adjutant for PIRA southern command] he strongly suggested to me that the horse had been killed within hours of his kidnap. The horse had been completely demented after the kidnap. It had badly damaged its left leg in the horse box and they had to kill it very quickly. If Shergar was out of control, killing the horse might not have been that easy. The idea that it could be done with a single clinical shot to the head might not be the case at all.[15]

O'Callaghan alleged that Shergar was machine-gunned to death and buried in Aughnasheelin in Co. Leitrim, the home place of John Joe McGirl. If so, no trace of the animal has ever been found. When a BBC investigation team went there in 2018 to investigate, locals professed no knowledge of the horse and said that even if they did know Shergar's fate, they would not be inclined to share it.[16]

The practical difficulties of handling a thoroughbred stallion forced Mallon to revert to the riskier strategy of kidnapping human beings. His next plan would have calamitous repercussions for the Provisional IRA, however.

On 7 August 1983, seven men entered the Roundwood estate owned by Galen Weston, an Anglo-Canadian businessman married to the Irish fashion model Hilary Frayne. The Weston family owned Associated British Foods, and Galen's brother Garry was its chairman. Galen Weston had bought the 350-acre Roundwood estate in 1968 as his permanent home in Ireland.

The gang were dressed in boiler suits, balaclavas and gloves, and armed with a Gustav sub-machine gun, two Schmeisser sub-machine guns, two Armalite rifles and a Webley pistol. It was a formidable arsenal to bear against a man who was most likely to be unarmed.[17] These were some of the most effective IRA henchmen south of the border and there was much optimism for a successful operation. But they were walking into a trap; the plan had been revealed by a high-level informer.

Seán O'Callaghan claimed he was the one who tipped off gardaí about this imminent abduction. The informer had given his garda handlers the names of the IRA gang Mallon had put together for the Shergar kidnapping, and the same crew was planning this one. Special Branch officers informed Weston and his wife about the planned attack. As it turned out, the couple were not due to be in Ireland anyway. They were on holiday in Britain, where Weston spent some of his time playing polo with his friend, the heir to the throne, Prince Charles.

Special Branch officers had also tapped the phones of active members of the IRA Dublin Brigade. They picked up chatter that the IRA's target was having his or her gates painted. Garda surveillance on suspected targets revealed that the gates to Weston's property were being refurbished.[18]

When the gang arrived at Roundwood on a beautiful summer Sunday morning, they saw a car in the driveway and assumed the owner was at home. A blue Hi-ace van, the type commonly used by workmen, was also there. Two men kept watch as the other five drove on to the courtyard. Nothing looked suspicious, but the blue van had actually been hired by a Special Branch team who hid out all night at the location.

Detective Sergeant Nacie Rice, who would also be present at Derrada Wood, had been on many such operations, waiting and watching for events that might or might not happen.[19] Rice has confirmed gardaí were there because of a tip-off, but that it had not come from O'Callaghan. There was no guarantee the information they had received was correct, but when the alarm and the phone in the house went dead in the middle of the night, they knew a confrontation was at hand.

Five members of the gang entered the coach house yard and were within metres of a wall behind which Detective Sergeant Dermot Jennings was concealed. He was in imminent danger. 'Gardaí! Drop your guns,' Rice called out. Two of the gang shouted, 'Come out, ye bastards!' and started firing. They missed Rice but hit a wooden door, which splintered from the bullet impacts.

A blizzard of gunfire followed, but the Special Branch officers were in solid defensive positions. They had reconnoitred the premises in advance and occupied the best vantage points. Hundreds of rounds were expended in the fire fight, which gardaí reckoned lasted between seven and eight minutes.

Holidaymakers camped nearby were woken to the sound of the gun battle. One heard a man crying in pain, 'like a wolf howling'.[20] Four of the five IRA men were shot. One, Peter Gerard Lynch (thirty-three) from Derry, was wounded so badly that a garda whispered an Act of Contrition in his ear. He survived, as did the others. Rice believes the gang were lucky that the detectives had acted with restraint in the circumstances. 'Well when you think of it, there were three of them injured, none life threatening. They were probably better armed than we were. They were quite prepared to fire on us. I would say we were quite professional and restrained in our response to the incident. I wonder if it had happened in any other jurisdiction would the incident have been dealt with similarly.'

The five terrorists, Lynch, Gerry Fitzgerald – who later revealed the fate of Shergar to O'Callaghan – John Stewart, John Hunter and Nicky Kehoe, were given sentences of between ten and fourteen years at the Special Criminal Court in November 1983. The men shouted 'Up the Provos' as they were led away from the dock after sentencing, and Gerry Adams gave them a wave from the public gallery.[21]

It was another disaster in a year of disasters for the Provos in the Republic, following on from the arrest of nine activists, including three members of the Sinn Féin ard comhairle (national executive) at a house in Drumcondra in Dublin.[22] To compound the IRA's embarrassment, Weston's very public appearance with the Prince of Wales exposed some amateurish intelligence work in their planning.

Weston played down the kidnapping angle, saying he thought the gang was planning a robbery. 'The estate is run as a farm but there are some nice paintings and furniture in the house – I suppose they were after that,' he said, perhaps naively. In reality, the gang were after him and his millions.

Shergar and Weston had been two very public failures by the IRA, but it would not deter them from trying again. In the North they would have one notable success and that would provide the manpower for a third and even more dangerous operation south of the border.

In September 1983 thirty-eight Provisional IRA prisoners broke out of the maximum-security Long Kesh prison outside Belfast. It was the largest prison break in British and Irish history and the largest in post-war Europe. The H-Blocks, or the Maze, as it was more commonly known, were a prison within a detention camp within a British army barracks, designed to hold paramilitary prisoners from both communities, though in reality the large majority were republicans. It had 5.5-metre-high concrete walls, impervious to everything except an air strike, plus a series of three electronically operated steel gates, and a five-metre barbed-wire fence which encircled the 2,000-metre perimeter. Watchtowers were manned by army snipers. It was Europe's most impregnable fortress, or so the British believed.

The hunger strikes had been called off on 3 October 1981. Three days later James Prior, the then secretary of state for Northern Ireland, granted most of the republican prisoners' demands. The British government believed it had prevailed over the Maze prisoners and was prepared to be magnanimous in victory. The prisoners had other ideas.

The aftermath of the hunger strikes ought to have been a time of intense bitterness, yet a strange, improbable peace descended on the Maze. In early 1982 the IRA inmates decided to accept the prison regime. There would be no more dirty protests or hunger strikes. This was accepted with some relief by the prison officers, who loathed the IRA as much as the IRA loathed them. Between the ending of special category status in 1976, after which republican prisoners were treated as common criminals, and the beginning of the second hunger strike in March 1981, republican paramilitaries killed nineteen prison officers.

Suddenly the officers in Long Kesh were finding republican prisoners surprisingly amenable. Exemption from prison work had been one of the five demands of the hunger strikers, yet the republican inmates now agreed to work. Some of the most senior prisoners, those serving long sentences, became 'orderlies' – given menial jobs around the jail to occupy their time. Gerry Kelly, who was serving two life sentences for the Old Bailey bombing of 1973, and Brendan McFarlane were among them. Kelly would go on to become an MLA in the Stormont chamber, a junior minister and one of Sinn Féin's most senior politicians and peace negotiators.

Sunday was chosen for the escape plan because it was the quietest day in the Maze, with no visitors or activities. After lunch seven prisoners, six armed with pistols, entered the control room. The signal to overcome the prison guards was given by McFarlane, who shouted the word 'bumper' – prison slang for floor polish. The ringleaders also included Kelly and Tony McAllister. They quickly overpowered twenty-three officers in H7 and locked them in a room.

Kelly pointed a gun through the grilles of the command centre at prison officer John Adams, who had access to a panic button, an intercom, a radio and a telephone. 'Don't f**ing move, this is an IRA operation. If anybody phones here, you ask what the problem is. If anybody asks what the problem is you tell them it is being sorted,' Kelly told Adams. 'Your life depends on it.'[23] Despite the warning, Adams attempted to reach for a truncheon and was shot in the head.

The prisoners stripped the prison officers and donned their uniforms. The conveyance that they had planned would take them out of the prison was a food lorry which had a regular delivery schedule. When the lorry arrived as anticipated, the escaping prisoners held the driver, David McLoughlin, at gunpoint and told him to drive out of the prison at their command. Kelly lay in the footwell of the cab, concealed from view, with a gun pointed upwards at the driver.

All thirty-eight prisoners clambered into the back of the lorry. Everything went to plan until the third gate hove into view. The operation was twenty minutes late and they ran into a change of shift. Some of the prisoners rushed the tally lodge, where prison officers clocked in and out, and made as many as twenty-four men lie on the floor.

The prison officers decided to fight back and a mêlée ensued. The prisoners who had guns were reluctant to shoot, for fear of raising the alarm. Prisoners who did not have guns stabbed their captives with screwdrivers and chisels from the prison workshop.

The plan simply to drive out of the Maze with the prisoners in the back was thwarted by two parked cars in front of the main gate. They belonged to police officers. The lorry ground to a halt; prisoners jumped out of the rear and ran off in all different directions. One prison officer was shot in the leg as he gave chase.

The British prime minister, Margaret Thatcher, was furious about the escape. 'It is a very grave incident indeed, the most serious in our prison history,' she said during a visit to Canada. Republicans were jubilant. They had turned the defeat of the hunger strikes into a victory and embarrassed the British government on the international stage.

Yet the mass escape was not quite the unalloyed triumph it would later be presented as in republican mythology. The violence involved tarnished the tale of audacious derring-do. One prison officer, James Ferris, was stabbed three times and died of a heart attack at the scene. Three others were seriously injured after being stabbed. John Adams took years to recover.

Three prisoners did not even make it out of the main gate before being recaptured. Four men were found hiding in the

River Lagan, just half a mile from the prison, and appre-
hended. Three more were caught at a police checkpoint less
than twenty-four hours afterwards. Half of the prisoners
were recaptured within a few days of the escape. The other
half got away. Among them were future Derrada Wood suspects Brendan McFarlane, Tony McAllister, Gerard 'Blute'
McDonnell and Seamus McElwaine, who all escaped
together. They were among seven prisoners who hijacked
two cars and a van from a farmyard.[24]

McElwaine exhorted McFarlane to get rid of the cars as
they were sure to encounter roadblocks. They stopped at an
isolated house at Dromore, Co. Down, and held a terrified
couple and their three children hostage. Coincidentally, the
Protestant family involved were also named McFarlane. The
escapees made the family swear on a bible that they wouldn't
inform the RUC for seventy-two hours. They then left on
foot and, using a compass, followed the railway line south for
three days until they reached the republican stronghold of
south Armagh and a safe house.

McDonnell asked for a local republican to be summoned.
The local man arranged for three cars to bring the escapees
over the border. Soon they would be in the care of John Joe
McGirl and his network of safe houses. And soon enough
too, some of them would allegedly become de facto prison
officers themselves, guarding a hostage in the jail they had
built for him among the trees of Derrada Wood.

8. Ballinamore

The War of Independence came to Leitrim in January 1920. Nationally it had been a sporadic affair for the first year, but in early 1920 the IRA struck hard at British forces in Ireland. Richard Mulcahy, its chief of staff, believed the Irish public had to be 'led gently into war' and that public opinion would be critical to any successful campaign. The widespread burning of Royal Irish Constabulary (RIC) barracks was the first escalation, but many communities were still unprepared for the violence that would follow.

In Leitrim an ambush was set up at Edentenny, roughly a mile outside Ballinamore, on 16 January. A wall was built across the road and trees were toppled. Then shots were fired at a Constable Carbery outside the RIC barracks. Next, flares were sent up in an attempt to lure British army personnel from Mohill, ten miles away, to come to the rescue of the barracks in Ballinamore. The soldiers resisted the bait, and the planned ambush never happened.

This incident is described in a book by Fr Dan Gallogly, a noted local historian, published in 1991.[1] 'The reaction of the town's people was prompt and unequivocal,' he writes.

Gallogly reproduces a letter published by the *Roscommon Herald* on 29 January. It said:

We the undersigned responsible and law-abiding residents of Ballinamore and vicinity condemn in the most emphatic manner the organised conspiracy and attempt to murder the members of the police force on Sunday 16th Inst. From what has come to our knowledge we are convinced that this conspiracy was arranged over a wide area. Those who took part in felling trees, building walls and in any other manner assisting are all guilty of attempt to murder. We congratulate the members of the police force in repelling that attack and we are very pleased that no member of the police force was injured. We appreciate very much the action of the police in causing no unnecessary panic and doing no damage whatever to person or property. We respectfully request the clergy to strongly denounce the outrage.

(signed)

Joseph Cafferty, P. Nicholson, James Moran, James Mulligan and A. Kiernan Solicitors, Tom Darcy, John T. Healy, J. Mulvihall, A. McAllister, W. H. McAde, Charles Dolan MB, Patrick Kiernan, T. Conlan, John McAllister, Marian [illegible], G. G. Davison, W. B. [illegible], Thomas R. O'Beirnes, Francis McAvinia, Hugh McGlynn, Francis McHugh, James Flynn, Francis Creamer, Patrick O'Farrell, James Wynne, J. O'Brien, Edward Cafferty, [illegible], Michael McGrail, Philip McLoughlin, F. Youell CPS, Thomas Beirne, P. J. McFarland, J. Price, Wm. Ruthledge, Patrick McGovern, John [illegible], John Cox, Tom Roddy, [illegible], James Donnelly, Francis [illegible], Michael Creamer, Hugh Reynolds, Thomas Tiernan, Patrick O'Rourke, James Gallagher, John Reilly, Francis Green, Patrick Martin, Edward Delehide.[2]

The fifty-one signatories included 'virtually all of the businessmen' of Ballinamore. The letter, Gallogly continues,

was in effect a declaration of loyalty to the police by the town, as well as an intimation to the young men conducting the armed struggle that they were not prepared to go with them down the road of physical force. The armed struggle in the area was the work, mostly, of the sons and daughters of small farmers in the hinterland of the town and the people who were prepared to shelter them, especially in Aughnasheelin.

Over one hundred years later, the people of Ballinamore would say that nothing much has changed in this regard. Contrary to popular perception, the great majority have always been on the side of An Garda Síochána, the defence forces and the institutions of the state. They have never been radical or militant in their politics – in fact, quite the opposite. It was and it remains a heartland of rural conservatism, committed to community life, business, progress, farming, education, the Church and the local Gaelic football club, of which they are inordinately proud.

The proof is in the electoral record. Ballinamore had its own TD for most of the twentieth century, and that TD was a member of Cumann na nGaedheal/Fine Gael, historically Ireland's most conservative political party. One of its foundational principles was law and order, and the defence of the state and its institutions against subversion.

Two general elections were held in 1927. In the second, Patrick (Paddy) Reynolds, representing Cumann na nGaedheal, was elected to the Dáil for the constituency of Sligo-Leitrim.[3] His power base was Ballinamore. It was the beginning of a political dynasty that is still represented today on Leitrim County Council through his granddaughter, Ita Reynolds Flynn, who was elected cathaoirleach in June 2022.

Paddy Reynolds was originally from the townland of Gorvagh, roughly halfway between Mohill and Ballinamore.

He began his working life as a primary-school teacher. Mary Reynolds (née Smyth) grew up a few miles outside of Ballinamore. They were going out together when Mary decided to emigrate to America. Paddy left his teaching post and followed her. In New York they opened a bar in the teeming Bowery district: 'a sort of speakeasy', says Ita.[4]

The couple's first two children were born there. The bar did well and the family prospered. In the mid-1920s they moved back to Leitrim and bought a farm in Drumreilly parish, near Mary's birthplace. After an outbreak of TB in their dairy herd, they moved into Ballinamore, where they opened a pub, shop and hardware business on the corner of Main Street and St Brigid's Street. Paddy Reynolds's life was cut short in horrifying circumstances: during the general election campaign of 1932 he was killed by a constituent in Fenagh, a few miles from the town. Joseph Leddy, a former member of the RIC who had swopped sides during the War of Independence, shot the TD after a heated argument.

Leddy had apparently been canvassing for a rival candidate, and Reynolds felt he was owed a vote because Leddy had been awarded a Free State pension and the TD believed he'd helped him get it. Leddy insisted it was General Seán MacEoin from Longford who'd swung it for him. As Reynolds left his property with a bodyguard, Detective Garda Patrick McGeehan from Donegal, Leddy fired twice from a shotgun. Both men died at the scene. Paddy Reynolds left behind seven children.[5]

The timing of the shooting precipitated one of the most acute crises that the fragile democratic state had to contend with. Fianna Fáil won seventy-two seats – five short of a majority – in the February 1932 general election, supplanting, with the support of the Labour Party, the Cumann na nGaedheal government that had held power for ten years. The handover of power was delayed by three weeks to facilitate the by-election triggered by Reynolds's death. In this power vacuum Fianna Fáil feared that those army officers who had been loyal to the Cumann na nGaedheal government would stage a coup because they feared losing their commissions and pensions. According to the future taoiseach Seán Lemass, members of the outgoing cabinet were willing to go along with it, but the leader of the government, William T. Cosgrave, would not countenance it and democracy prevailed.

Mary Reynolds was nominated to replace her late husband and was duly elected to the Dáil. She lost out in the snap election of January 1933, but was re-elected in 1937 and would hold her seat thereafter in the general elections of 1938, 1943, 1944, 1948, 1951 (topping the poll), 1954 and 1957. She retired from public life with the dissolution of the 16th Dáil in the autumn of 1961. 'This tall, dignified woman dressed in sombre black would become the grand lady of Leitrim politics down to her retirement,' writes Gallogly.[6] 'She rode out some of Fine Gael's worst days electorally to hold onto her seat, increasing her vote steadily.'

One of her sons, Pat Joe, was eleven when his father was murdered. 'He never spoke about it,' recalls Pat Joe's son, Gerry, brother of Ita. Raised in the family business and steeped in politics from childhood, Pat Joe Reynolds was first elected to Leitrim County Council in 1942. He was the natural choice to succeed his mother in the general election of 1961. But Leitrim was a perennial pawn when it came to the redrawing of constituency boundaries, and by then the county had been carved up between Sligo and Roscommon, leaving him shorn of a tranche of his south Leitrim voters.

Pat Joe managed to win the seat in Roscommon-Leitrim, however, and retained it in 1965. He lost it in 1969 but regained it in 1973, and three years later was appointed a junior minister. In 1977 he lost his seat again, another Fine Gael casualty of the historic Fianna Fáil landslide. Reynolds was subsequently elected to the Seanad and served as its cathaoirleach for four years between 1983 and 1987.[7]

Gerry Reynolds in turn picked up the family baton, topping the poll in the 1985 local elections, entering the Seanad in 1987 and the Dáil in 1989. He lost his seat in 1992 and returned to the Seanad before being re-elected a TD in 1997. Five years later he was edged out in Sligo-Leitrim. When the county was carved up again ahead of the 2007 general election, Reynolds decided to pivot away from national politics and continue his service at local level. He remained on Leitrim County Council until 2014. Ita Reynolds Flynn was elected to the council in 2019.

Ballinamore has, therefore, been the home base for a dynasty that has represented the party of law and order for almost a century. The party that began as Cumann na nGaedheal and became Fine Gael was given a seat in Dáil Éireann by the people of Ballinamore, and further afield, in fifteen general elections between 1927 and 1997.

By contrast, John Joe McGirl, Sinn Féin's most high-profile figure in the region, also based in Ballinamore, was successful in just one general election. He topped the poll in Sligo-Leitrim in 1957 with 7,007 first preference votes; Mary Reynolds was second on 5,962. In 1961 McGirl's tally collapsed to 2,487, and he finished ninth out of ten candidates. It would be a further twenty-plus years before he'd contest another general election, polling 2,772 votes in February 1982, and 2,627 in 1987, his final campaign.[8]

The electoral record is a compelling illustration of the chasm between myth and reality: fifteen general elections won by a candidate from Ballinamore representing Fine Gael, versus one won by a candidate representing Sinn Féin. Its reputation as a 'Provo town', as the 'republican stronghold' of popular caricature, is entirely misleading. Time and time again, the people of the town came out in support of the state, the gardaí, and the family they were proud to return to Dáil Éireann for three generations. John Joe McGirl's political career in the town was dwarfed by the Reynolds dynasty. The people had spoken and their verdict was clear.

But the myth persisted and it would be consolidated by the tragedy at Derrada Wood.

One of the many reporters in Ballinamore covering the Tidey kidnapping was Eugene McGloin of the *Sunday Independent*. In his piece two days after the shootings, McGloin referred to the black flags that had been flown in the town in the summer of 1981 as one hunger striker after another died. 'One shopkeeper,' he reported, 'estimates that most of his business colleagues flew black flags to commemorate hunger strike deaths solely through fear. No black flags flew yesterday for the murdered members of the gardaí and army. Local fears don't end there either. Ballinamore is a haven of English tourists engaged in fishing holidays.'[9]

On 23 May 1981 a touring bus hired by a group of anglers from Sheffield was burnt out where it was parked in the town, by a local Sinn Féin/IRA agitator. It was presumed to be some sort of retaliation against English people after the first hunger strike deaths earlier that month. The arson had been committed while the town was sleeping, and gardaí could never get enough evidence to pin it on the main suspect.

Later that same day a new group of anglers from Sheffield, about thirty in all, landed by boat in Dun Laoghaire for their vacation.[10] Much to their surprise there was no bus to bring them to Leitrim: the transport company had pulled out following the news from Ballinamore earlier that morning. The touring party went back to England.

Bord Fáilte, now Fáilte Ireland, had spent a lot of money in previous years promoting angling tourism on behalf of lakeland counties such as Leitrim and Longford. The arson attack in Ballinamore set back every local business. A businessman speaking anonymously to McGloin said: 'That burning caused tourist cancellations, not just here, but in other counties as well. We were just getting back to normal.'

The economic consequences of terrorism were evidently viewed within militant republicanism as a superfluous consideration, but they loomed large for any community hoping to develop itself economically through business and employment. Leitrim had always been a vale of tears when it came to poverty and emigration, as Gallogly notes in *Sliabh an Iarainn Slopes*:

> The English officials who first came into contact with Leitrim in [the] late sixteenth and early seventeenth century all commented unfavourably on it. They spoke of 'the woods and fastness of Leitrim'. Sir Conyers Clifford, governor of Connaught in the 1590s, said it was 'the least valuable of all the counties in Ireland'. Another official commented that none but devils could live in such a hell. Only about a third of the land was inhabited; the rest was

mountain, lakes, bog and swamp with great belts of primeval forest and shrubbery.[11]

In 1841 its pre-famine population was 155,297. By the time of the 1971 census this had plummeted to 28,360. Therefore, when the Industrial Development Authority announced in 1972 that a new textiles factory would be opening in Ballinamore, the news was widely welcomed. But there was a caveat: the company was based in Northern Ireland and its shareholders were highly sensitive to political turbulence. They needed reassurance it would be spared a terrorist attack by the local IRA.

Gerry Reynolds recalls: 'I remember my father saying to me that to get them [the company] to agree to come, he had to get John Joe to come to a meeting and give them an undertaking that nothing would ever happen to the factory from a terrorist perspective.'[12] Which apparently McGirl did, although his potential to sabotage the local economy must have been unsettling.

Within a decade, McGirl and his acolytes would be driving ordinary English anglers away from the town and its environs.

Pat Joe Reynolds and John Joe McGirl were born just four months apart during the Irish War of Independence – Reynolds in November 1920, McGirl in March 1921, the most eventful month of the war in Leitrim when the Sheemore and Selton Hill ambushes took place. Their respective pubs were only a hundred yards apart on Ballinamore's Main Street but, in political terms, they were at opposite ends of the spectrum.

McGirl joined the IRA at the age of sixteen in 1937. In 1939 he was jailed for six months for a blatant act of intimidation in his home parish of Aughnasheelin. The parish council, led by Fr James O'Reilly, had banned IRA fundraising dances in the town hall. This was not unusual. The IRA had been a proscribed organization since 1936. Fr O'Reilly's actions incurred the wrath of local republicans, however. They resolved that if they could not use the hall, nobody else would either.

In April 1939 a concert was arranged in aid of church funds. Six republicans, including McGirl, felled trees on the way to the hall to block access to the public. A garda came along on his bicycle, but McGirl and another young man broke the spokes in his wheels with kicks, and pulled buttons from his tunic. He and the five others were arrested and given nine months in jail.[13] It would be the first of many prison terms on both sides of the border.

McGirl was in jail in 1957 when he topped the poll in the Sligo-Leitrim constituency. It was at the beginning of the IRA's border campaign and feelings were running high. He believed that the deaths of Seán South and Fergal O'Hanlon in that year's abortive raid on the RUC barracks at Brooke-borough had galvanized support in Sligo-Leitrim.[14] It was a sensational result but a one-off. McGirl was never a TD again.

In 1960 he was elected as a county councillor for the Balli-namore ward. The border campaign was proving to be increasingly unpopular and Sinn Féin's national vote declined from 65,640 in 1957 to 36,393 in the 1961 general election. McGirl lost his seat. His 2,487 first preferences were only about a third of what he'd received in 1957.

Shortly afterwards McGirl was involved in an incident for which he would earn nationwide notoriety. On 20 November 1961 he was stopped while driving his hearse on the old Sligo–Dublin road between Jamestown and Drumsna in

Co. Leitrim. Gardaí found twenty-nine rounds of .42 automatic ammunition and thirty-three rounds of .45 automatic ammunition in a tin box on the floor of the hearse.[15]

There was no coffin in the vehicle, but the bitter irony of having death-dealing bullets in a hearse was not lost on the judge. McGirl was sentenced to two years in jail for carrying ammunition without a licence and to four months' imprisonment for failing to give an account of his movements.

A defiant McGirl told the Special Criminal Court that the Offences Against the State Act was introduced to 'kill republicanism'. He added: 'This vicious act was designed to give coercion full power and to strip the victims – Irish republicans – of the most elementary human rights.'

McGirl lost his seat on Leitrim County Council in the 1967 local elections. He was a prisoner in the Maze in 1974 when he regained it on the first count with 737 votes (the quota was 672), another sympathy vote. He held the seat from then until his death in 1989, including a short spell as chairman.

After Bobby Sands died on hunger strike in 1981, a couple of local republicans visited every business in Ballinamore, requesting that the owners close on the day of his funeral and put up a black flag on their premises. Most proprietors would have been Reynolds voters or Fianna Fáil supporters, yet most reluctantly complied.

'Nearly everybody closed the first day,' recalls Gerry Reynolds, whose father was a senator at the time. 'He agonized over putting up the black flags and closing the shop. But he did.' Gerry was twenty; Ita was in secondary school. She remembers every shop in the town closing. 'You were afraid not to,' she says.

'There was intimidation,' Gerry agrees. 'Like, when my father gave in and put the flag up the first day and closed, that was not like him; that was very uncharacteristic of him. The tensions were so high, you know, that I'd say he gave into it against his better judgement. Because my father, with his father being shot and the whole intimidation thing, he usually faced that head-on.'

Gerry recalls that he was working behind the counter of the family hardware store after the second hunger striker died. 'A Sinn Féin activist came in and announced, "All shops are closing at three o'clock." Three to six or something like that. "And put up the black flags." So my father says, "Well I'm not closing anyway." ' Words were exchanged; the visitor issued a warning that if the shop didn't close, there would be trouble.

'So I was behind the counter,' remembers Reynolds, 'and I leaped out from behind the counter and I says to him, "I'll tell you what now, when you pay us the money you owe us, five hundred quid, you can come in and say whatever you like. Otherwise get to fuck out now and never come back."'

The Fine Gael/Labour coalition government of 1973–7 had clamped down hard on the escalating terrorist campaign in the Republic. Led by Liam Cosgrave, and with uncompromising figures such as Paddy Cooney and Conor Cruise O'Brien in the cabinet, it was viscerally disliked by the republican movement. As a government backbencher, Pat Joe Reynolds felt the collateral hostility.

It even trickled down to his son, then a boarder in Garbally College in Ballinasloe. A talented sportsman, Gerry Reynolds was a member of the Garbally rugby team that played in the 1976 Connacht Schools Junior Cup final. A few days before the game he was summoned to the president's office. 'There's two guards standing there [with] this letter saying that if Gerry Reynolds plays in this "foreign game" he'll be assassinated. Unsigned, obviously.'

The school authorities contacted his father. 'And he says, play away.' The final was in the Sportsground in Galway. The dressing rooms were three or four hundred metres away from the pitch. 'I was full back. And I walked down to the Junior Cup final with a guard each side of me and the team in front of me.' Pat Joe Reynolds attended the match, accompanied by Cooney, the minister for justice, in a gesture of solidarity.

When Pat Joe became a junior minister in 1976, he and his family were regularly targeted for intimidation. 'They picketed the bar every Saturday night or every second Saturday night,' recalls Ita. 'They'd arrive at seven or eight o'clock and they'd stay for two hours. And they'd have big posters and stand outside the house and say, "IRA all the way, fuck the Queen and the UDA." That was the chant.' Gerry: 'And, "British collaborator Reynolds out."'

In the family home across the road from the bar, Reynolds would hold a constituency clinic on Saturday evenings, which was also picketed. Ita got into the habit of staying with her cousins on Church Street on Saturday nights. 'I remember being terrified. I used to hate to see [the picketers], and they'd have the balaclavas and the whole lot. In the end I used to go up and stay in Auntie Nelly's. I couldn't cope with that at all.'

John Joe McGirl, they say, never showed his face at these pickets. But the pickets wouldn't have gone ahead without his say-so, Gerry believes. Instead it was more of a 'rent-a-crowd', usually numbering somewhere between twenty and thirty, including a small number of locals and some outsiders. They were far outnumbered by the crowds that would turn up in support of the family.

The Reynolds bar and lounge would be packed on Saturday nights. 'You couldn't get into it,' recalls Gerry. 'They came from all over, local people and staunch Fine Gael people from south Leitrim and west Cavan. And they got great satisfaction walking past [the picket].'

The family home faced onto the street. One night a brick was fired through the front window, with a note threatening that the house would be bombed the next time. On another occasion a firebomb was thrown at a storage shed behind their hardware premises further up St Brigid's Street.

'It was some sort of incendiary device,' he remembers. 'It was at night-time. Somebody must've seen it and the fire brigade was called. There was a bit of damage done but it didn't ignite, thank God.'

Walter P. Toolan was a solicitor of long standing in the town. He took over a practice in 1944 on High Street, just fifty yards or so up from the Reynoldses. His son, Brian, joined the practice in due course. The family firm has been run for many years now by Gabriel Toolan, younger brother of Brian. Gabriel acknowledges that, when it came to the IRA, many people in the town were afraid to put their heads above the parapet.

'It was a very dark time. The Troubles in the North and the spillover in the South blighted that whole era. The vicious and at times indiscriminate cycle of bombing atrocities and murders on all sides – in hindsight it can appear as if the perpetrators were seeking to outdo each other in depravity,' he says. 'So it's perhaps somewhat understandable that many people would not want to attract attention to themselves.

However, it's in such an atmosphere of fear that evil can freely prosper.'[16]

Walter P. Toolan had been obdurate when the pressure came on locally in the summer of 1981. 'At the time of the hunger strikes,' Gabriel remembers, 'the word was put out that all businesses were to fly black flags. My father did not. But in point of fact, he had a feeling of respect for the hunger strikers, the impossible position they had found themselves in. However, his feeling of respect was a personal consideration, and he did not take kindly to being directed to take any course of action which was not of his own volition and initiative.'

On many occasions Walter P. Toolan had offered support to Pat Joe Reynolds and his family. They went back a long way. As a junior minister, Reynolds had a state car and garda detective drivers. Its tyres were slashed and paintwork scraped a number of times. The family had to accept police protection. 'The guards used to come in and they'd stay nights,' says Ita. 'They used to say that [my father] was fearless. And my mother [Tess] was never afraid either. She kept it going [at home]. He'd be gone to Dublin, she was running the show in Ballinamore. She was great.'

Gerry agrees: 'She was tough as nails. There was no hiding place – she was in the bar, like, in a public place, and people used to come in and abuse her. But she didn't give in.'

For years she had allowed the Sinn Féin newspaper *An Phoblacht* to be sold in the bar every Saturday night. Many customers bought it out of civility to the local seller. 'At that time you'd pass no remarks,' says Ita. It had never been an issue until eventually the hostility became intolerable. 'My mother met [the seller] at the door one night and says to him, "Now, enough is enough. Never come back with that paper." And they stopped it. They never came back.' When Pat Joe lost his seat in the 1977 general election, Ita's reaction was one of relief. 'I remember to this day thanking God that he wasn't elected. Because I didn't want it [the intimidation] to continue. I thought it would stop, and it did stop after that.'

John Joe McGirl was watching his local GAA team, Aughnasheelin, play in the Leitrim junior final at Páirc Seán Mac Diarmada in Carrick-on-Shannon when the Maze jailbreak happened in September 1983. His team lost, but the news came through as the game was ending. He was jubilant, and he was ready: McGirl had assiduously built up a network of safe houses in south Leitrim.

Previous garda searches nationwide had revealed to the IRA which safe houses remained unknown to the authorities, and many of them were in Leitrim. Being poor, underpopulated and isolated were the conditions that drove many natives away; but it was those same conditions that attracted republican fugitives into this backwater.

'The whole of Leitrim was safe but especially south Leitrim with its woods and small fields. There was freedom in Leitrim,' one IRA veteran remembers.[17]

McGirl set about arranging safe houses for any Maze prisoners who made it across the border. He sourced support locally, and at one stage up to twelve escapees were living around the rural hinterland of Ballinamore. One woman offered to take in four. She was an aunt of Miréad Farrell, the IRA member who would be shot dead by the SAS in Gibraltar in 1988.

McFarlane, McElwaine, McDonnell and McAllister were among those who found refuge in the county. Gerry Kelly and Dermot Finucane, the brother of murdered solicitor Pat Finucane, were others. They were guided by members of the

South Armagh Brigade along the southern side of the border until they got to Ballinamore. They were then taken into McGirl's pub, where they were introduced to a 'well-dressed gentleman' who turned out to be the proprietor. He took them to a safe house in the surrounding hills.

The clock was now ticking on the conspiracy that would unfold some eight weeks later, and five miles away from Ballinamore. The town would soon become indelibly identified with crimes that had nothing to do with its people who, going back to 1920, had demonstrated their loyalty to the police, to democracy and to the rule of law.

9. The Man Before the Storm

Don Tidey began his working life at twenty-one, when he joined the Marks & Spencer management training programme in 1956. Nine years later, while working as a deputy manager in the chain's Hammersmith branch, he benefited from one of the many chance encounters in his life that would profoundly affect his future. It was common practice for M&S head-office buyers to be sent out to branches to observe what was happening on the shop floor. Tidey's was one of around eighty stores in London and the man from head office could have gone to any one of those; it happened to be his. After the visiting buyer had spent a week in Hammersmith, Tidey sat down with him for an informal coffee and chat. Had he found the front line of the business more demanding than expected, Tidey wondered. On the contrary, the head-office delegate replied, he knew what it was like to work at the coal face. He had gained experience while working in Ireland with an emerging chain called Dunnes Stores.

Co. Down-born Ben Dunne, who had started the business in 1944, had been approved by M&S to carry selected St Michael merchandise in his stores. M&S had one store on the island of Ireland, on Royal Avenue in Belfast, and it attracted many visitors from the Republic. M&S management saw there was an opportunity to sell its merchandise south of the border. Since Dunne was attempting to mirror the M&S formula, it made sense to sell its products through his shops. Tidey's visitor had at one time headed up a major buying department within Dunnes Stores. The buyer eventually returned to the UK to rejoin M&S, but Ben Dunne sometimes contacted him to ask if he could recommend any promising executives who might be willing to come to Ireland.

Some months later, the buyer contacted Tidey to say Dunne had been in touch again looking for recommendations. Was he interested? Tidey responded that he had not thought about it but asked for a telephone number for Ben Dunne anyway. The buyer told him that Dunne was best contacted at his Cork residence at weekends. Tidey thought about it some more and decided to make the call. He rang Ben Dunne one Sunday night at home. Out of that conversation came an invitation from Dunne to spend three days in Ireland looking at the business and getting to know each other. By the end of his stay, Tidey had decided to move to Ireland. He returned to London and resigned from M&S.

'I could see in Dunnes a growth opportunity where I could exercise all the skills that were required at that time in the organization.'[1]

So Tidey and his wife Janice, known as Jan, and their two young boys, Alistair and Andrew, moved to Dublin in 1965 to begin their new adventure. He knew very little about the country. That would soon change.

Don Tidey was born on 26 September 1935. His parents were full-time officers of the Salvation Army doing pastoral and administrative work in Hackney, east London, where he stayed until the Second World War broke out in September 1939. The Luftwaffe bombed the East End of London and the densely populated docklands area. In 1940 the British government set up Operation Pied Piper, a scheme to evacuate schoolchildren from urban areas.

Evacuation resulted in a lot of sadness and anxiety for millions of British children, but Tidey was fortunate to be placed with relatives forty miles south of London in rural Sussex where, with parental visitation, he was to remain until the end of the war. Burgess Hill, which is now a commuter town for London, was at the time a much smaller community. His new home was only ten miles from the English Channel. From there he could see the German planes coming in overhead to bomb London every night. School was regularly interrupted by lengthy spells in the town's air-raid shelters.

The Battle of Britain in 1940 was followed later that year by the Blitz, when the Luftwaffe attempted to break British resistance with a ferocious bombing campaign that lasted into the summer of 1941. The bombers were eventually replaced with unmanned V1 and V2 rockets in 1944 and 1945.

Tidey vividly remembers the fins of the V1s, which could be tracked in the sky en route to the capital. The missiles would often fall short in the surrounding countryside and be sought out by the local children. 'We went for souvenirs,' he recalls. The V2 rockets flew at a much higher altitude, but Tidey remembers planes flying so low he could see the German crews as they strafed the area.

Near the climax of the war, as the Allies prepared for Operation Overlord, the planned assault on occupied western Europe, Tidey saw the growing legions of British, American and Canadian troops pass by his front door on their way to what would be the D-Day invasion of the Normandy beaches in June 1944. The Americans played baseball on the carefully preserved cricket green. Many of the women in the local villages had not seen their menfolk for years and some would never see them again. The US and Canadian troops immediately caught the eye of many of them. Tidey noticed that the troops brought a product from North America that most English women had not seen before – nylon stockings – and which proved an instant fashion hit. It was an early lesson for the future retail executive.

He had a boy's wooden rifle and would stand to attention as convoys of tanks, artillery and troops made their way to the coast. He peeled potatoes for them and sampled their chewing gum – a rare treat for British children. As D-Day approached, the woods where children played were covered in camouflage to conceal the tanks and armoured vehicles being readied for the invasion.

The war ended a year later in 1945. No child who lived through it was unaffected and Tidey was no different.

After the war his family moved to Brighton. He passed the entrance exam to get into the highly regarded Brighton, Hove and Sussex Grammar School. It offered a wide range of sports at which Tidey excelled.

The school also had a Combined Cadet Force contingent, which stimulated a continued fascination with military life. The CCF had its roots in Victorian Britain, when public schools and universities were encouraged to set up volunteer corps that would serve as a pathway into the armed forces.

Tidey was an enthusiastic cadet and immersed himself throughout his teens in the military training and annual camps with the regular army, often with the Brigade of Guards regiments. 'I was more trained than the average soldier who was in the forces.'

At seventeen, as a sergeant in the CCF, he was selected to represent it at the coronation of Queen Elizabeth II in June 1953, standing guard on the Victoria Memorial outside

Buckingham Palace. 'I had a very privileged view of the comings and goings of the royal procession, looking along Pall Mall,' he says.

He turned eighteen later that year and was immediately called up to serve his compulsory two years' national service in the army. From there he went to the Mons Officer Cadet Academy in Aldershot and was commissioned as a second lieutenant in the Royal Army Service Corps (RASC) about a fortnight before his nineteenth birthday. Subsequently he was selected to attend the Army School of Physical Training in Aldershot and qualified as a regimental fitness instructor. He also qualified as an amateur boxing judge and referee.

He finished national service in 1956 and took up his position in Marks & Spencer. He followed up national service with nine years of service in the Territorial Army (the reserve). This required regular attendance during the year, and a two-week camp with the professional army.

He was also selected to attend the Royal Military College of Science in Wiltshire, where he completed a course in logistics. He had the opportunity to fly with the RAF on training flights. These flights involved dispatching field guns, smaller vehicles and other logistical items, all suspended on eight parachutes and dropped from the hold of a Blackburn Beverley freight aircraft by a crew of eight soldiers under his command.

In 1963, at the age of twenty-eight, he was promoted to the rank of captain in the Territorial Army, in 47 Infantry Brigade in Chelsea, west London and carried the title of BRASCO (Brigade Royal Army Service Corps Officer). He held that rank for two years before he went to Ireland in 1965, which was the end of his military obligations. But all of this training and experience and discipline in uniform would come back to help him survive his ordeal eighteen years later.

It was the old military and music hall song 'It's a Long Way to Tipperary' that first alerted the young Don Tidey to Ireland. He had searched for Tipperary on a map. 'My relatives had been in the trenches in the First World War with Irish soldiers, and I was aware of that,' he says. 'I found out about Tipperary long before I knew I was to come to Ireland. But I knew no more than most English people about Ireland.'

The family soon settled in. 'I managed to make friendships and was quickly assimilated into the social round. I have never been a big social man, but certainly visited the homes of Irish people, where we were well received and had a lovely time.'

Tidey recalls that Jan was particularly accomplished on the social scene. 'She was a west-of-England girl, and west-of-England people are very nice English people, and so it made my assimilation into Ireland much easier. She got on very well with the wives of the management of Dunnes and took naturally to Irish people. The Dunnes Stores staff gradually got accustomed to me as I made my way around the twenty-six counties beginning to effect change for the benefit of the company and the employees.'

In 1966 he was invited to join Ben Dunne Sr on one of his regular visits to America. Dunne was always warmly received by the directors of the leading retail groups in New York and it allowed Tidey to look closely at their operations and most recent innovations.

Tidey also travelled internationally with Ben's son Frank, who was the managing director of Dunnes Stores. 'We embarked on an extended journey into Canada, Scandinavia, France and Germany, noting the latest trends and developments in retailing, particularly out-of-town shopping complexes.'

In February 1966 he was invited by Dunne to visit a site on the perimeter of Dublin city. It was a field of four and a half acres with two factory-size sheds of 35,000 square feet each. Tidey looked quizzically at Dunne. The boss responded, 'I've bought it!' It was the site that would, by the end of that year, become the Cornelscourt Shopping Centre. Tidey would be responsible for this pioneering project for the southside suburbs, far removed from the traditional city-centre retail locations of the time. Suburban shopping centres, though common in North America, were only just emerging in Ireland and the UK.

'We immediately set about getting the buildings ready for occupation and converting the balance of the site into car parking and we had the great excitement of opening the completed complex in October 1966,' Tidey says. In opening when they did, they stole a march on the new Stillorgan Shopping Centre, which opened some weeks later.

He would spend three more years working alongside Dunne before another chance connection brought him into the orbit of the Weston business dynasty. The original patriarch was Garfield Weston, a Canadian who in the 1920s established a successful bakery chain and food-products business in his native country before embarking on an international expansion programme. A decade later he had exported his business model to Britain. In Northern Ireland he acquired a bakery company, with shops extending throughout the region, which traded as Stewarts during the war and into the 1960s, by which time it needed reinvestment and new management. Weston had a large family and two of his sons, Garry and Galen, were involved in the empire. Garry was the chairman of Associated British Foods (ABF), Stewarts' parent company. While Galen had been appointed chairman of Stewarts, he also had come south in the early 1960s and started a supermarket company in the Republic called Powers.

Garfield and Galen Weston owned properties in rural Ireland, including Galen's Roundwood estate in Co. Wicklow. As Tidey tells it, Garfield and Galen were passing Cornelscourt one busy Friday night in the summer of 1969 and found themselves stuck in traffic outside the shopping centre. 'And he [Garfield] said to Galen, "What's Ben doing there? I've been held up every time I come back to Ireland and pass by here." And Galen said, "Ah, he's brought a Marks & Spencer man over who's been organizing the company for the last four or five years and he was responsible for opening this with Ben." And Garfield turned round and said to Galen, "Why isn't he working for you?"'

A few days later Don and Jan Tidey were being hosted by Galen and his wife Hilary at Roundwood. Stewarts in the North required a strong manager to revitalize the operation and Weston decided that Don Tidey was the man he needed. Tidey needed to consider this carefully. Dunnes Stores was by then a successful company in the Republic of Ireland. The political and economic situation in Northern Ireland looked uncertain and threatening. Still, Tidey recognized a career opportunity and agreed to become the managing director of Stewarts Northern Ireland.

In his four years in Ireland Tidey had never been north of the border. His first trip was memorable and would provide him with an insight into what was to come. 'On the twelfth of July [1969] – a date that will resonate with Irish people – I was on the Enterprise [train] going up to Belfast,' he recalls. 'As we came into Belfast main station, I leaned out the window and I could see smoke coming from the west of the city.' He was met at the station by the retiring managing director of Stewarts. 'And I said, "Eh, bit noisy up here I can see?" And he said, "Yes, there's trouble in the west of the city today – it's the twelfth of July."' Stewarts' headquarters was in east Belfast near the shipyards.

A month later the Troubles began with the Battle of the Bogside in Derry and riots in Belfast. It could hardly have been a more difficult time for a stranger to Northern Ireland to begin trying to rejuvenate a flagging business. Undaunted, Tidey threw himself into the challenge. Soon enough, he began turning Stewarts towards profitability.

The Westons were impressed by Tidey's resourcefulness in such demanding circumstances and he was offered the managing directorship of Powers supermarkets in the Republic, alongside his work with Stewarts. His travel schedule was now relentless, constantly moving between stores in the Republic and across Northern Ireland.

In 1972 Galen Weston bought out the Quinnsworth chain of supermarkets from Leitrim businessman Pat Quinn, and the Power chain was rebranded under the Quinnsworth banner. 'I sat with Pat Quinn and Galen Weston and we decided to latch on to the formula of Quinnsworth, which Pat had built as the housewives' friend, but which wasn't making any money,' says Tidey. 'We subsequently acquired the Five Star retail chain and some of the better H. Williams stores. It was all action.'

Pat Quinn once told a newspaper that Tidey was the 'most dynamic executive in the supermarket business'. Tidey, in turn, describes Quinn as an 'immensely popular individual, outgoing with a charming personality, but he couldn't make money out of what he set out to do. He was very happy to sell to us.'

Quinnsworth had hired Des O'Meara Associates as its advertising agency. Tidey was impressed by Maurice Pratt, one of the agency's executives, and asked him to join the company to become the personification of the Quinnsworth brand and replace Pat Quinn in that role. During his time in America, Pat Quinn had observed how the Westons pioneered the concept of an agreeable front man becoming the public face of a business that needed promoting. Pratt was handsome and engaging and became a fixture on Irish television in the early 1980s with the slogan, 'That's real value!'

Tidey was constantly commuting between Belfast and Dublin during those years. The Troubles were at their height, yet Stewarts continued to invest in Northern Ireland. It acquired a food discount company, Crazy Prices, which eventually entered the Republic – a forerunner to the entry of German discounters Lidl and Aldi. In the first five years of the 1970s, when the violence was at its worst, Tidey opened superstores in Derriaghy outside Belfast, Glengormley, Bangor and Newtownards. 'Derriaghy was a terrific success despite being bombed in that period. We repaired it and carried on trading. We then followed it with similar combinations of Stewarts and Penneys in the other three places.'

Penneys, which was first established in Mary Street in Dublin, would go on to become one of ABF's most successful companies, trading under the name Primark elsewhere. Tidey was asked to join the board in its first formative year and take responsibility for store expansion until Penneys' managing director Arthur Ryan was able to assemble an experienced team of executives.

No matter how terrible the violence became in Northern Ireland, the mantra was to continue trading and continue expanding. 'We lost stores and we lost people continuously from paramilitary activity. I remember getting phone calls in the middle of the night to be told another property had just been bombed. I remember being called to the Oldpark Road at around 3 a.m., nearly killing myself driving past burnt-out buses crossing Belfast in the dark to get to the location. There I would find the army, the police and some of my staff all trying to sort out the situation with the neighbouring domestic properties, where the residents were looking at the considerable damage to their lovely homes. This was repeated in other locations.'

Around that time he was approached to become managing director of an emerging supermarket chain in the west of England, Ford and Lock. 'I had intended leaving Ireland to concentrate fully on that project, but Galen Weston persuaded me to stay on with responsibility for the Irish operations,' he says. 'But they allowed me to join Ford and Lock so I was at that time running companies in Northern Ireland, the Republic of Ireland and in the west of England.

'My wife had loyally been through four years of living in Belfast with all its trauma, and my three children were brought up in that sad and dangerous environment. As it happened, her widowed father was living in England so we moved to Exeter, where the headquarters of Ford and Lock were situated. It was all the same to me because each week I was travelling between our offices in England, Northern Ireland and the Republic.'

In 1979 Ford and Lock was bought out by a competitor, and the Tideys returned to Ireland. They bought a house in Woodtown at the foot of the Dublin Mountains. It was an exclusive development of ten homes below the well-known historical landmark, the Hellfire Club. It gave them the privacy and rural setting that the family sought in counterbalance to the hectic demands of Tidey's working life.

He tried to make space in his busy days for a brisk run in the nearby hills. When time allowed, he played squash and tennis at the Fitzwilliam Lawn Tennis Club and the Castle Golf Club in Rathfarnham. Having lived through the worst years of the Troubles in the North, Tidey and his family loved the serenity of their new home. They attached themselves to Whitechurch, the local Church of Ireland parish. Alistair and Andrew attended Campbell College in Belfast as boarders to complete their A levels while their daughter Susan went to Alexandra College, Milltown.

The family's enjoyment of their new home was to be tragically short lived, however. They were in Woodtown just ten months when Jan became seriously ill with leukaemia; she passed away in July 1980 at the age of thirty-eight. Tidey was now a widower with three children. His housekeeper and some of the directors' wives helped him manage his home life. 'We enjoyed nineteen years of happy marriage,' says Tidey. 'Above all, she had a quality about her which was above normal, while at the same time she knew how to have a good time with our Irish friends.

'I was away a lot, travelling not only in Ireland but by then to our interests in the Far East. I was particularly concerned for my daughter Susan, who was just ten. Jan had the ability to cope with a family situation and education and make a life for us when I had all of that on my agenda. She was a very accomplished person. When she died, it hurt.'

10. With the Life of a Man at Stake

On the morning of 24 November 1983, Don Tidey did not stick to his usual routine. Most days he would be up before 5.45 a.m., running with his dogs up to the Hellfire Club before returning to wake up his household and to take thirteen-year-old Susan to school. On this morning he got up later because he had been at a business dinner the night before and had not arrived home until midnight. He left the house at approximately 8.15 with nineteen-year-old Alistair driving in his car behind. They had driven no more than 200 metres past the gate when he noticed a garda coming towards the car. It occurred to Tidey that the garda, with his hat slightly askew and in a badly fitting coat, was unusually 'scruffy-looking'.

A little further away a mustard-coloured Ford Escort and a beige Ford Cortina, both with blue lights flashing, were parked at the T-junction where the road out of Woodtown Way joined Stocking Lane. Two more uniformed gardaí were standing alongside the cars. It seemed they had set up a checkpoint.

No sooner had Tidey assimilated the fleeting impression of a dishevelled garda than the man was standing at his driver's door. Tidey rolled down the window. The garda asked his name. When Tidey replied, the man pulled a handgun from inside his coat, pointed it at Tidey's head, and ordered him out of the car. Tidey would subsequently learn that other terrorists were concealed in the bushes on both sides of the road.

The kidnapper pulled Tidey out of his car. With a gun to his face, Tidey couldn't attempt to resist. His terrified daughter was screaming. Finally, he was dragged from the car by several kidnappers and hauled into the back of the Cortina. To ensure that he would not be visible, they shoved him violently into the gap between the front and rear seats and sat on him. They bruised his ribs badly, a pain that would remain with him through his forthcoming ordeal. The criminals also beat him on the back of his head with the butts of their weapons.

Susan was pulled from the car by another kidnapper, who threw her up against a fence before ordering her to lie on the ground, facing away from the cars. He handed custody duties over to an accomplice in a balaclava. Alistair was also ordered out of his car onto the road at gunpoint. He complied and emerged with his hands up; whereupon he was rifle-butted to the ground and kicked in the legs. One of the kidnap gang fired shots to complete the intimidation.

The car containing Tidey was driven away while his own car was also driven off by one of the hooded men. It was later found half a mile away with its tyres slashed. Two other cars drove away towards Tallaght. One of them later collided with a motorist on the Old Bawn Road. With the men gone, Susan and Alistair dashed to a nearby house from where phone calls were made to the gardaí.[1]

Tidey, meanwhile, had a hood placed over his head and was ordered not to speak. The excruciating pain combined with the shock had left him nauseous. With the car speeding along bad roads and virtually bouncing off the ground, he began to vomit violently. After a lengthy period of panicked driving – he could not recall exactly for how long – the car slowed to a halt. He was taken out. Wherever he was, it was quiet. His senses told him it was farmland; he'd been taken from an urban to a rural environment.

Soon he was shaking with the cold as a biting November wind cut through the fine business shirt he was wearing beneath his suit jacket. His kidnappers improvised some insulation by trying to wrap clumps of hay around him. Then the interrogation began.

They had found Tidey's diary/contacts book on his person. They demanded to know about some of the names in the book – who they were, where they lived. The kidnappers stood behind their hostage at all times. They removed his hood only to get him to read information in the book and explain it. They demanded to know which of the directors in his company would pay a ransom.

Tidey later recalled: 'I did not know what to expect at that stage. I was told that I had been kidnapped and that there would be a ransom demand made for me. To that end, they needed information, which subsequently they secured from my diary. It was at this point they told me in no uncertain terms that my life was in my own hands and that if I attempted to do anything hazardous they would have no hesitation in dealing with me if their operation was put in jeopardy.'[2]

The farmland episode may have taken place in rural Kildare. The kidnappers' cars were found abandoned in Maynooth later that day. The Escort was burnt out, the Cortina was left intact.

Tidey was transferred to a red Commer van. The gang had two other vehicles at their disposal, a yellow Mini and a brown Renault. The convoy headed off on what seemed to the hostage a cross-country journey. By now he was disorientated and losing track of time. His legs were chained, his hands manacled and a blindfold was strapped across his eyes.

Some hours later, the van stopped at another location. Tidey was taken out and pushed forward into a marching pace. Soon he found himself in fields. He was still blindfolded, hooded and handcuffed. He was pulled forward by a kidnapper who had a grip on the handcuffs. The terrain became hard going; the ground was rough and the pace slackened. He could see nothing and hear very little.

It was nightfall before they started on what turned out to be the final leg of the journey. Tidey was bundled into another vehicle. He later recalled a lot of high-speed driving around multiple bends during which he was tossed and turned by the motion. Finally, the vehicle slowed to a halt. Now Tidey was back in open terrain once more. The night was bitterly cold; he was soon trembling from exposure. He was force-marched across fields, stumbling over rough winter fields and feeling the groundwater seeping into his shoes.

Next he sensed he was surrounded by trees; the branches were in his face and pressing against his arms and torso as he was pushed forward. Eventually he was pulled to a halt. The gang had stopped marching. The first of what would be twenty-three days in captivity was over.

Word spread quickly among neighbours about the shocking crime that had just been perpetrated on the Tidey family. Revd Horace McKinley had just come from a school service and was planning to visit some of his parishioners in hospital. He remembers it as a cold day; he had returned home earlier to put on a heavier coat.

He was only just in the door when the phone rang with news that his friend and parishioner had been abducted. His shock was accentuated by bafflement. There had been a feeling that the Provisional IRA's failed kidnapping of Galen Weston in August might have deterred them from trying it again. The wholesale condemnation included criticism of the damage they were doing to the Irish economy by such actions.

McKinley said: 'I thought because of the Quinnsworth network, they surely wouldn't strike at someone who was a major employer. It was hitting people's jobs. I thought he [Tidey] was less vulnerable.'[3]

Revd McKinley was one of the first visitors to the Tidey home that morning. He sought to comfort the distressed siblings, Susan and Alistair. Andrew was making his way home from Belfast, where he was working for Stewarts. Soon after, gardaí arrived to take statements and begin the search that would become the talk of Ireland over the next three weeks.

A publicity drive was deemed essential in the hunt for victim and gang. The public needed to be alerted, in the hope that someone might spot the stolen cars or notice activity that looked suspicious. The dramatic events of the morning were reported on RTÉ's lunchtime news bulletins; the story was also splashed across the evening newspapers and the following morning's daily editions.

An early appeal for information attracted hundreds of phone calls. Rathfarnham garda station became the centre of operations. In the first day alone thousands of offers of help were received from the public. Roadblocks were set up around the country but there was no initial pattern to the search.

In the first week of Tidey's captivity, gardaí received neither public information nor private intelligence about the location of the gang. Revd McKinley visited Tidey's family every evening and agreed to speak to the media on their behalf. He quickly became a public figure in the ongoing story. 'I got a lot of calls late at night from crackpots. I got one who said he [Tidey] was on a trawler, another that he was down a lead mine. When events like this happen you realize there is a whole other underworld out there. I passed all of the information on to the guards.'

This wasn't just a crisis for the Tidey family. The pressure was being felt by Fine Gael and Labour Party ministers in the cabinet too. On 1 December the minister for education, Gemma Hussey, wrote in her diary:

> Garret [FitzGerald] told me he had spoken to Margaret Thatcher in the middle of the night while she was flying over India. He has spoken to her about the whole question of whether or not there was ransom money being paid in England for Don Tidey, who has been kidnapped, and about whom there is not one word of good news and we are all sick with worry.[4]

The assumption from the start was that it was another terrorist job by the Provisional IRA. But in that first week there was absolute radio silence from the captors – or so the family thought. The lack of information about their father agitated the nerves of his already distressed children, who were still grieving the loss of their mother and were now facing the very real prospect of being orphaned.

Seven days after his father was seized, Andrew, the eldest sibling, spoke to RTÉ News in a bid to keep the story in the public consciousness. 'We have now had to live for a week without my father and the strain has been quite terrible,' he said. 'The greatest worry is the silence. Every time the phone rings, your hopes are raised and then when it isn't the kidnappers, they are dashed.'

Susan Tidey was also interviewed. She was strikingly composed; she said her friends had helped her recover from the trauma of a week earlier. She then looked at the camera and directly addressed her father's captors: 'Let him go, please. Let him come home. We are fine and he doesn't have to worry about us, but we are worrying for him.'[5]

At this stage, neither the children nor the gardaí knew that someone in the criminal organization had in fact been in touch. On Sunday, 27 November, an IRA operative had telephoned the London offices of Associated British Foods and was put through to an executive. The caller, who had a Northern Ireland accent, was blunt in his terms: 'We want £5 million. Mr Tidey is a dead man if this reaches the police.'[6]

Garry Weston, chairman of ABF, decided to contact the Metropolitan Police, despite the warning. Weston also decided that Des McSherry, Quinnsworth's head of security and a former garda, should travel to Derry to liaise with various republican contacts who might have information about the kidnapping.

The phoned ransom demand was not conveyed by ABF to either the British or Irish governments but gardaí quickly found out about it anyway. ABF was sternly informed by official sources in Ireland that it was government policy never to pay a ransom. Three days later McSherry was prevented by police at Dublin airport from boarding a chartered flight for London. He was taken to Whitehall garda station, near the airport, and questioned for almost twelve hours. He had been under surveillance, as had many of the executives at Quinnsworth, out of concern that ABF might attempt a solo run and pay the ransom irrespective of garda or government policy.

Senior police officers were unhappy with ABF's manoeuvrings and leaked to newspapers the information about McSherry's questioning. It was a veiled reprimand to the parent company, a message to co-operate with the authorities in Dublin.[7]

The £5 million ransom demand was also made public by gardaí on 2 December, accompanied by an explicit warning that the payment of this sum 'cannot be countenanced', and that they would block any move by ABF to make it.[8]

After being briefed by senior gardaí, FitzGerald wrote urgently to Thatcher, complaining that ABF was preparing to make a ransom payment of between $1 million and $2 million into a Swiss bank account. 'It is vital to both our governments,' the taoiseach warned, 'that this money not be paid. Can you help in any way to ensure this?'[9]

Thatcher had long suspected that Irish governments were incompetent at best and ambivalent at worst when it came to dealing with PIRA terrorism. But any resentment she felt had to be parked, given the exigencies of the moment. The British prime minister replied to FitzGerald on 7 December: 'I need hardly say that I feel as strongly as you that it is vital that a ransom should not be paid in a kidnapping case. The apparent involvement of terrorists in this case adds to our resolve.'

She reiterated this stance in public via spokespeople. The Tory peer Lord Elton, an undersecretary at the Home Office, emphasized her position to the House of Lords. London was utterly opposed to paying ransoms to terrorist organizations, he stated. 'Should that question arise within this jurisdiction in the present instance, all concerned have been asked to respect this policy and to act only after consultation with appropriate authorities.'[10]

Michael Noonan, the minister for justice, acknowledged the emotional pressure on families and companies to pay the money for the sake of their loved ones. The natural instinct, he told the Dáil, was to pay the ransom to ensure the life of a kidnap victim. But this would only lead to a vicious cycle.

> The payment of a ransom would be likely to encourage others to resort to the same tactics. The level of money usually sought by way of ransom is such [that] the government could not acquiesce in the idea of it falling into the hands of paramilitary or other subversive groups. The probable cost in human life and human suffering does not need to be spelled out.[11]

Garry Weston was torn on the matter. Publicly he conceded that he would comply with the government's wishes, but privately he must have been torn. Just three months earlier he'd had to deal with the fright of the attempted abduction of his younger brother Galen; now he was facing the disappearance of his chief executive in Ireland and the accompanying extortion demands. Paying the money would solve this awful crisis.

Ten days after Tidey was snatched, Weston publicized his dilemma. 'With the life of a man at stake – one who is an admired and respected colleague – we stand ready to consider whatever is open to us to secure his safe release,' he said. This seemed to leave the door ajar for some sort of negotiation with the criminals. 'But,' he added, 'notwithstanding our personal activities and concern, we feel we are bound, as must always be the case, by the overriding policy of the governments concerned. I have been told that the security authorities of both British and Irish governments are doing all in their power to secure the outcome which we all so earnestly wish for.'[12]

On the weekend of 3–4 December Quinnsworth executives, using televisions mounted in their stores, released a video-taped appeal to their customers asking for any information that might help in the search.

A few days later, the newly elected Sinn Féin leader Gerry Adams was in Galway city to lead a commemoration for Liam Mellows, one of four anti-treaty leaders who had been executed without trial by the new Free State government during the Civil War. His visit to Galway came just a day after the IRA shot dead Edgar Graham, an elected Ulster Unionist Party assembly member and Queen's University Belfast law lecturer.

Adams was repeatedly challenged about that shooting, and about the kidnapping of Don Tidey. He resorted to the evasive semantics with which the Irish public would soon become all too familiar: 'I would not condone the kidnapping though I also would refuse to condemn it,' he said. 'I would hope he is released but I think it is a matter between his firm and the people, whoever they are, who have kidnapped him.'[13] Adams, who always denied being in the IRA but who in reality had been a member of its Army Council since 1977, presumably knew full well that 'the people' who had taken Tidey hostage were his own criminals.

Nightly prayers were offered for Tidey's safe return in Whitechurch. The congregation, which usually numbered between fifty and a hundred, lit candles and recited psalms. The Tidey siblings often attended and were surrounded by well-wishers. Dr Henry McAdoo, the Church of

Ireland Archbishop of Dublin, made a public appeal to the terrorists' humanity. 'You have everything to gain as human beings by setting free an innocent man,' he implored. 'I ask the kidnappers to have a change of heart. Let Mr Tidey go so he can return to his family. His children have suffered enough.'[14]

All of the publicity surrounding this emergency served to pile pressure on An Garda Síochána, the Department of Justice and the government as a whole. It was not just the life of an innocent man that was at stake. The ability of the state to defend itself against a fanatical internal enemy was now being called into question. How come terrorists were able so brazenly to challenge the security forces, and damage the country's business interests and its broader economy? And how come they were, so far, getting away with it? Where was Tidey – and could he be saved?

Nationally the feeling grew daily that the state was in a race against time to rescue the victim, and to prove it still had the capacity to maintain law and order. The pressure on the gardaí mounted with every passing day.

11. Closing in on Leitrim

The first lead in the investigation came with the discovery of a second burnt-out Ford Escort – this one red – in Celbridge three days after the kidnapping. Detectives were able to trace the car back to a garage in Tralee, Horan's, and to establish that it had been hired two days before the crime by Billy Kelly, a veteran subversive from Belfast who was periodically resident in Kerry and who had served lengthy periods in prison.

At his subsequent trial Kelly would claim that he had left his paramilitary past behind him, but on this occasion felt he had to comply with a demand from members of the IRA that he hire the car and leave it outside his house with the keys in the ignition. 'I'd be afraid for my wife and children and my own safety,' he stated.[1]

The car was driven away on the night of 23 November, but Kelly had made a critical mistake. When questioned by detectives, he could not explain why he hadn't reported it as stolen. The registration plates had been destroyed when the car was torched in Celbridge, but it was identified and traced by its engine and chassis numbers. Inside it were three partially charred garda uniforms which were traced to a raid on Fenit garda station in Kerry some seven months previously.

The reason the car had been burnt out before it could be used in the kidnapping, according to Seán O'Callaghan, was that it had been crashed en route. In his 1998 memoir *The Informer*, O'Callaghan claimed it was he who assembled the

Key locations before and after the Tidey kidnapping

Tralee, 22 November: Ford Escort is hired from Horan's garage for use in the kidnapping.

Celbridge, 23 November: The IRA gang switches cars to be used for the kidnapping.

Woodtown, 24 November: Kidnapping of Don Tidey near his Dublin home.

Maynooth, 24 November: The kidnappers abandon their cars near Maynooth, and Tidey is transferred to a van.

Ballinamore, mid-December: HQ for the largest manhunt in the history of the state.

Derrada Wood, 24 November – 16 December: Don Tidey is kept here for twenty-three days.

Ballycroy, 20 December: Three gardaí are tied up at a checkpoint by two members of the kidnap gang.

Claremorris, 21 December: Two of the Tidey kidnappers and an associate escape from a house.

team that would be involved in the kidnapping of Tidey.[2] Kevin Mallon had anticipated gardaí would search in Kerry for the hostage, O'Callaghan said, so he chose Leitrim as the end destination instead.

The crash of the red Ford Escort led to a switch of vehicles for the criminals. The changeover was spotted by an eyewitness who recognized a car at the scene as belonging to a prominent IRA man who lived locally and who was subsequently brought in for questioning. According to Superintendent John Courtney, one of the chief investigating officers, the IRA man cracked in the interviews and corroborated what O'Callaghan had been told by IRA colleagues: the kidnap gang had taken Don Tidey to Leitrim.[3]

Detectives also worked off the intelligence gleaned from the attempted kidnapping of Galen Weston the previous August. They knew that the IRA was resorting to abductions in order to raise money, and had set up a unit for this purpose. They believed the planning for the Weston and Tidey operations had been conducted in a house in south Dublin.

The investigation expanded into raids on the homes of well-known IRA sympathizers throughout the country. Coincidentally, gardaí were also hunting for one of the most notorious psychopaths unleashed by the violence in Northern Ireland, Dominic 'Mad Dog' McGlinchey. He was wanted on both sides of the border in connection with a series of atrocities.

McGlinchey had fallen out with the IRA after becoming chief of staff in 1982 of the rival Irish National Liberation Army. He was an early garda suspect in the Tidey kidnapping before it became clear that this was the work of the IRA.

For a brief, terrifying moment, the two groups overlapped.

On 2 December, a raid on the house of prominent Sinn Féin supporters John Hartnett and his wife in the east Cork town of Carrigtwohill brought Garda John Dennehy and Sergeant Tim Bowe face-to-face with the INLA leader. Moving through the house, Dennehy came to the bathroom. There he was confronted by a man with a machine gun and a woman also pointing a weapon at him and threatening to shoot him dead. It was Dominic McGlinchey and his wife Mary.

They ordered the gardaí down on the floor. Dennehy and Bowe were faced with what they believed was a life-or-death situation. They knew that McGlinchey was capable of murder; his wife's demeanour and verbal threats suggested she was similarly dangerous.[4]

Mrs Hartnett then intervened. Dennehy recounted the story in a 2005 documentary for TG4. 'When the lady of the house came on the scene and told Mrs McGlinchey, who had a gun over us at the time, that she didn't want to see any blood on her carpet, that eased it a small bit,' he said.[5] The two gardaí were bound and gagged and stripped of their uniforms. McGlinchey and his wife escaped. Hartnett, seventy-seven, was given a three-year suspended sentence in 1985 relating to the false imprisonment of gardaí at his house. The judge Liam Hamilton described him as an 'old fool' who should have known better than to harbour two people 'masquerading as republicans and nationalists' but who were nothing more than 'criminals and terrorists'.

Information that Tidey was being held in Leitrim came from another source too. Freddie Scappaticci from Belfast, the son of an Italian immigrant, had been interned in 1971; he rejoined the IRA on his release in 1974. Four years later he became a paid informer of the British security forces and one of their top sources of intelligence in Northern Ireland.

Scappaticci became the head of the IRA's internal security department, dubbed the 'Nutting Squad' because of the extreme violence it inflicted on suspects, up to and including murder. He was known as an egomaniac with an explosive temper. At the same time as he was beating, kneecapping and murdering suspected informers with impunity, he was supplying his handlers in the British army's Force Research Unit (FRU) with critical information about IRA operations.

The extraordinary revelation that Scappaticci was an informer only came to light in 2003, much to the horror of those within the IRA who had wondered for decades if there was a mole at the top of the organization. According to his handler, a man known by the pseudonym Martin Ingram, whose real name was Ian Hurst, Scappaticci supplied information to the FRU about the attempted Galen Weston kidnapping and the whereabouts of Don Tidey. That information was passed on to the RUC and then to the gardaí. Scappaticci died unmourned in April 2023, his sordid double life still the subject of much speculation and controversy.[6]

With all this intelligence pointing towards Leitrim, detectives in the Special Branch and the Security Task Force, along with uniformed gardaí, began combing a triangle of land in the north of the county, crossing into Sligo, Donegal and up to the Fermanagh border. They had the right county but the wrong location.

Surveillance was intensified on known subversives in the south Leitrim area. Three or four miles outside of Ballinamore, in the mountain parish of Aughnasheelin where John Joe McGirl had grown up and much of his extended family still resided, garda night-time surveillance teams picked up a lot of suspicious movements by known IRA activists.

According to an extended report broadcast in January 1984 on *Today Tonight*, RTÉ's flagship current affairs show, one of the surveillance teams spotted two known terrorists from Northern Ireland: the Maze escapees Brendan McFarlane and Gerard McDonnell.[7] They were seen running from a farmhouse. This was a significant breakthrough in terms of narrowing down the location of the kidnap gang within the county.

Inevitably, McGirl's movements in and out of Ballinamore were also being monitored. Garda sources and local speculation suggested that McGirl was seen buying tinned food and groceries, perhaps including cartons of North Connacht Farmers milk, in shops in the town. This was deemed to be unusual, both because of the quantities he was purchasing and because he was engaging in such domestic transactions at all. He was not, apparently, in the habit of doing the shopping.

When the security forces eventually descended on Ballinamore in the third week of the search, local rumour spread like wildfire that it was because McGirl had been seen loading up his car with groceries and driving away to the location that would soon become nationally known as Derrada Wood.

McGirl may also have been responsible for offering up the critical breakthrough. According to Security Task Force detectives who had access to the garda intelligence as it was being gathered day by day, McGirl had been in contact with a prominent republican over the border in Co. Fermanagh. In that third week McGirl, according to detectives, had made a phone call to this republican in which he discussed problems relating to the ongoing hostage situation, including logistics and support, and the mounting pressure from the security forces. But the callee's phone had been tapped by the RUC.[8] The call was recorded and analysed by RUC detectives, who then passed on this priceless intelligence to An Garda Síochána.

This tip-off may have been decisive in terms of identifying the location. Tidey was surely being held hostage somewhere in McGirl's hinterland beyond the town. This RUC intervention was kept under wraps by their southern counterparts. But in 2001 the journalist Liz Walsh published *The Final Beat*, a book about gardaí who had been killed in the line of duty during the Troubles, from Richard Fallon to Jerry McCabe and Gary Sheehan. In her chapter on Sheehan, Walsh writes:

> Officially, gardaí say it was good detective work, and not information supplied by an IRA informer, that led them to Derrada Wood. They also point to the fact that they had been monitoring, covertly and overtly, the movements of all known republicans and republican sympathizers in the area. But this author has learned that the RUC Special Branch in Belfast had also supplied information to the gardaí that Tidey was being held at Ballinamore. The RUC got the tip-off either directly from an IRA informer or through a communication interception, most likely a telephone tap.[9]

Gardaí were also monitoring the movements of a local woman who was married to a well-known republican. She was known to make hot dinners for men on the run. 'She didn't ask questions. Around that time, she was making more dinners than normal. Somebody would come and collect the dinners,' said one republican source. 'When the gardaí and army started to come around, local republicans felt it was either her or somebody linked with her that said something locally as to where they [the kidnappers and Tidey] were.'[10]

These and other tip-offs accumulated into a pool of intelligence that convinced the security forces to concentrate their search on the rural hinterland that had a long-standing reputation for active Sinn Féin/IRA support. More than two weeks after Don Tidey had been kidnapped, all roads led to Ballinamore and its environs.

The overall leader of the search operation was Chief Superintendent Jim (J. J.) McNally, head of the Cavan-Monaghan division and a forty-year veteran. His many years in border policing meant he had a reservoir of knowledge about the republican movement, its people, its methodologies and its crimes. He was contemptuous of those who had perpetrated atrocities, and of those who justified them.

With the Tidey kidnapping making daily headlines, and senior gardaí under intense pressure to resolve it, McNally was determined both to find the hostage and capture the kidnappers. But there was too much terrain to cover for one police force. The army would have to be drafted into the search in order to get more boots on the ground. It would become the largest joint operation between gardaí and military in the history of the Irish state.

Things were about to get busy in Ballinamore garda station. Sligo native Joe Feely had been transferred there in March of 1983, aged twenty-three. He had graduated from Templemore training college two years earlier. His first posting was to Carrickmacross, where he worked alongside Detective Garda Jim Sheehan, among others.

Feely recalls being in Ballinamore district court on the morning of Friday, 9 December, and returning to the station after what was a brief session. 'John O'Donnell, who was the sergeant at the time, said, "Lads, get your raincoats, ye have to go over on duty to Carrigallen." And that was the first of it. He didn't even specify what it was but I think we did come to the conclusion the Don Tidey thing was behind it.'[11]

Ten miles from Ballinamore, Carrigallen sits close to the Cavan and Longford borders. Feely was sent to a checkpoint on the Longford border. 'There was an emphasis on searching every car, searching [car] boots,' he says. 'That first night when we were relieved, a bus came from Dublin and dropped off lads at my checkpoint. We were on a country road, up at Moyne Cross I think it was, and it was pitch dark. And this guard down from Dublin, he was a real Dub, he wasn't used to this set-up, he was looking for street lights! I could see him when I was pulling away, he was terrified of having to stay there, even though there was army lads with him. It was a new experience for him to be stuck in the middle of the countryside, with no lights, no nothing around it.'

The following morning Feely and his colleagues were ordered back to Carrigallen community hall. To their surprise, they found the premises swarming with gardaí and soldiers. Their hunch was proved accurate in a briefing by a senior officer: they were indeed looking for Don Tidey.

Gardaí and soldiers would be split up into search parties, codenamed Rudolph 1 up to Rudolph 10. 'And each Rudolph consisted of a local guard, because they had local knowledge, maybe eight or nine more guards, a sergeant or an inspector, and an army patrol with maybe a corporal and eight or nine soldiers. That would be your search party,' says Feely.

'We were given a little map on an A4 sheet and we were to go out searching each day. We'd pick a point, we'd go into a field and we'd fan out and do a pretty thorough search. It was done seriously but it was all new to us, and it was quite enjoyable – for the first couple of days anyway. There was food brought out to us on site, sandwiches and tea. There was a real buzz around the town, helicopters, army units, and you felt you were the centre of attention.

'You'd be back watching television that night and it was all over the [news] so you felt you were in the middle of what was happening.'

In an interview for *Today Tonight*, which was broadcast the night before Tidey was found, Chief Superintendent McNally explained the practical challenges of covering the terrain in question. As far back as the 1960s, a report commissioned by the Fianna Fáil government had concluded that much of rural Leitrim was fit for nothing except forestry. The land wasn't good enough to support families on their small farms and the population trend was continuing to show the young generations leaving in their droves. New forests of pine were being planted on a regular basis.

McNally described it as 'mountainous country, more rough than usual. The woods aren't the old-type woods, it's all new wood that's overgrown.'[12] The sweep of land covered by the search teams included mountain and bog, ditch and drain, field and forest, nearly all of it done in rain, or with the threat of rain, and with the permanent presence of water underfoot. Every garda had his regulation wellingtons and a covering cape that was supposed to be waterproof.

Searching concluded each day at dusk, around 4 p.m. For the first couple of days, Feely recalls, the local garda in each party had to report back to the station in Cavan town, where a room had been commandeered to co-ordinate the search operation. 'The chief was there and they had a big map up on the wall, an Ordnance Survey map, and each search party had to outline where they had searched that day and whether they got it all completed. If they had, they were given a new area, and if they hadn't they had to finish off that area before they went to a new area.'

On this point, Feely is well aware that the Garda Síochána suffered a serious hit to its reputation after the whole saga was over. His recollection is that the search operation was methodical and thorough. 'I actually thought it was quite organized. Each area had a local [garda] who knew what to expect there. Like, were lads trained for searches like that? Maybe not, but the majority of them were young hardy bucks. The soldiers as well. Were they prepared for shots to be fired at them? Nobody was. But it wasn't badly organized.'

After the first few days in Cavan garda station, the headquarters of the operation was moved to the secondary school in Ballinamore, St Felim's College. Pupils and teachers were given early Christmas holidays to make way for the takeover by the security forces. The school's football field became a landing pad for helicopters. The local hotels, B&Bs and guesthouses were suddenly full of visitors, including reporters and photographers and film crews from the national newspapers and RTÉ.

Soldiers poured in from the army's Western Command. Five hundred men of the 58th Battalion, from Finner Camp in Donegal, arrived. A similar number came from the 6th Infantry Battalion based in Athlone. The roads to and from the town were clogged with jeeps and armoured personnel carriers. A 90mm anti-tank gun was driven down Main Street one day, looking like something from a war movie. A helicopter buzzed intermittently overhead. Armed soldiers were coming and going on the streets and in the shops. The overall impression was that of an army marching off to war against an unseen enemy.

And still all this manpower wasn't enough to cover the

great sweep of countryside that needed to be combed for dozens of miles in each direction of the town. So Garda Commissioner Larry Wren, in concert with his most senior officers, made the decision to augment the numbers from a new source of personnel: the garda training college in Templemore.

The class that had begun its training in September 1983 had ninety-eight recruits. They were midway through their twenty-two-week term. They were studying the law as it would pertain to their police work; they were being put through their paces in PE, and given swimming lessons and instruction in self-defence; they were drilled and marched on the square. But nothing could have prepared them for what was about to come.

12. 'If you get it wrong, you're dead'

Gary Sheehan was a member of the garda recruit class of September 1983. He was the third generation of his family to join the force, an unbroken record of service going back to the foundation of the state. Gary's grandfather Tom Sheehan, born in 1905, left the army in late 1923 to join the new state's police force, An Garda Síochána, and served until his retirement in 1968. By then his son, Jim, was over a decade in the force.

At twenty-three when he signed up, Gary was older than most of his fellow trainees.[1] On the morning of 13 December 1983 they were told to pack up and prepare to leave on two buses. They were billeted in two hotels in Cavan town, twenty-five miles from Ballinamore. Early the next morning they were taken to the town and allocated to the Rudolph search parties.

Sergeant Major (retired) P. J. Higgins, then a twenty-four-year-old corporal, remembers the two busloads of garda recruits landing in St Felim's Square that morning. Higgins had been on the search for a couple of days. From Moate, he was a neighbour of the Bradleys, the family into which his colleague Paddy Kelly had married. 'Jack Bradley was noted for the vegetables he used to rear,' says Higgins. 'He always won [at the annual show] because his carrots and parsnips were huge. Paddy used to help him grow them, and that's how I came in contact with Paddy first.'

When Higgins joined the army they became comrades as

well as friends. They were both based in Custume Barracks. He recalls being at home in bed in Moate on the previous Sunday night when the front door was hit with a loud, urgent knocking. It was an army colleague. Higgins was wanted for a company of soldiers that would be leaving Athlone in a couple of hours. The chap told him to bring enough warm clothes for seventy-two hours. They would be assembling on the square in Custume at 2 a.m.[2]

'We were all there at two,' recalls Higgins. 'We went to our stores, drew our weapons and formed up in the square. I think we left around four o'clock on the Monday morning. John McManus was the company sergeant and I was his company clerk, so we checked everybody off, loaded them up into the back of about ten of the old Bedford trucks and headed to Ballinamore. About two hours later we're on the town square.' A couple of days later, 'the two busloads of recruits from Templemore landed'.

For four days he combed the land in one of the Rudolph groups. Corporal Higgins carried a Gustav sub-machine gun, the soldiers carried FN rifles, the garda detectives Uzi sub-machine guns. Members of the Army Rangers, the special forces unit, carried Heckler & Koch sub-machine guns. Higgins remembers long days in miserable conditions. 'Woods, bogs, fields, rushes, streams, everything.'

The soldiers had no wet gear. 'When you went into a wood you came out soaked. You were always on your hunkers, you couldn't stand up because it was so dense, the branches of the trees were growing out so low at the bottom, so you had to kneel down. And if you hit a tree, all the raindrops came straight down on top of you.'

They were being assailed by water from the bottom up as well as the top down. 'Walking on top of bog, your foot would go down into this spongy ground and your feet'd be soaking. Within an hour of getting there you were soaking, that's the way you were for the day. You'd be sinking down into these drains. It was rough terrain all right.'

When darkness fell they'd be loaded up in the Bedfords and taken to Seán Connolly Barracks in Longford where they slept for the night. 'And when we got back to Longford, we had no change of clothes,' says Higgins. 'We had pot-bellied stoves with turf fires in them. We had to take our clothes off, dry them in front of the stoves, get up the next morning, get something to eat, be on the road for five, be in Ballinamore for six, the briefing started at half six or seven, and we were back in a search team at eight. And we were searching all the way through to four in the afternoon and then back up to Longford. You got your dinner at six, back over to your pot-bellied stove and try and dry out your socks and your clothes, and that was it.'

On the Thursday evening, 15 December, after four days on the trail, Higgins and colleagues were brought back to Athlone for a bit of rest and recuperation. He would not be involved on the Friday. 'And I'll never forget it: I met Paddy Kelly at the bottom of the new accommodation block [in Custume Barracks] and I said to him, "What are you doing here?" This was about eight o'clock at night. "Oh," he said – he never called me by my rank, it was Gossoon – he said, "Gossoon, I'm going up to Ballinamore. What do I need?"

'Well, I said, "Paddy, take my advice, leave the army boots at home and bring a pair of top boots. Wellingtons." And he said, "Gossoon, sure I won't be needing wellingtons, won't I be driving?"

'So Paddy didn't actually think he was going to be searching. We spoke for a few minutes and he asked me where I was going and I said, "I'm going home to get a hot shower and a hot meal and chill out."'

Detective Garda (retired) Eugene O'Sullivan had been on the Tidey case from day one. From Ballinskelligs, south Kerry, he had joined An Garda Síochána in 1977, aged twenty-three. Having worked in England for a couple of years, he remembers the day he entered Templemore because it involved a flight from London to Dublin and a rail journey to Tipperary.

But he remembers the day for another reason. 'I was getting a taxi from Busáras to Heuston station and I passed the scene of a Provisional IRA murder, in Timmons's pub on the quays. It was the seventh of September, a man called John Lawlor was executed by a man called Jimmy Gavin. There was an internal row [within] the Provisional IRA at the time. So that always left a mark on me.'[3] In 1980 he joined the Security Task Force, the recently established detective unit that was designed to be mobile, proactive and quick to respond.

A few years later the STF would morph into the Emergency Response Unit. At the time, he explains, its job was 'ultimately, the security of the state'. Criminal networks with money and manpower, be they in narcotics or terrorism, were deemed too dangerous to be left to routine policing; the STF was created to target them.

Operating out of Dublin Castle and with about fifty or sixty officers, it would respond to the intelligence coming in from garda patrols and surveillance, and mobilize with rapid response actions. It could have members in any part of the country at any given time. It always had a unit on the border, moving anywhere along it from Dundalk to the top of Donegal.

'It was quite effective in that we were out there, we knew who we were dealing with, we were stopping them, we were searching them, we were just making it difficult for them,' O'Sullivan says.

On the day of the kidnapping, O'Sullivan was parading for duty in Dublin Castle. 'Suddenly the radios crackled with [news of] activities in south Co. Dublin. There had been an abduction and there was a scramble to get into cars and get going.'

It was too late; the kidnappers had made good use of their head start. 'We did get out around the city but I suppose we were behind the curve in that they had switched cars,' O'Sullivan says. 'I know that one of the cars was switched at Connolly's Folly near Celbridge. That was one of the staging points. We think that when they switched cars they went directly from Connolly's Folly to Derrada, [although] there's no evidence to back that up.'

The STF went checking on 'the local Provisional suspects' in the south of the city. 'Were they at home, were their cars missing, that type of thing would kick in. Obviously the [kidnap] operation had been well planned but every operation leaves traces. It can be somebody's presence, or absence. It can be a car missing, a car going in a particular direction, the clothes somebody is wearing, any of those things.'

John Joe McGirl was one such suspect. He had been on the STF's radar for a long time. 'I actually stopped him on the road [previously] with one of my colleagues, and he was quite a belligerent little man,' says O'Sullivan. 'I think he regarded us basically with the same contempt he would have had for the security forces across the [border].'

Detectives were familiar with his car, as they were with most of the cars being driven by known subversives. They would habitually memorize the make, the colour and number plate. This meant O'Sullivan and his colleague recognized the vehicle approaching them on the Dublin to Leitrim road that day. 'McGirl had on him little messages written on cigarette papers. They were smuggled out of prison, so we confiscated those. They would have been messages from prisoners in Portlaoise to families outside.'

The hunt for Tidey brought several STF members from Dublin to the border region. They were conducting searches and surveillance, targeting the usual array of sympathizers and suspects. 'Going to their houses, setting up checkpoints, gathering intelligence, just basically making life awkward for their movements,' says O'Sullivan. 'But suddenly all the emphasis switched to Ballinamore. The latest information was that [Tidey] was in the Ballinamore area, without being specific.'

With so many security personnel from so many different sources in the Leitrim town, problems arose that would be analysed at length in the debate afterwards about what went wrong and why. But it didn't need the benefit of hindsight to spot them. 'To me, there appeared to be no proper chain of command,' says O'Sullivan. 'You had a mixture of army, uniformed guards, Task Force detectives, local detectives, and then the recruits from Templemore. There seemed to be a mish-mash, [people] divided up into different groups, different call signs.'

On top of that, communications technology was not nearly as sophisticated as it would later become. 'Radios were not as functional as they are now. The topography of the area I don't think lent itself to good radio communications. And it happened at the worst possible time, weather-wise.'

On Friday morning, McGirl was arrested under Section 30 of the Offences Against the State Act and held for forty-eight hours. Three other republican activists were also rounded up: McGirl's son-in-law Martin Donnelly, from Tyrone; Denis Downing, also from Tyrone; and Patrick Rehill from Cavan.

In 1974 Donnelly had been sentenced to five years in Long Kesh for possession of explosives. He moved south of the border after his release and married McGirl's daughter, Áine. Downing had spent time in Portlaoise prison after a timing device was found on his property in Ballinamore. Rehill, working with McGirl, was one of the main republican organizers in south Leitrim.[4]

By Friday afternoon the Rudolph 5 search party was making slow progress through the tangled undergrowth of another wood on another upland that had yet to be ticked off the Ordnance Survey map. And then, in a small clearing between trees, recruit garda Tom Barrett spotted something: a dome-shaped black polythene tent. Frozen to the spot, he then saw a man holding a long gun and another man kneeling, also holding a gun. The moment had come; the violence was imminent; the tragedy of Derrada Wood was about to unfold.

In Connolly Barracks, some thirty-five miles away, the army signals section would have been listening to the radio traffic among troops on the ground around Ballinamore. The radio operators in the barracks would therefore have heard almost immediately that there had been bursts of gunfire at Derrada. Lieutenant Colonel (retired) Kieran Dalton was a twenty-seven-year-old army captain based in Longford at the time. Originally from Mallow, Co. Cork, Dalton had joined

Óglaigh na hÉireann in 1975. On that Friday, Captain Dalton was in the barracks when word came through over the radio that there were casualties.

Initially, however, the gravity of the situation was not known beyond the immediate vicinity of the shooting. 'As the evening progressed, the information began to emerge that this was much more serious than first anticipated,' Dalton recalled in December 2022.[5]

Then confirmation came through that there had been fatalities and that one of them was a soldier based in Custume Barracks. A priority for army command in Athlone was to inform Paddy Kelly's wife, once the casualty was verified. 'But then, of course, it emerged that Private Kelly's father and mother were living in Ballinamuck in Longford, so we got the call here to say, "Look, there's an urgency to get a message to his parents because he is going to be named on the nine o'clock news." That sticks in my brain: the nine o'clock news.'

Learning how to deliver the news of a death to a family was part of an officer's training. 'The protocol is that an officer should do it if the deceased was killed on duty. Is it something you can learn? You might learn it only by doing it.' Dalton was summoned to the office of the second in command at Connolly Barracks and given the home address of Michael and Mary Kelly. Ballinamuck in north Longford borders Leitrim and Cavan. It is a twenty-minute drive from Longford town. Dalton, in full uniform, was taken by a driver to the location. 'When we arrived I dispatched the driver for the priest in Ballinamuck. I knocked on the door, came in, and my recollection is that it was quite a dark room, because it was a winter's night, and the couple were at the table. An elderly couple, I would say, humble people. I sat down and I hit them with this bombshell.'

It was rare for the family of an Irish soldier to receive such terrible news. Dalton recalls: 'There was a certain question in the exchange as to whether I had the wrong information because they had a son [Jim] in UNIFIL [in Lebanon] at the time. Another recollection is that there may have been no [need to worry] about the nine o'clock news after all because I remember not seeing a television in the room. So not only was I bringing them this terrible news, I would say it was the first time they even realized what had unfolded a few miles up the road.'

Shortly afterwards the priest arrived and Dalton departed. He went on to have a long military career, serving at home and abroad before retiring in 2014. But that visit to Ballinamuck on 16 December 1983 has stayed with him. 'Let me put it this way: I haven't forgotten it.'

Sergeant Major Higgins has never forgotten those days either. On the evening of the fifteenth he had no idea that his conversation with Paddy Kelly in Custume Barracks would be their last. He went home to Moate that night and enjoyed a hot shower and a hot meal. The next afternoon he was relaxing at home when the phone rang; it was someone in the barracks; he was wanted back in; there had been a fatality in the search for Tidey; reinforcements were needed to go back to Ballinamore.

They travelled from Athlone to Longford and stayed in Connolly Barracks that night in preparation for another day of searching on the Saturday. At this stage he didn't know the identity of the dead soldier; it wasn't until Saturday morning that he was told it was his great friend and colleague.

Almost forty years later, the emotion of that moment still catches him. 'It's an awful feeling,' he says, struggling for words. 'To lose a soldier, in that scenario, and even the guys in the Leb, you can't describe what it does to you. It absolutely tears your whole being apart.'

Joe Feely cannot remember for sure if it was the Thursday or Friday morning, but on one of those days he was instructed to guide a bus driver who didn't know the area down towards Derrada. The bus was full of garda recruits. 'I was told to drop them lads off at some checkpoint or whatever. I got on the bus, I was last on, and who was I beside? Only Gary Sheehan.' In his first posting in Carrickmacross Feely had become friendly with the Sheehan family, Gary included. 'We got chatting for a few minutes. "How're you doing? Long time no see," it was as simple as that.'[6]

When word came through of the identity of the slain recruit, it stunned Feely and all those involved in the search. It stunned everyone. The shock rippled outwards from Gary Sheehan's family to his friends, his colleagues in Templemore, the people of Carrickmacross and Monaghan, the whole of the police force, the entire nation.

Sheehan's death sparked a charged debate about the rights and wrongs of deploying trainees in the search. But at the time, says Higgins, there was no real concern that the exercise would result in violence, and especially not in the murder of gardaí or soldiers.

'Nobody told us that it could be a do-or-die situation,' he recalls. 'It was a routine search of land and woods. OK, we were told that if we came across somebody they were likely to be armed. But, even if they were armed, we didn't expect them to kill a soldier or guard.

'Like, we never thought for one single second, not one of us, that the IRA would kill an Irish soldier. We were naive, we were trusting. That was probably a rude awakening for the

Irish defence forces. And that naivety changed after Ballinamore. Everything changed – the line of thought, the
training, the preparation and planning – forever more.'

Eugene O'Sullivan believes the gardaí were also a bit naive,
given the mounting evidence of the dangers they faced, such
as the terrorist murders of Detective Garda John Morley and
Garda Henry Byrne in Roscommon in July 1980. The garda
mindset might have been outdated, not in terms of the dangers posed by armed fanatics – 'we were under no illusions
about that' – but in terms of being reluctant to meet fire with
fire.

The vast majority of gardaí were unarmed and in general
the force's culture was non-confrontational, in keeping with
a fifty-year tradition of conciliatory, community policing.
Violent death among the civilian population was rare; murder
was so aberrant as to be virtually inconceivable. But terrorism and the Troubles had changed that culture of profound
respect for the sanctity of human life.

To this day, the retired detective still struggles to understand how anyone can decide to end another person's life.
'No guard that I know ever wanted to go out and shoot anybody or kill anybody. It's just not in our nature. And it
probably has cost us over the years. It probably cost John
Morley and Henry Byrne.' How so? 'In that they hesitated. I
mean, I hesitated in Derrada. I had the advantage and I lost
it. Or we had the advantage and we lost it because the shout
went out on the radio, "Don't shoot at the blue car, a guard
has been taken hostage." [Then] a blue car comes round the
corner and we hesitate.

'If we opened fire we probably would've nailed that gang.
But we didn't. And a man jumps out with an Armalite and
just sprays us with gunfire.'

Naturally, any police force has to abide by the rules of a civilized society. 'It's the way it has to be,' O'Sullivan agrees. 'There have to be rules and regulations for police officers. But, of course, the advantage that people [have] who examine these situations afterwards is that they can sit down in perfect conditions and analyse it blow by blow, whereas [when] you're out there, you have to make a split – a less than split-second decision.

'If you get it wrong, you're dead. You get it right, you could still be dead. But that's the way it is. I think we all accept that.'

Kieran Dalton believes that, from an operational point of view, the rescue of Don Tidey was 'a remarkable achievement'. Given the amount of terrain that had to be covered, and the nature of that terrain, he considers that even finding Tidey was an exceptional feat.

'You could be in a field and you would not know what's in the field next door because of the ditches, the overgrowth, the closeness of the ground. It's not like other parts of the country where you have swathes of meadow and cornfields and ploughed fields. This is close country. [Finding Tidey in] that overgrowth, in deepest winter, it was a remarkable achievement.'

The nature of the terrain the search teams had to cover was one thing; the scale of it was another. 'My understanding is that whatever information the guards were working with wasn't specific,' says Dalton. 'This had been ongoing for five days and they had been crossing all that territory and so, to hit on the right location in Leitrim, in the entirety of Leitrim, was in my view remarkable.

'The other thing I think is important is the weather and time of day – a very overcast, wet, cloudy day. They've been searching all morning, and they hit this point at that time. That's why I think there were a number of factors that made it quite remarkable they came across this hide.

'The objective of the search was to find the hostage and they did that, although it was achieved at enormous cost.'

The Sheehan and Kelly families bore that cost and have been bearing it for forty years. The passage of time, says P. J. Higgins, has eased the pain for him personally, but Paddy Kelly is still vivid in his memory. He wants him honoured and remembered for the soldier and the man he was.

'I would describe him as the best friend anyone could ever have. If you were stuck or you were in need, Paddy Kelly was the man for you. He was old fashioned, a country guy, and had a heart of gold.'

One memory sticks out from an overseas tour of duty. 'I was in the Leb with Paddy Kelly in 1980/81. We were in a place just outside Tibnin. And I remember, Paddy used to always say to me, "Listen, Gossoon, calm down. Calm down there now!"

'He was the man who mentored me. When I joined the army first, a young cocky guy from Moate, he used to say to me, "Now, Gossoon, you just polish the boots and shave and wash yourself and keep yourself clean and we'll get through this." That's what he used to say: "Look after your boots now, young Higgins. Keep yourself shaved and look after your boots."'

PART TWO
A Common Enemy?

13. Harrods

In the garda station in Cavan town on Friday evening, Don Tidey phoned home. It was the call his children had been waiting on for twenty-three days. He had an emotional conversation with Susan in particular. After a shower and a change of clothes, and a debrief with senior gardaí, the travelling party set off for Dublin, a two-hour drive. Eugene O'Sullivan was at the wheel; Tidey was flanked in the back seat by Detective Superintendent Bill Somers and Detective Sergeant Tom Conroy. Trailing the garda car was an RTÉ crew with its precious film footage of the events of that day. They were under pressure to make the nine o'clock news. On the outskirts of Dublin, somewhere around Blanchardstown, the tape was handed over to a motorcycle courier to fast-track it to Montrose.

When they reached the gates of his home in Woodtown, Tidey in the back seat kept his head down to avoid the waiting journalists and photographers standing outside in the pouring rain. It was only when Garret FitzGerald and Michael Noonan later swept past them in state cars that the press pack realized Tidey was already home.

That evening the IRA issued a statement with its usual disclaimer when operations went wrong: the ultimate responsibility for the deaths of Private Kelly and Recruit Garda Sheehan lay with Britain and her partition of Ireland. 'Free

9. The iconic image of Don Tidey at Ballyconnell garda station following his rescue, escorted by detectives Eugene O'Sullivan, Tom Conroy and Bill Somers.

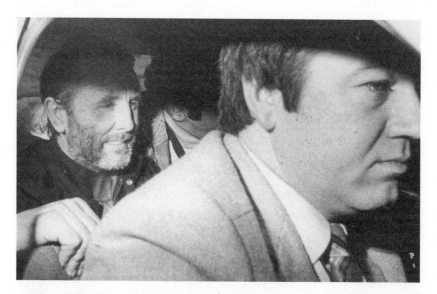

10. Don Tidey in the back of a garda car, about to be taken home after his long ordeal.

11. On the day after his release, accompanied by his three children Andrew (left), Susan and Alistair, Don Tidey gave a short press conference outside his Dublin home.

State governments' were an accessory to partition by refusing to pressurize the British to leave Northern Ireland.[1] Therefore, they too were responsible.

The statement admitted the abduction of Tidey but denied the IRA had intended to target the Republic's security forces. It begrudgingly recognized that the killing of Irish security personnel was a public relations disaster and therefore the 'British government will now rub its hands and watch with glee as the Free State government reacts to us'.

Gerry Adams added to the sense of national outrage by saying the IRA gang who murdered Kelly and Sheehan were 'doing their duty'. Adams was careful, though, to add that the killings were an 'isolated incident . . . and not an attempt to overthrow the Dublin government'.[2] He then planted a malevolent rumour that was perpetuated for decades afterwards by Sinn Féin/IRA supporters: Adams said that Sheehan and Kelly may have been killed by 'friendly fire'.

Garda and army eyewitnesses at the scene that day knew this was untrue. Ballistics evidence is now able to prove it definitively. 'Friendly fire' was only possible if there had been a shoot-out in the woods. There was no shoot-out. Neither gardaí nor the army fired a shot during the fatal incident.

Moreover, Adams's suggestion was directly contradicted by the IRA's own statement, which expressly admitted that its members opened fire on gardaí and army. 'In the fatal shoot-out they were acting in defence of their lives and had in their minds the [Security] Task Force's attempted massacre of IRA volunteers at Roundwood [during the failed Weston kidnapping] and the killing of Eamon Byrne in Dublin,' they said. 'The situation and atmosphere had been hyped up by massive searches and dragnets and by the Dublin government's encouragement to Mr Tidey's company who refused to pay. The fatal shootings were clearly distinct from, say, a premeditated ambush on the Task Force or Free State army which would be an attack on the institutions of the state. We regret the deaths and injuries.'[3]

In an interview with *An Phoblacht* in early January an unnamed IRA spokesman claimed it had been the Irish army that fired first and 'our volunteers responded in defence of their lives'. Again, this was false.

The IRA amplified the alternative narrative by bizarrely suggesting that Tidey was beaten up and then trailed about the media by members of the Security Task Force.[4] Sinn Féin's newspaper also carried an admission from the IRA that the purpose of the Tidey kidnapping was to raise money and was justified because a 'large injection of funds to escalate the armed struggle will shorten the duration of the British presence in Ireland'.

Negotiations had gone on between Associated British Foods and the IRA, but these were thwarted by Thatcher and FitzGerald. It was therefore the fault of the Irish and British governments that a garda and a soldier had been killed. This self-exculpating logic was augmented by a claim that Tidey had been targeted because he was part of the establishment, and the proof of this was the taoiseach visiting his home. 'Tidey has been elevated to the status of a saint, but his company is in Ireland to exploit our people and we were only exacting from it some dues,' *An Phoblacht* said. Tidey had no political affiliations in Ireland whatsoever.

After his first night's sleep in the comfort of his own bed since 23 November, Tidey emerged from his home on Saturday at lunchtime and walked to the end of his road to speak to the waiting press. Wearing a wool cardigan, check shirt and a pair of slacks, his beard now neatly trimmed, he looked more like an off-duty supermarket executive and less like the haunted captive he had been.

He had intended only making a statement to thank those who'd rescued him and said he would not be taking questions. He ended up doing both. 'How do you feel, Mr Tidey?' he was asked. 'I might ask you, "How do I look?"' he replied in a moment of levity.

Aside from some scratches on his cheeks, he showed little evidence of the trauma he had been through. In Cavan garda station the day before, a doctor who'd examined him declared Tidey to be in remarkable shape. 'I am blessed with a strong constitution and I feel that I can stay that way.'[5] His faith had helped keep him going, he added. 'I prayed very hard they [those searching for him] would be given the grace and strength of the Lord to cope with the situation which would, in most people's judgement, be dramatic.'

The news that a soldier and a young garda had been killed filled him with the 'utmost sadness'. He sent his prayers to their families. 'I hope that the same wonderful sufficiency of God's grace which supported me and my family will be provided to them at this time of great sorrow.'

He had survived from moment to moment unsure whether he would live or die. He spoke of his sensory deprivation, of being constantly blindfolded, about a bandage being wrapped tightly around his ears so he could hear nothing. He pointed to his head. 'As such, all I have got to show for it is a couple of very sore ears which the specialists may look at tomorrow.'

Tidey was accompanied by his three children and was visibly proud of how well they had coped. 'I am only learning in the few hours I have been back [about] the responsible role my two sons have taken in the period I have been away,' he said, looking at Andrew and Alistair with admiration. 'They have demonstrated great courage and great initiative. As far as my daughter is concerned, for a young lady of thirteen she has acquitted herself in such a way that I, as a father, am naturally proud and very thankful.'

Tidey then leaned over to give Susan a hug and the press got their shot of a family happily reunited after a terrible ordeal. The photograph made the front pages of the early editions of the evening newspapers.

But the light that came from the darkness of Derrada was quickly extinguished by another IRA atrocity that took place at almost exactly the same time as Don Tidey was speaking to the press.

At 1.21 p.m. on 17 December 1983 an IRA unit detonated a bomb outside Harrods in Knightsbridge, London's most famous department store. With all its cosmopolitan wealth and prestige, Knightsbridge was socially and economically the antithesis of a remote hillside wood in Co. Leitrim. Yet it was deemed just as appropriate a locale for an act of terror. IRA members parked a car bomb at Harrods' side entrance on Hans Crescent. A 1972 blue Austin 1300 was primed with between eleven and fourteen kilos of explosives. The gang then telephoned a warning to the local Samaritans at 12.44 p.m. stating there were bombs in Harrods and in the vicinity of the store. They gave the number plate of the blue Austin.

The warning came too late for six police officers who were approaching the car. Two were killed instantly when it exploded; a third died of his wounds on Christmas Day. Three bystanders were also killed. A fourth police officer lost both legs and part of a hand in the blast. A sniffer dog with them was so badly injured it had to be put down.

12. An IRA bomb in Hyde Park in July 1982 killed four soldiers and seven horses. This image of dead horses is one of the defining photographs of the Troubles.

13. The Harrods bomb occurred a day after Recruit Garda Gary Sheehan and Private Patrick Kelly were killed at Derrada Wood. Six people died in the London explosion.

14. The juxtaposition of relief due to the liberation of Don Tidey and horror arising from the Harrods bomb made many front pages. *(This headline, written shortly after the bomb exploded, reflects initial confusion about the death toll.)*

More than ninety people in total were injured. The blast destroyed twenty-four cars and shattered windows on five floors of the department store. Eyewitnesses spoke of glass falling on their heads like hailstones. One woman lay on the ground with shards of glass protruding from her stomach as her eleven-year-old daughter screamed for help.

Blood mixed with rainwater in the gutters of Hans Crescent. All that was left of the Austin was the two front wheels. Debris from it was found on the top of a six-storey building nearby. The indiscriminate nature of the bomb meant several Irish people in London were injured in the blast, including a Dublin-born police officer, William Kane.

It was the third major bomb attack in London by the IRA in eighteen months. On 20 July 1982 it detonated explosive devices in Hyde Park and Regent's Park. The Hyde Park car bomb was particularly gothic. It consisted of eleven kilograms of gelignite and fourteen kilograms of nails. The bomb was designed so that the nails would become projectiles capable of piercing flesh and causing mortal injury. It exploded as soldiers of the Household Cavalry passed by on their way to the changing of the guard.

Four soldiers from the Blues and Royals were killed and seven horses were either killed or put down. The attack produced some of the most harrowing photographs of the Troubles. The sight of the dead mounts lying in pools of blood outraged the animal-loving British public. It also embarrassed many people in Ireland, given the country's famed love for horses.

The second attack, at 12.44 p.m., targeted the Royal Green Jackets' military band which was performing in Regent's Park. Seven bandsmen were killed and eight civilians were injured.

The Hyde Park and Regent's Park bombs had been aimed

at military targets. The Harrods bomb was a murderous attack on innocent civilians in the run-up to Christmas. For the second time in as many days the IRA was forced to offer a partial apology. It admitted its members carried out the attack but made an unusual disclaimer: it had not been authorized by its Army Council.

The IRA's protestations did nothing to dim the fury of the public on both sides of the Irish Sea. Harrods would join Birmingham, Guildford, Claudy, La Mon, Bloody Friday and several other bomb attacks in the grim catalogue of IRA atrocities against civilians.

FitzGerald sent a message of sympathy to Thatcher after the Harrods attack, which pointedly included a reference to the 'tragic murder of two members of the security forces' in Ireland the day before. In linking the Harrods atrocity with the murders of Sheehan and Kelly, the taoiseach was identifying the IRA as a common enemy of both countries. His comments appeared to have an impact on the British prime minister, who hitherto had been downright sceptical about the Republic's attempts to combat terrorism. The deaths of Kelly and Sheehan brought home to her that the Republic was being targeted by the same terrorists.

The consequences of what happened in 1983 would be long lasting. After the Enniskillen bomb of 1987, the journalist Ed Moloney observed:

There can be little doubt that the Harrods/Tidey episode laid the foundations for the Anglo-Irish Agreement [of 1985]. The deaths at the hands of the IRA of Irish security force personnel in the Ballinamore woods [sic], and of English policemen and civilians in Knightsbridge, dramatically brought home to both governments the lesson that they faced a common enemy. This added urgency and direction to the then intergovernmental conversations and in the nine months leading to Hillsborough it was a recurring theme in the negotiations. It only needed Sinn Féin's electoral success in the north and the threat of success in the south to add the necessary catalyst for a common alliance and strategy to defeat the IRA.[6]

14. Meeting Fire with Fire

The failure of the Irish security forces to apprehend the killers of Private Kelly and Recruit Garda Sheehan fed a growing anxiety about the fundamental challenge now posed by organized terrorism on the island. It led many people to question the capacity of An Garda Síochána to take on the IRA. It was clear from the events at Derrada Wood that gardaí had underestimated the ruthlessness of violent republicanism.

The public unease was compounded by the way Dominic McGlinchey had escaped gardaí during the kidnap crisis. McGlinchey's public notoriety was further amplified in November 1983 when he admitted to the *Sunday Tribune* editor, Vincent Browne, that he had been personally responsible for at least thirty deaths.[1]

McGlinchey had been released from Portlaoise prison in January 1982. He was immediately arrested with a view to extraditing him to Northern Ireland for the murder of a woman, but he jumped bail and went on the run. On the night after Don Tidey was freed, and fifteen days after he'd escaped from the house in Carrigtwohill, McGlinchey, his wife Mary and three men took three gardaí prisoners near Enniscorthy.[2] His actions once again demonstrated the vulnerability of an unarmed police force faced by ruthless fanatics, but still no Irish government would contemplate arming all gardaí.

Michael Noonan robustly defended the conduct of both gardaí and army at Derrada. Firstly, he pointed out, the gardaí had succeeded in tracking down the whereabouts of the IRA gang. Secondly, they had achieved their main aim – to free Tidey unharmed, albeit at a tragic cost.

The cordon at Ballinamore had covered an area of 300 square miles and had a perimeter of more than sixty miles, Noonan said. All roads leading out of the area were monitored by armed checkpoints, but a comprehensive sweep of the area, he asserted, was 'totally beyond the resources of the Garda and the army and, I would stress again, the gardaí did not know that the kidnappers were inside that circle, so there was a limit to what numbers should be committed to the task'. Therefore, it had been essential to use recruit gardaí from Templemore in the search as the regular force alone could not be expected to cover such a vast area.

Noonan dismissed arguments that the recruits should never have been put in that position. 'The nature of the terrain, especially in the particular area where the kidnappers were hiding out, was such that the recruit gardaí, because of their exceptional physical fitness, more than played their part.'[3]

Both the minister for justice and Garda Commissioner Larry Wren were willing to give senior personnel at Derrada the benefit of the doubt because of the difficulties they'd faced. No such latitude was given to the officers in charge of the botched raid on the kidnappers' hideout at Claremorris. Seven of the officers present had been armed, yet still the gang got away. Wren made a rare public admission: the senior gardaí involved would be disciplined. The failure of the operation could neither be 'justified nor defended' and there would be consequences, he said in response to questions from journalists.

The commissioner gave a staunch if qualified defence of

the Ballinamore operation. Gardaí had had 'no positive, concrete information on where Mr Tidey was held', he told the *Sunday Press* in an interview in January 1984, and had stumbled across the hide.

'There has been much suggestion in the media that we are not sufficiently trained to deal with this type of counter-guerrilla activity. This misunderstands the situation,' Wren claimed. 'We are not trained at all to deal with intensive searches like the Tidey operation. Our main role is the traditional one of crime prevention and intelligence. We are not a counter-guerrilla group.'

The *Press* journalist Seán Flynn put it to Wren that the 'embarrassing failure' at Ballinamore was compounded by 'appalling police work at Claremorris'. Wren did not demur. 'In my mind so many questions about it [Claremorris] remain unanswered – so many obvious questions. Why was the front of the house not covered? Why was no resistance offered?'

In the end, however, only one officer was disciplined: Detective Sergeant Patrick Tuohy, who had been in charge of the operation. Tuohy claimed he had carried out his instructions, and denied responsibility for the kidnappers having escaped. He was initially demoted from detective sergeant back to sergeant in uniform.

Farcically, having been accused of mismanagement, his demotion was in turn mismanaged. Tuohy and the other gardaí involved in the Claremorris incident had been interviewed by a deputy commissioner. Tuohy said he believed the interview was merely a fact-finding exercise, but that it became a disciplinary tribunal unbeknownst to him. Incredibly, garda management had not given him a reason for his demotion and therefore he had no grounds on which he could appeal.

Tuohy obtained a High Court interim injunction stopping

the garda commissioner from acting against him, but it proved a temporary reprieve. Wren was determined to make an example of him.[4] The next time, the commissioner followed the correct procedure, and Tuohy was demoted from plain-clothes detective to uniform.

Rather than accept a decision he said would humiliate him in the eyes of a community he had served for twenty years, Tuohy retired later in 1984 at the age of fifty-two.[5]

The lessons of Derrada and Claremorris were absorbed by the Security Task Force. In future engagements they met force with force.

On 18 March 1984, gardaí tracked McGlinchey to a cottage in Crussa outside Newmarket-on-Fergus in Co. Clare. He had chosen a republican safe house that was under surveillance by gardaí. His two children were spotted in the company of a well-known republican activist in Shannon, who was herself under surveillance. A quarter of the population of Shannon had been refugees from the Troubles and there was a strong republican enclave in the town. McGlinchey's choice of sanctuary was a 'fatal blunder', one officer said afterwards, and may even have been a consequence of the fact that he had run out of places to stay.

Some forty Special Branch men surrounded the cottage at dawn. They called on him and three other activists present to surrender. McGlinchey responded with a burst of gunfire from the roof of the cottage. A blizzard of shooting followed, in which a police car was sprayed with bullets and a garda was hit in the shoulder.

A garda negotiator told McGlinchey he could fire away, but the army would be called in. McGlinchey asked for a priest. One was provided, and he and the three others were led away.[6]

McGlinchey was wanted for questioning in relation to the 1977 murder of Mrs Hester McMullan, whose home in Toomebridge, Co. Antrim, had been riddled with bullets. The target was her son, Joseph, a member of the RUC reserve. The Irish government successfully argued in court that the death of Mrs McMullan was not a 'political' offence, as she had been a civilian not a member of the security forces. Within eighteen hours of his arrest in Clare McGlinchey became the first republican terrorist extradited to Northern Ireland to face multiple charges there. He was later extradited back to the South.[7] Arresting Ireland's most wanted man was a victory for policing after the stain of Claremorris.

The capture of McGlinchey was the first tangible evidence of a hardened attitude towards terrorism by the security forces.

The events at Derrada also forced a reckoning within the IRA. Their kidnap strategy was supposed to yield big sums of easy money. Instead it had unleashed a huge level of public opprobrium and a whole new campaign of pressure and surveillance from the police. The Tidey debacle proved to be the end of Kevin Mallon's short and disastrous tenure as IRA director of operations. Mallon had been sceptical of Adams's electoral strategy and could have made a lot of trouble for the Sinn Féin president, but the kidnapping fiascos marginalized him.

'It was Adams's great fortune that Mallon self-destructed and that he did not have to confront him,' Ed Moloney wrote in his book *A Secret History of the IRA*.[8] Moloney later recalled, 'I remember two things about the aftermath of Tidey. One was a phone call with Jim Prior, the then secretary of state for Northern Ireland, on the Sunday of Tidey's release and he could hardly conceal his delight at the damage the IRA's own goal had caused Adams & Co., and the sympathy he now expected from Dublin.

'The other was: earlier that day I had a session with Adams and [Danny] Morrison. Adams was blazing with anger at what had happened, and it was then I realized from an off-hand remark that Mallon had been the architect of the Tidey operation and that his IRA career was at an end. So as own goals went, it was a biggie.'[9]

The three kidnappings of 1983 had ended in calamitous failure, but to admit as much publicly risked a split in the republican movement. 'Certain types of IRA action certainly produced political problems for Sinn Féin, and where they occur we would be privately critical,' said Morrison, the party's director of publicity, shortly before Christmas in 1983.[10]

Phil Flynn, the vice-president of Sinn Féin, was also general secretary of the Local Government and Public Services Union. The Irish government refused to deal with him. In response to the public outrage over Harrods and Derrada, Flynn took the unprecedented step of issuing a statement condemning both IRA actions. In 1984 he resigned as Sinn Féin vice-president.

Reflecting on the events of forty years ago, the former Labour Party leader Dick Spring confirmed that his party's refusal to meet Sinn Féin representatives was the reason it would not deal with Flynn as a trade unionist. 'Even though it is very difficult to recall the security situation and the threat to the government from the PIRA in the 1980s in comparison to the relative calm in present-day Ireland and the abandonment of a military campaign by the PIRA, I am confident that there was total rejection of the terrorist/

military campaign that was being waged at the time,' says Spring. 'It was very firm government policy that no tolerance would be shown towards the murderous campaign of the PIRA. The refusal to meet Sinn Féin representatives was primarily to do with Philip Flynn. I believe it was perfectly understandable that government ministers refused to meet him while he was VP of an organization that had a policy to undermine the stability of our state.'[11]

The public distancing from Sinn Féin/IRA continued at other official levels. The Irish army was withdrawn from all St Patrick's Day parades where there were Sinn Féin delegates on the viewing platform. For the same reason, the army based at Connolly Barracks in Longford declined to participate in the 1984 St Patrick's Day town parade, and the event was cancelled.

In the immediate aftermath of Derrada and Harrods, the Irish government considered going even further, and banning Sinn Féin entirely. The party's spokespeople were already banned from the RTÉ airwaves, a decision that had been upheld by the Supreme Court. Chief Justice Tom O'Higgins stated that the broadcasting ban was justified as Sinn Féin was an 'evil and dangerous organization whose object was to overthrow the state and its institutions, if necessary by force'.[12]

There would have been widespread support for the proscribing of Sinn Féin in December 1983. Even Fianna Fáil leader Charles Haughey, well capable of lubricating republican sentiment when it suited his political needs, said he would support the government if it moved to ban the party.

Proscribing the organization would have made it illegal to be a member of Sinn Féin, which had polled a respectable 7 per cent in the Dublin Central by-election, held the day before Tidey was seized. It would have allowed for the confiscation of all the party's assets, the banning of its public meetings and the jailing of its members.

Such a move might also have had unintended consequences, however. Sinn Féin was not registered as a political party in the Republic, a state it did not recognize, though it contested elections there. Its thirty councillors sat as independents and would not be subject to a ban.[13]

More significantly, a ban on Sinn Féin might have driven the party underground and made it harder to monitor its members, especially those involved in the IRA, such as John Joe McGirl. The surveillance on his movements had provided valuable information in finding the location where Tidey was being held.

For that reason, gardaí advised against the banning of the party, and that advice was accepted by the government.

15. In the Line of Duty

The funerals of Private Kelly and Recruit Garda Sheehan took place three hours apart in Moate and Carrickmacross on Monday, 19 December 1983. They were both national events. Thousands of people travelled from all parts of the country to pay their respects. Many hundreds of thousands watched and listened to the coverage broadcast on RTÉ television and radio.

Ranks of soldiers and gardaí formed up in the official guards of honour. Dozens of politicians from across the political parties were present. The taoiseach and President Patrick Hillary attended both ceremonies, symbolically representing a nation in mourning. The Christmas lights in Moate and Carrickmacross were extinguished for the duration.

15. Patrick Kelly   16. Gary Sheehan

'A nation's shame was reflected in the tears of thousands of mourners at two funerals yesterday,' wrote Máirtín Mac Cormaic in the *Irish Independent*. 'Even God seemed to weep as the rain poured down from dark skies over the fresh graves of a young garda in Monaghan and a veteran soldier in Westmeath. The shame of last Friday's tragic events on a bleak hillside in Leitrim united Irishmen and women of all religious and political views. We were all represented.'[1]

Private Kelly's remains had been removed from Our Lady's Hospital in Navan on Sunday afternoon, two days after he was killed. His cortège passed through Mullingar, where thousands of people lined the streets. When it arrived in Moate it was met by an army detachment. Six of his comrades attached to 6th Infantry Battalion Transport Company at Custume Barracks carried his coffin into St Patrick's Church.[2] It was draped with a tricolour and sitting on top was the soldier's beret and belt. The narrow church was filled to overflowing.

The presence of the taoiseach alongside Charles Haughey and Dick Spring demonstrated that political differences were nothing compared to the shared revulsion at these killings. Most of the members of the cabinet attended too, along with the serried ranks of army high command and civic leaders from across Irish society.

The chief concelebrant in Moate was Dr Colm O'Reilly, the Bishop of Ardagh and Clonmacnoise. In his homily he said it was 'profoundly disturbing that the feast of Christmas, the very feast which announced peace on Earth, should be accompanied by some of the most savage attacks on peace that we have known in these troubled years'.[3]

The Irish army was not an aggressive army, Bishop O'Reilly added. It was one engaged in peace-making around the world. How ironic, then, that a soldier should be at greater risk in a wood in Co. Leitrim than in places like Lebanon or Cyprus.

In words directed at republican supporters, he said the army deserved 'one hundred per cent co-operation from every citizen of his country'. He concluded:

> It is a sad comment on our country that peace should have become so difficult to maintain at home. Patrick Kelly died as he lived in the work of making peace by setting free a man unjustly held captive. He was serving his country no less truly than those who fought for the freedom of our country and for the rights of Irish people in the history of our patriotic struggle in the past.[4]

The plaintive sight of Private Kelly's widow Caitriona in the front pew with two of her four children, David and Michael, was the sharpest reminder of the true impact of the events at Derrada Wood. (Her two other children, four-year-old Patrick and baby Andrew, were at home with measles.) All of Private Kelly's siblings – Geraldine, Teresa, Bernadette, Mary Anne, Michael, Peter and William John – were in attendance. His brother Sergeant Jim Kelly was flown home from the Lebanon.

Behind them, Private Kelly's parents sat with Caitriona's brothers and sisters. The hostage whom the soldier had died rescuing sent a wreath with the message: 'From Don Tidey and family'.

The coffin was carried out of the church by military policemen wearing black armbands. Afterwards, the usually undemonstrative taoiseach put his arms around Caitriona. Garret FitzGerald looked like he was on the verge of tears himself.[5]

The cortège proceeded through the streets of Moate with soldiers flanking the hearse. The band of the Western

Command followed, with muffled drumbeat and funeral music. Private Kelly's last journey ended at Tubber cemetery across the county border in Co. Offaly. It was raining and bitterly cold as the Last Post and Reveille were played by buglers and the coffin was lowered into the ground.

At the request of Private Kelly's widow, no volley of shots was fired at the graveside. Instead the guard of honour, standing to attention, reversed arms in a mute gesture of tribute.

For the young Kelly children it was a bewildering theatre of grief. Just four days previously their father had departed their home on what was supposed to be a routine job of work. Now he was dead and this hitherto anonymous family was the focus of national grieving. Things would never be the same again, as David recalled.

'What I really noticed was the coffin, with the tricolour and the beret and the belt. I remember watching it pass by, and the sheer amount of people on both sides of the road. Local people say it was the biggest funeral ever in the town. We went by car out to Tubber, [to] Kilcurley Cemetery. Tubber means a lot to me because that's where my parents met [in the local dancehall]. They got married in Tubber Church; it was where they had me christened and it's where they're both buried. So that little village has a lot of meaning for me.'[6]

Michael can remember his aunt holding his hand and the volume of people on the streets. 'I remember seeing the coffin going down, it was absolutely surreal,' he recalls. His mother had been reluctant to let him view the body at Navan general hospital. 'I wish she had,' Michael says now, 'because I think it might have helped me in terms of closure, you know? But I heard that the two families were there, the Sheehans and the Kellys side by side.'[7]

*

Three generations of service to the state were reflected in Gary Sheehan's funeral as dusk settled over Carrickmacross. His body had also been taken from Navan hospital, and once again the public came out in towns along the route to its final destination. As the cortège entered Carrickmacross, it stopped outside the family home on Kingscourt Road. Garda recruits lined the passage all the way to St Joseph's Church for the funeral Mass.

The church accommodates 1,500 people and every seat was taken, while hundreds more stood outside. Two RUC officers in plain clothes were present to pay their respects on behalf of the Northern Ireland police service.

The Sheehans were embedded in almost every aspect of town life. Jim was not only a respected local detective, but also a member of the bridge club and Nuremore Golf Club. Gary had been a member of Carrickmacross Emmets' GAA club; he and his younger siblings had gone to schools in the town. There were guards of honour from the St Louis Convent, which Jennifer was attending and where Gráinne had been a past pupil, and from the Patrician Brothers High School, where Gary had been head boy in his final year and which David had also attended.

The coffin was draped in the tricolour and bore his garda cap on top. It was carried into the church by six of his colleagues. Three buglers from the Garda Band played the 'Royal Salute to the Blessed Sacrament'.[8] Though it was midwinter, a tortoiseshell butterfly was spotted flitting across the coffin. The first reading was delivered by Gráinne; the second by Gary's girlfriend Ann Flannery.

Joseph Duffy, the Bishop of Clogher, delivered a forceful sermon directed not only at the perpetrators but also at the ambivalence among some people in Irish society to political violence. He believed uncritical veneration of those involved in the Easter Rising and the War of Independence had given a new generation the impetus to resort to paramilitary actions.

'The gun is not the way forward,' Duffy declared. 'We have all sinned in glamorizing the use of arms in Irish history. If we look more closely at our history – and I suggest we should do this – we get a different picture. We see the gun as a tyranny, as a destructive wasteful instrument of division and hatred.'[9]

Afterwards, the cortège was led by the Garda Band with forty trainees from Templemore marching behind it. The walk to the cemetery was about a mile. After the coffin was lowered into the ground, Garda Commissioner Wren presented the cap and the flag that had adorned the coffin to Gary's parents.

'We were very, very proud of him,' Jim Sheehan told the *Irish Independent* after his son's death. 'He was such a happy lad and contented with what he was doing. I think it was a stupid way to die.'

Don Tidey's friend Revd Horace McKinley attended Gary Sheehan's funeral and visited Private Kelly's widow some weeks afterwards. He also went to see Detective Sergeant Donal Kelleher in the Mater Hospital, where he was recovering from his bullet wounds.

A Christian minister preaches the triumph of good over evil, of the light overcoming the darkness, he says, but he was challenged by the terrible consequences that came with the freeing of his friend. He remembers how depressed he felt making the return journey from visiting the grieving families. 'I will never forget those two journeys home because it was so dark, and [I was] worrying about the country. What had we come to?'

*

The scenes broadcast on national television of a country in mourning, of the shattered communities in Moate and Carrickmacross, of the families broken-hearted and bereft, generated deep unease among many republican sympathizers in Monaghan. The consequences of their ideology had landed on their own doorstep. A native son of the county was now a victim of that ideology.

Carrickmacross was a border town where Sinn Féin was well organized. Two years previously, silent parades had been held on Friday evenings in support of the hunger strikers. Shops and pubs in the town shut – some voluntarily, others out of fear – during the funerals of the hunger strikers. There was resistance to demands from the local H-Block committee that schools should also be closed.

There had been demonstrations in Carrickmacross and in many towns throughout Monaghan after the newly elected TD Kieran Doherty died on hunger strike in the Maze prison in August 1981. Doherty had polled highest of any of the H-Block candidates in the June 1981 Irish general election, with 10,063 first preference votes.

Carrickmacross, in short, was a not untypical border town in terms of containing a nucleus of republican activists and a wider base of passive sympathizers. It would also have had a silent majority that rejected the cult of violence.

The killing of Gary Sheehan gave many passive supporters pause for thought. It brought home to them what many victims of the Troubles elsewhere were suffering. That much was evident when RTÉ's *Today Tonight* programme interviewed people in the town immediately after the killing.

'I noticed on Friday evening there was a lot of anger and a lot of people felt they had kept their mouths shut for too long,' local teacher Bill Cotter said. 'I went into one of the local bars on Friday evening and there were local farmers having a pint. When they heard the news, they were tremendously angry about the whole thing. They were certainly in a mood where the people who allowed this sort of thing to happen shouldn't be listened to any more.'[10]

Gerard Martin, a schoolfriend of Gary Sheehan, also spoke on camera. 'The town may have felt united around the time of the H-Blocks, but the town is much more united now with a much different feeling in a completely opposite direction,' he said. 'A lot of people who are apolitical have finally decided that they have taken enough.'[11]

Though there were many garda recruits from Templemore at Gary Sheehan's funeral, his classmates were not there. They were still searching forlornly and, as it turned out, pointlessly in Derrada Wood and its environs. Their colleague's killers were long gone.

A day after having the muzzle of an assault rifle prodded into his back and being forced to walk as a hostage behind Provo gunmen, Paul Gillen was back out searching again. 'We were young guys and had a job to do and we just got on with it,' he says. 'We were part of the group and the job wasn't finished. In some ways we were already battle-hardened and replacing us wasn't a great idea.'[12]

By the time they left, a week after the shooting, their uniforms had been shredded from briars and brambles and many were longing for the Christmas comforts of home. The class took a detour via Carrickmacross on their way back to Templemore. 'It was grim that we never got to that funeral because we were working,' Sheehan's classmate Paul Gillen remembered. 'We went to his grave and formed a hollow square around it.'[13]

The garda class of September 1983 passed out on 9

February 1984. Black gloves replaced the white dress gloves traditionally worn on parade by those graduating. The first Gary Sheehan Memorial Prize for 'diligence and ability' was awarded.[14]

The inquest into the deaths of the two men took place at Carrick-on-Shannon courthouse on 13 March 1984. In his evidence, Private Paddy Shine recalled entering the wood with Private Kelly at about 2 p.m.[15] They were providing armed cover to the recruit gardaí.

The trees in the wood were young, no more than five to six feet in height, but the undergrowth was thick. The recruit gardaí climbed over an embankment and disappeared into the undergrowth. Shine heard a garda recruit call out that there was a man in front of them with a rifle and he wasn't answering. They were about to cross the embankment when the kidnappers opened fire.

'Private Kelly fell backwards off the embankment onto the small trees. I saw blood on his left cheek,' Shine testified. 'I was a yard from him at this stage. I dived down for cover under the embankment. Private Kelly called my name, "Paddy". I heard a thump. I knew it was a grenade, so I put my hand over my head.'

Garda Inspector Seamus O'Hanlon recalled hearing a loud bang of gunfire and shortly afterwards seeing gardaí coming out of the woods with their hands in the air. He ordered anybody else in the wood to leave.

O'Hanlon said he went into the trees and found the body of Gary Sheehan, whom he had known for fourteen years. Gary had a large wound in his head and was dead. The bodies were removed from the wood at 12.10 p.m. on Saturday and taken to Navan hospital. At 2.40 p.m., almost exactly twenty-four hours after they were shot, O'Hanlon formally identified the bodies of both men to the state pathologist Professor John Harbison.

The twelve-person jury returned verdicts in accordance with the medical evidence – that Private Kelly received bullet wounds to the neck, head, chest and legs and died from shock and haemorrhage, and that Garda Sheehan suffered fatal bullet wounds to the head and chest. Significantly, the inquest found that both men's wounds were consistent with being shot from in front and not, as republicans alleged, from 'friendly fire', which would have come from behind.

Questions persisted for months afterwards about the wisdom of deploying unarmed young recruits in the search operation. Eugene O'Sullivan, the detective who came under fire at the Ford Granada shoot-out, is among those who believe it was the wrong call by garda management.

'Gary Sheehan should never have been there,' he argues. 'A garda recruit should not have been involved. Private Kelly – I'm not quite sure what the army take is, but at least he had some chance, he was an armed soldier. Gary Sheehan had nothing. I don't know, did he even have a baton?

'It would never happen now. But at the time, risk assessment wasn't really a thing. It was just, you know, someone would go to the back of the house, someone to the front of the house, that type of thing. Obviously there was huge risk in this. But that was the way things were done then. Practices, training, intelligence gathering, communications, air support and logistics have improved dramatically since.'[16]

On the other hand, O'Sullivan can see the reasoning behind the decision. 'What recruits always bring [is] enthusiasm, they're mad to get out and get involved, and they brought that enthusiasm with them. But unfortunately, Gary Sheehan paid for it with his life.'

O'Sullivan's colleague Joe Feely argues that the decision can be justified in terms of what they were being asked to do. He also respects the alternative viewpoint as articulated by O'Sullivan. 'Them young lads were physically far more capable of doing a search like that,' he reasons. 'Maybe it was unfair because they were untrained in anything, but there was no garda trained in searching. It was a very basic search: walk in a line, look behind the bush, look in the drains, anything unusual you see take a note of it, call over the sergeant, keep going.

'After two or three days of it I can well remember the older guards and soldiers scooting around the edges of the roads because they didn't want to be going in getting pine needles down their necks and the rain and all that. But [with] the recruits, it'd be done properly. They were fitter and far better able to cover the ground than a lot of the older fellas. I honestly believe that if it wasn't [for the] young lads that were there at the time, I don't think they [Tidey and the gang] would have been found.'17

Retired assistant commissioner Jim Wall, who was an inspector at Templemore training college at the time, also believes the use of recruits at Derrada was the right decision. 'They were madly enthusiastic. I said it to them afterwards: "I would have gone through the gates of hell with them behind me." They searched Wednesday, Thursday and they found him [Tidey] at dinner time on Friday.

'If you had gone through Derrada and seen the conditions, you'd see what they did. We had great faith in them. They were enthusiastic like all fellows starting out. I'd have had no hesitation in going back and doing it again.'

16. No Com-mint

Within a few days of the killings at Derrada Wood, it was clear the kidnappers had vanished. Many gardaí and soldiers resented spending their Christmas in Leitrim knowing that it was more for the optics than any valid security purpose. The number of search personnel steadily dwindled, and on 30 December the last checkpoints were lifted.

The media had long departed by then. RTÉ's Brendan O'Brien had, like many of his peers, travelled to the town when it was clear the search for Don Tidey was intensifying. For him, the operation left behind a lot of unanswered questions. How did the kidnappers, who were vastly outnumbered, manage to shoot their way to safety? How had they escaped the so-called 'ring of steel'? Why had they chosen Leitrim? O'Brien was determined to get to the truth of what happened.

On the fateful Friday afternoon he had been on the verge of beating every other journalist there to the big news. He received exclusive information that Tidey had just been found and freed. To check his information, the RTÉ reporter had to go through official channels. He put it to the garda press office, which flatly denied the claim.

'After that episode I never again used the garda commissioner's press officer for important information,' O'Brien said. 'I had learned a useful lesson about trust in the garda commissioner's office, i.e. not to trust it, and continued to use my new source to good effect for a number of years ahead.'[1]

O'Brien spent weeks compiling a major report for *Today*

Tonight. It was broadcast on 11 January 1984. He forensically detailed how the search and rescue operation was conducted and named the suspects wanted by the gardaí.

He began by recalling how gardaí were able to narrow the search when their night-time surveillance team spotted the two senior Maze escapees in Aughnasheelin between a week and ten days before Tidey was found. O'Brien named them as Brendan McFarlane and Gerard McDonnell.

O'Brien told viewers that the exact location where Tidey was being held had been given to a garda sergeant by a woman who pointed to Derrada Wood roughly an hour before the rescue happened and said: 'That's an IRA hill.'

His report gave a minute-by-minute account of the shooting and its aftermath. He revealed that the kidnappers escaped on foot through Ardmoneen Wood and that one who knew the area – O'Brien did not identify him – got away on Friday night.

O'Brien did name another suspected member of the gang – Oliver McKiernan from Newtownbutler, Co. Fermanagh. McKiernan had been sentenced to five years in Portlaoise prison in April 1973 for having batteries and wires under his control near the Cavan–Fermanagh border. He was one of nineteen republican inmates who escaped from Portlaoise in August 1974. He had been hiding out under an assumed name while living in a mobile home in Aghacashel, beside Aughnasheelin. This meant he had local knowledge of the terrain.

The fourth suspected member of the gang was named by O'Brien as Tony McAllister, the Maze escapee who had been serving fifteen years for the murder of a soldier in 1979. O'Brien did not include Seamus McElwaine as one of the suspects, though local republicans are convinced he was involved.

The RTÉ report detailed a litany of errors in the rescue operation that allowed the gang to escape:

- The numbers of security personnel involved on the ground at any one time after Tidey was located were closer to 300 than the oft-quoted figure of 2,000.
- Multiple garda and army reinforcements had arrived on the wrong side of the wood after the shooting, having been given the wrong co-ordinates.
- The radio operator at Garda base who knew the terrain best was gone to lunch when the firing began.
- It was 11 p.m. on 16 December before the ten Rudolph search teams were reallocated to checkpoints in the wider cordon area. This gave the gang an eight-and-a-half-hour head start.

At a time when most Irish people had only a handful of TV channels to choose from, O'Brien's report secured a vast audience. The revelations generated an enormous reaction, much of it critical because of the failings in the search that had been laid bare. It was raised in the Dáil and dominated discussions about the Tidey kidnapping for weeks afterwards. O'Brien recalls:

'The garda commissioner didn't deny the *Today Tonight* version, based as it was on top-grade contacts which I had cultivated within the garda/army operation team. Instead, the commissioner's office was mostly focused on finding out who my sources were ... and I was quizzed to that effect after the embarrassed commissioner appeared live on the *Today Tonight* programme. Naturally I didn't divulge any names or info about my sources.'

The RTÉ journalist's other mission was to ascertain the

level of support for the IRA in Co. Leitrim. 'Overall, I was there to test my feeling and knowledge of the area . . . that this was sort of "Provo territory" where IRA activists, including Maze escapers, could operate with local support, tacit or direct, involving storage of arms, cross-border arms smuggling etc. I had acquired significant contacts about IRA activity in those parts prior to the Don Tidey kidnap.'

Garda contacts had told O'Brien the hideout was serviced from outside by local activists, and that the full support team could have numbered up to ten. Fifteen people had been taken in for questioning afterwards. Four of them lived in and around Ballinamore, the rest in the vicinity of Drumcroman Wood.

'Many people here have no love for the gardaí. It is the kind of country where John Joe McGirl picks up votes,' O'Brien concluded. He was not able to record an interview with McGirl because of the Sinn Féin/IRA broadcasting ban.

The programme included a series of interviews, or more correctly encounters, between O'Brien and locals who lived in the vicinity of Derrada Wood. The main set piece was filmed after Sunday Mass outside St Brigid's Church in Corraleehan parish, which encompasses Derrada.

Just two days after the shooting, local priest Fr Con Dolan had used his Sunday sermon to criticize sympathizers who had supported the kidnap gang and then helped them to escape. Those who had done so were guilty by association of the mortal sin of murder, he said. 'Each one of us must answer for ourselves before God – whether in any way, over the past number of years, we have been ambivalent in our attitude to murder or violence; if we have assisted, promoted, condoned or supported, even in a remote way, murder or violence or those who organize or perpetrate these crimes.'

He added that those who had facilitated the IRA gang bore responsibility not only for the murder of two men but also indirectly for the wounding of their fellow parishioner, John Gerard Wrynne, who had been married in the church just a few months previously.

The priest may have hoped his sermon would persuade some people in the community to stop turning a blind eye but, if it did, they were keeping that change of heart to themselves.

A few weeks later Brendan O'Brien and the television crew were waiting outside the church. The congregation exited at the end of Mass and many of them, mostly men, sat on the wall outside for a chat and a smoke. O'Brien approached with his microphone and went from one person to the next.

17. St Brigid's Church, Corraleehan. In 2003 a Sinn Féin memorial was erected outside the church, which is less than a mile from Derrada Wood.

BRENDAN O'BRIEN: What do you think about the whole business of the Tidey kidnap?

MASS-GOER 1: [*Says nothing and shakes his head.*]

BO'B: What about this man here? Why are you walking away? Would you have phoned the gardaí if you knew anything?

MG 2: I have nothing to say at all about it. I don't wish to comment on it at all.

BO'B: Would you have informed the gardaí?

MG 3: I have been asked that question several times already.

BO'B: Would you?

MG 3: I don't know whether I would or not.

BO'B: Would you have phoned the gardaí if you knew something suspicious was going on?

MG 4: I have no comment to make at all.

BO'B: Would you have informed the gardaí if you knew somebody was being held kidnap around the place?

MG 4: I said no comment.

BO'B: Would you have informed the gardaí?

MG 5: I have no comment, no comment whatsoever.

BO'B: Why not? Do you support Sinn Féin?

MG 5: No comment.

BO'B (*to a child*): Would you inform the gardaí?

CHILD (*laughing*): No way.

BO'B: Would you sir, would you inform the gardaí?

MG 6: No comment to make.

BO'B: You said you wouldn't inform the gardaí. Why not?

MG 6: No comment to make.

BO'B: What about you, sir, would you inform the gardaí?

MG 7: No comment.

BO'B: Why not? Was it not the right thing to do?

MG 7: I couldn't say. I don't know what is the right thing to say.

BO'B: What do you think is the right thing to say?

MG 7: Well, I couldn't tell ya.

It wasn't just the men of the parish who would not tell. O'Brien also spoke to Rose Curnan, whose husband John had been arrested in connection with the kidnapping. The couple owned the wood where Tidey had been found.

ROSE CURNAN: I didn't know there was a hideout there at all. I didn't know anything, nothing. Could I go about my business, could I do my work like every other person around here? My home was searched four times. It all happened before Tidey was found. The one thing I can say is that my nerves are gone and I'm not in the best of health.

BO'B: Supposing you had heard something specific, what would you have done?

RC: I would have done nothing.

BO'B: Would you have called the gardaí?

RC: No, I wouldn't.

Fr Dolan reiterated to O'Brien and to a national television audience what he had told his parishioners: 'I think people should examine their conscience about any support they would have given, not just over the events which led to the murder, but also over the past number of years their attitudes towards violence and murder and towards those who perpetrated these crimes.'

The programme was the talk of Ireland for weeks afterwards. For many of the men who had risked their lives rescuing Tidey, it confirmed their worst prejudices about the locals in Leitrim. These were the 'quiet, unhelpful people' as observed by the former head of the murder squad, Chief Superintendent John Courtney, in his book *It Was Murder!*

Retired Deputy Commissioner Nacie Rice was a detective sergeant in 1983. 'That famous RTÉ programme still reverberates with me,' he says now. 'To this day, even if it was a shortcut to somewhere, I would drive around rather than through Ballinamore.'[2]

In the almost four weeks between Derrada and the RTÉ broadcast there had been national revulsion at the killing of a young garda and a soldier. Now here was the spectacle of a Mass-going community seemingly turning their backs on the forces of law and order, and even common decency.

Perhaps some of those interviewed had republican sympathies, or at least a hostility towards the state, which they regarded as having done them no favours. Many people in the area lived lives that were remote from the centres of power, not just geographically but economically and socially and culturally too. Many were annoyed that their lives had been upended for almost two weeks; some had had their houses searched several times.

Rose Curnan's attitude to gardaí was surely coloured by the fact that she had been arrested and questioned in relation to the kidnapping and that her husband was still in garda custody. She told *An Phoblacht* that Special Branch detectives had dragged her by the arms and legs out of the house and put her children under house arrest. While in garda custody in Clones, Co. Monaghan, she was 'abused and subject to foul and obscene language about herself and the people of Ballinamore', the newspaper claimed.[3]

Many locals would have resented the exposure their area was getting in the national media. The early 1980s saw the beginning of a culture war between what became known as 'the Dublin 4 set' and rural Ireland. The Dublin 4 set was so named after the postcode of the affluent south Dublin suburb. Dublin 4 was a perceived nexus of politicians, economists, academics and media types who were liberal-minded, contemptuous of the Catholic Church and of traditional republicanism. It was characterized by a loathing of the IRA.

The RTÉ campus was located in the heart of Dublin 4. To some locals in rural areas an RTÉ man like O'Brien would have epitomized a Dublin 4 outsider. That, along with some inherent sympathy for the IRA, may have been behind their reticence when he started asking questions outside Sunday Mass that morning.

There was also a cultural resistance to being seen as 'an informer', or to go against the herd in an intimate community where everybody knew everybody else. The hatred of the informer was deep in the Irish psyche. An IRA slogan of the 1970s, 'Whatever you say, say nothing', was worked into a poem of the same name by Seamus Heaney, in which he referred to the reticence of northern people.[4] He was referring in particular to the 'wee Six' – the six counties of Northern Ireland – but it could equally apply to communities along the border with a strong republican identity.

Silence and discretion were necessary defence mechanisms in a society where a significant number of people secretly supported violent republicanism. But most basically of all, in the exigency of the moment, with a camera poked in their faces for the first time in their lives, perhaps many were lost for words and simply did not know what to say.

*

Irrespective of their political views – and some may have been apathetic about politics in general – people in places like Corraleehan and Aughnasheelin would have felt genuine regret and sadness for the Sheehan and Kelly families. One veteran garda who worked there is adamant that these were good and decent people, reared for generations in rural hardship on terrible land. They probably never thought about the reality of IRA violence until they were confronted close-up by its awful consequences.[5] Death and suffering due to political violence happened somewhere else, to people they didn't know.

There was a similar gap of comprehension between the people of urban and suburban Ireland, and those outside Corraleehan Church that day. For this appalled audience, watching from the living rooms of their three-bed semi-detached homes with all mod cons, this exchange with O'Brien was almost akin to an intrepid explorer making contact with a tribe that few people knew even existed until that moment. This was the deep interior of the border countryside.

Adding to that sense of otherness was the manner in which these folk pronounced the word 'comment'. In their vernacular it was pronounced 'com-mint', as in 'No com-mint'. It became the subject of much comical banter nationally, as Leitrim people living in Dublin and elsewhere would experience thereafter. It was a focus of local banter too, not least in the pubs and marts and shops.

The parish priest in Ballinamore, Canon Terry McManus, was not amused. Local altar boys nicknamed him 'Billy Whizz' – a character from the *Beano* comic – because of the speed with which he paced up and down the altar rails dispensing communion. Canon McManus was equally as forceful as Fr Dolan in calling out the ambivalence that allowed an IRA kidnap gang to exist in the midst of their community for more than three weeks. He told the Co. Leitrim Vocational Education Committee that local people must condemn the killings unequivocally. He also protested that the incident had unfairly tarnished the reputation of Ballinamore people as being supporters of violence when in fact the kidnappers were from outside the area, and those who supported them locally were a small minority – and not actually from the town either.[6]

The local Chamber of Commerce, community council and angling-and-tourism committee issued a joint statement in the immediate aftermath of the shooting. The town had always endeavoured to make visitors welcome, they said. Community organizations such as the GAA, the theatre festival, the drama society and the golf club made Ballinamore the 'envy of many other towns in the north-west'. The town had suffered from the recession, which was made worse by cross-border shopping. 'It would be regrettable if the events of the past week should undermine the work of so many dedicated people.'[7] The statement, though, was open to the accusation of being mealy-mouthed, because it contained not a word of condemnation against the kidnappers.

O'Brien's report noted that Ballinamore had hardly recovered from the burning of the English anglers' tourist bus two and a half years earlier. He further noted that many Leitrim politicians appeared to be ambivalent about the IRA – John Joe McGirl had been unanimously voted in as the Leitrim County Council chairman for 1980–81 and had used his office to campaign for the hunger strikers. Fianna Fáil councillor Joe Mooney, father of the popular RTÉ broadcaster Paschal Mooney, had shared a platform with Gerry Adams.

The RTÉ reporter wanted to gauge the mood of the people

of Ballinamore as well as that of Corraleehan. Many of the townspeople gathered together for the *Today Tonight* cameras in the local hall. The encounter didn't go well. O'Brien was determined to pursue the theme of ambivalence – did the locals support the IRA or were they prepared to turn a blind eye to republican violence in their midst? He challenged the gathering as to why, for instance, every business in the town had closed during the hunger strike funerals. Who had ordered the closure?

> BO'B TO JOSIE CRYAN (local Fianna Fáil cumann chairman): As a member of Fianna Fáil, do you believe that people should simply condemn the Provisional IRA and should they also condemn Sinn Féin?
>
> JC: Each general election I have gone out and canvassed from door to door asking people to vote for Fianna Fáil. I suppose in doing that, I am asking them to condemn these other parties just as I ask them to condemn Fine Gael.
>
> BO'B: Let's not fudge it. What I am asking you is do you condemn Sinn Féin?
>
> JC: I would condemn the present Sinn Féin. Fianna Fáil came from the original Sinn Féin which I believe in.
>
> BO'B: Isn't that the problem? You originated from Sinn Féin which was a physical force movement at one time. How can you then ask people to condemn the present physical force Sinn Féin?
>
> JC: This is a different thing for the Irish people. Yes, I condemn it. I think that with the change in leadership in Sinn Féin, there seems to be a change in attitude as regards the Free State, the authorities, the guards and the army. As you know, the two young men were shot out there.

O'Brien also interviewed the local solicitor Brian Toolan, who had criticized the absence of any condemnation of the IRA in the Chamber of Commerce statement. He was the son of Walter P. Toolan, who had refused to put out the black flag during the hunger strikes in 1981. Brian Toolan told O'Brien, he believed he was speaking for the silent majority in Ballinamore.

> BT: We are all aware the position of the Provisionals/Sinn Féin is the Armalite in one hand and the ballot box in the other. The majority of people in this area don't have Armalites. People are afraid to speak out, 90 per cent of the people would be totally against the IRA and totally against the Provisional IRA.
>
> BO'B: Why have you decided to speak out?
>
> BT: I think the time has come now for people who were hesitant in the past to speak out, otherwise this area, which has great tourist potential and is a very scenic area, will be totally destroyed and the country itself will be totally destroyed and we will have the hell that people have to put up with in Northern Ireland.
>
> BO'B: So, what would you like to see the leaders of this community do?
>
> BT: There should be a meeting held of all the community organizations to tell the extreme republican element they are not acceptable in this area and this community is not going to tolerate any repetition of the Tidey affair.

The 'extreme republican element' responded to Brian Toolan's comments a couple of nights later. On the ground floor of the family legal practice was a large plate-glass window with 'Walter P. Toolan & Son' engraved in gold lettering. It was smashed in with rocks. The glass in the two entrance doors was also broken, as was a smaller window in the waiting room. The attack was carried out in the dead of night.

'It clearly was a retaliation for Brian's interview with RTÉ,' says his brother Gabriel.[8] 'Obviously, being confronted with such open, aggressive and public hostility was challenging, particularly as no one else broke the silence in the town.'

Symbolically, there was another troubling dimension to the attack. 'My father [Walter P. Toolan] perceived the incident as a direct attack on the rule of law. The legal profession, by definition, is required to be an independent voice, willing to speak out without fear or favour, in the face of atrocity, tyranny or intimidation. When freedom of expression, particularly a considered opinion from a legal authority, is threatened with naked aggression, it is a real threat to an ordered society. This was how he saw it.'

As Gabriel Toolan remembers it, Walter P. called down to John Joe McGirl's premises after the attack. McGirl said he knew nothing about it. Many townspeople visited the Toolans to express their disgust at what had happened and to offer their support to the family. As ever, this was done in private. Few spoke out publicly on the Toolans' behalf.

17. Seething with Sedition

Many senior gardaí were unimpressed by these scenes from Corraleehan and Ballinamore. Here was visible proof of local ambivalence towards the IRA, Jack Marrinan, the general secretary of the Garda Representative Association (GRA), believed.[1] He called for an emergency meeting of the board of the association to discuss the programme.

Traders in the town had demonstrated a 'mealy-mouthedness' and a 'frightened response' to the threat of the IRA, Marrinan claimed. Others on the programme indicated support, which would be a 'source of encouragement to the gunmen and the terrorists'.

Marrinan did stress, though, that the views expressed on *Today Tonight* were at odds with his own experiences in Ballinamore town, where he had received nothing but friendliness and kindness from local people after the kidnapping. Brendan O'Brien also stressed that he and his team had been treated well by locals.

The *Today Tonight* programme certainly damaged the image of Leitrim in the eyes of a national audience and would have confirmed for many viewers that this was a hotbed of republican sympathizers and 'sneaking regarders'. The people of the county knew it was a much more complicated picture than that.

Philip McGovern, a communications graduate from the College of Commerce in Rathmines, made a thirty-six-minute film in response to the programme. McGovern's father was a doctor from Ballinamore, and he knew the town and county well. He began the film by reciting the multiple ways in which Leitrim was bottom of every social index in the country at the time. The county's population had halved from 56,000 to 28,000 since the foundation of the state. In the 1940s and 1950s, some 17,000 people had left. Leitrim had the lowest birth rate, the lowest marriage rate, the lowest female-to-male ratio and also the highest death rate, the highest percentage of bachelors and the highest unemployment rate.[2]

Three-quarters of all Leitrim farms were less than sixty acres in size and the county had lost two-thirds of its farming workforce in the previous fifty years. Consequently, the county was infected by what a report in 1971 from An Foras Talúntais, the state's agricultural research institute (now Teagasc), identified as the 'psychology of decline'.[3]

The businessman Joe McCartin, a Leitrim TD and an MEP for Connacht-Ulster, was interviewed for an article about local agriculture in the *Irish Farmers Journal* shortly after the Derrada shootings. Its reporter, Larry Sheedy, had decided to write about farming, migration and the local economy in this part of Leitrim. He described the long-running struggle with the land, and the elements: a struggle that often became a lost cause.

There was, wrote Sheedy,

the tragedy of whole families selling out to emigrate to America. Nobody took their places on the slopes of Slieve an Iarainn. Others looked to the Land Commission for holdings in Meath or Kildare, and a few got them. Others, still, went to England, cherishing a hope of coming back with money to invest in their own land and perhaps buy more with it. Their half-grip on the land while they drove a bus in Birmingham often gave nature a head start on its takeover bid.

At that point, the *Farmers Journal* reported, south Leitrim had fewer families, more old people and a small proportion of part-time jobs, all of which militated against having a pool of labour big enough to make progress in such adverse conditions.

On Slieve an Iarainn itself the roll call of houses runs like this: (a) an old woman alone; (b) three bachelor men; (c) a man in his sixties alone. It goes on like that till you come to the last of the houses. There is (x) an elderly couple; (y) a woman of maybe 90; (z) the heather and the forest. There were houses up there once but their families gave up an unequal battle.

McCartin told him that the problem was a combination of shallow topsoil, impervious subsoil which holds water up, steep slopes and high rainfall. 'Together,' wrote Sheedy, the conditions

amount to real, genuine hardship for a farmer even before you add the big stones. With a guarantee of six comparatively dry months, a lot of Leitrim land could be tackled with confidence. But heavy rain on gluey daub means that a wet April keeps you in a month too long, a wet summer damages prospects for hay or silage, and a wet autumn drives you in off the land a crucial month too soon. It's a battle you can fight all the days of your farming life.

The conclusion was that massive investment from the Irish state and the EEC would be needed to make agriculture a viable way of life in places like south Leitrim. Yet, as Sheedy explained,

> a fundamental problem is that Europe no longer needs this stubborn land for food. The potential of the good land is so immense that it is hard to make a case for the required investment. At the same time, Leitrim needs it for people and perhaps, in a perverse way, a new spotlight has been beamed, by the pre-Christmas events, on an area that is threatened with a barren future.[4]

Contained in his bleak but realistic analysis was the sense of alienation between these hard-scrabble farming communities and the machinery of the Irish state. Though the Leitrim land was bad and the weather hostile, the blame in human form was placed on the remote establishment in Dublin. This was the ideal climate in which to cultivate support for sworn enemies of that self-same establishment, such as the Provisional IRA.

Philip McGovern also picked up on that connection in his film. 'Leitrim's neglect had bred a sense of a mistrust of authority, resentment, a rich harvest of cynicism and a lack of confidence in political institutions. These are the conditions that are nurturing support for the Provisionals,' he argued.[5]

The same sentiments were expressed in the documentary by the veteran republican Cathal Goulding, who also identified deep-seated resentment as a driving force behind support locally for the IRA.

'They feel themselves as some sort of second-class citizens and the wrongs have never been redressed since the establishment of the state,' he said. 'This is the reason why the Provisionals are so strongly based in Leitrim, though I'm not saying they are numerically strong there. The Leitrim people may not join the Provisionals en masse, but they would support them en masse in that they would put them up and they would not tell on them and if they had anything to mind – be it guns or men, things like that, they'd mind them for them. They see these people as being in the same tradition as their forefathers.'

Most Leitrim people would have agreed with the arguments made in McGovern's documentary. There was resentment about the county's decline and about how it had been bounced around like a political football into different Dáil constituencies. In practice, though, Leitrim remained loyal to the established parties of Fianna Fáil and Fine Gael, which, as recently as the local elections in 1979, had garnered between them 88 per cent of the vote.

John Joe McGirl's failure to get the hunger striker Joe McDonnell elected for Sligo-Leitrim in the general election of June 1981 was an indication that Leitrim was not as strongly republican as the border counties of Cavan, Monaghan and Louth, where hunger strikers were elected. McGirl did not even stand in the November 1982 general election after the drubbing Sinn Féin received in the general election of February of that year, when the vote he received was less than half that achieved by McDonnell in 1981. McDonnell got 5,639 votes (11.8 per cent) in 1981; McGirl 2,772 or 6 per cent of the vote in February 1982.

Even in his Ballinamore heartland, McGirl was not a proven vote winner. He was the only Leitrim Sinn Féin councillor elected in the 1979 local election, the last one before the Tidey kidnapping. Tallies from the 1985 local election show that most of McGirl's support was concentrated in rural areas outside the town.[6]

In the aftermath of Derrada, Pat Joe Reynolds, by now the cathaoirleach of Seanad Éireann, pointed out how little support Sinn Féin had in the county. 'I want to emphasize that the evil perpetrators of these deeds do not find acceptance or approval in the area,' he said. 'This is borne out by the fact that in the last local elections a certain party got less than five per cent in the polls.'[7]

Reynolds confronted McGirl at the first Leitrim County Council meeting after the murders of Kelly and Sheehan. McGirl had brought a delegation from Belfast – three people who had been victims of plastic bullets fired by the security forces. He asked the council to pass a resolution condemning the use of plastic bullets in the North. Reynolds asked McGirl and his delegation what they thought of the real bullets that were fired in Derrada Wood.

McGirl did not address this matter. Nor did he express any regret over the loss of life or extend his sympathies to the Kelly and Sheehan families.[8] He referenced instead the killing of two IRA operatives, Brian Campbell and Colm McGirr, who had been shot dead by the SAS as they examined an IRA arms dump in Co. Tyrone a fortnight before Derrada. Why no condemnation from the council for those shootings, McGirl inquired.

His bravado at the council meeting in Carrick-on-Shannon did not extend as far as Ballinamore. A Christmas social event for local Sinn Féin supporters had been planned months earlier. It was to be held in the town's Commercial Hotel on 27 December. But it seemingly dawned on McGirl and his coterie that they could not brazen this one out. They cancelled the 'do' in the Commercial.

The Derrada crisis, the *Today Tonight* episode and enduring rumours that Shergar was buried in Leitrim gave rise to a satirical song written by traditional musician and folk song collector Fintan Vallely. 'The Ballad of Ballinamore' was recorded and made popular by Christy Moore in 1984 and was a staple of his live set for many years afterwards.[9]

The tune is the same as an old Irish rebel song 'The Man from the Daily Mail' and the sentiment is much the same. 'The Man from the Daily Mail' was a send-up of British media incomprehension about Ireland; 'The Ballad of Ballinamore' is about the perceived ignorance of the Dublin-based media regarding a place like rural Leitrim:

> Leitrim is seething with sedition,
> It's Sinn Féin through and through.
> All the task force have joined the local unit,
> The post office in the GHQ.
> They've a racetrack underground for training Shergar,
> 'No comment!' is all they'll say to me.
> Subversion here is bubblin', please take me back to Dublin,
> Said your man from RTÉ.

18. Locking the Stable Door

The garda investigation into the kidnapping of Don Tidey and the murders of Private Kelly and Recruit Garda Sheehan involved thousands of man hours and the pursuit of hundreds of leads. Some thirty people around Ballinamore were arrested, in what gardaí described as a 'sieving operation'. They also distributed 300 questionnaires to locals.

Most of this would have been unnecessary had gardaí captured the suspects at Derrada, or four days later in Claremorris. But the stable door had been left open at both locations, and now they were trying to catch horses that had bolted in all directions. About 600 soldiers and gardaí were deployed to search around Claremorris, to no avail.

Gardaí knew that at least three of the kidnappers were Maze prison escapees but this didn't help in finding them. Others were caught, convicted and jailed for their part in the kidnapping, though they were all peripheral figures.

John Curnan was the farmer who owned Derrada Wood. Like so many Leitrim people before him, he had previously emigrated to England to make a living. It was there he met his future wife, Rose. In December 1983 the couple were bringing up six children on eighteen acres of bad land.

Curnan, aged fifty-nine, was receiving disability benefit because of chest trouble and paralysis from a stroke. His family was already struggling to get by in reduced circumstances, and John's poor health exacerbated their situation.[1] He suffered from severe bronchitis, shingles and kidney trouble. A doctor who examined him in custody thought him a 'very frail man' who struggled with his breathing as a result of smoking sixty cigarettes a day. He was also on anti-anxiety tablets while his wife suffered from anxiety neurosis and had been hospitalized three times in the previous five months.[2]

The Leitrim farmer was sympathetic to 'the cause' and considered himself a republican. 'I vote for Sinn Féin, for John Joe McGirl. He is my man,' Curnan told gardaí after he was arrested. His republicanism had been of the passive type until a man called 'Sonny' started to appear at his farmhouse in Derrada some weeks before the Tidey kidnapping. Curnan believed Sonny to be an IRA man on the run from the North, but said he asked him no questions.[3]

A few days before the abduction, Sonny told Curnan that the IRA intended to kidnap a man in Dublin and bring him to the wood. The farmer kept the information to himself. He would look the other way. 'I was glad to be asked to do this and I agreed that I would,' he explained afterwards. 'When I heard on the radio that Don Tidey was kidnapped, I knew it was Sonny and the boys that did it.'

During the first week of December, Sonny came every day looking for two bottles of hot water. When Curnan realized the water was to make tea for the 'IRA boys in the wood', he complied. 'I gave them whatever help I could after that. I gave them hot water and food and I kept Sonny informed about the guards and army when the searches were going on. Sonny was in the IRA and him and the boys would shoot if they had to. I would not inform on the IRA. I am an Irishman.'

On the day before the hide was discovered, John and Rose Curnan went up to the wood to meet Sonny and found him cleaning a rifle. 'We were standing about twenty-five yards away from where Don Tidey was concealed in a bunker. I asked him [Sonny] how things were going, and he said all right. I told him I would tell him if there was any movement of the guards about the place.'

On the afternoon of Tidey's release, Rose Curnan was in the wood cutting timber with a chainsaw when she heard shots. She ran screaming from the wood and says she collapsed when she got home.

When the drama of the day had subsided, the couple were left to face the reality that two men were dead and that they were complicit. They said they had never dreamed it would come to this and felt guilt and remorse. Both were arrested and taken to Clones garda station.

'I am sorry now that I did not tell the guards where Don Tidey was hidden as I may have saved two lives,' John Curnan told detectives. He later claimed he had been mistreated by gardaí in custody. When he asked for a solicitor, Curnan alleged, he was told he could 'rot in hell or at Dundrum asylum'. He claimed he could hear his wife crying in an adjacent cell.[4]

Curnan was given a seven-year sentence by the Special Criminal Court, but five of those years were suspended on account of his ill-health. He died in 1996.

Charles Gilheaney, thirty-six, was a single farmer from Clogher, a few miles outside Ballinamore. In January 1984 Gilheaney was arrested and questioned and then charged with kidnapping Don Tidey.

While in custody in Clones, he was told that several armed men had been seen around his home in the days before the kidnapping. According to gardaí, he told them: 'OK, all right, the boys were at my house, but I will not make a statement until I see the man in charge.' He also told gardaí that he had nothing against them but would not become an informer.[5]

Gilheaney claimed he was head-butted several times and knocked about while in custody. He claimed he asked for a solicitor four or five times, but his request was not heeded. He successfully argued in court that gardaí had not followed the correct procedures during his period in custody. He was acquitted of the charge, as the statement he had made to gardaí was the only evidence against him.

Patrick Rehill, along with John Joe McGirl, was one of the chief facilitators of the kidnapping. Rehill was arrested on the morning that Tidey was found and questioned in Carrick-on-Shannon garda station. He denied knowing anything about the crime.

Detective Sergeant Leonard Ahern from the Special Detective Unit at Dublin Castle was one of the interviewers. At one stage Rehill kicked him hard on the shins under the table with his work boots. Ahern told Carrick-on-Shannon District Court: 'He never replied to any question that I asked him during the whole period he was detained other than to call me a Free State bastard. That didn't annoy me. I am used to this type of behaviour.' Rehill was fined £10 for assault.[6]

The second person to be jailed in connection with the Tidey kidnapping was William (Billy) Kelly, from Tralee, who had hired one of the cars used. Kelly was a forty-one-year-old house painter. He had been jailed for membership of the IRA in 1974 and released after two years. He claimed he was no longer a member of the IRA when he was asked to hire the car from Horan's garage two days before the kidnapping.

Kelly refused to tell the Special Criminal Court who had ordered him to hire the car because he said he was afraid for his wife and children and for his own safety. 'If I give any names, my life won't be worth living. I'd have to live in the shadows for the rest of my life.'[7] He also claimed not to know what the car was intended to be used for, but this was dismissed by the judge, Liam Hamilton.

Almost a year to the day after the kidnapping, Kelly was sentenced to three years in jail for the offence of aiding and abetting a kidnap gang. Kelly had been arrested in the company of Seán O'Callaghan, the informer, who was released without charge and later claimed it was he who had told gardaí that Tidey was being held near Ballinamore.

The last person jailed for the kidnapping was Michael Burke from Co. Cork. He had walked into Tralee garda station ten months after the kidnapping, on hearing that police were looking for him. He did not present himself out of any desire to expiate his guilt. Rather, he was apparently confident that the gardaí had nothing on him.

Presumably, then, he was surprised to find himself being picked out in an identity parade by Padraig Mooney, a neighbour of Tidey, as one of the kidnappers wearing a garda uniform at Stocking Lane on the morning of 24 November.[8] Among those who gave evidence at Burke's subsequent trial were Don Tidey, his son Alistair and daughter Susan, but the critical witness was Padraig Mooney.[9] He had come across the roadblock earlier that morning and studied the three men. The one wearing a garda uniform looked like a 'young, clean-shaven policeman', and had a pointed nose and peculiar eyes.

In two separate identity parades in Tralee garda station, Mooney had picked out Burke by putting a hand on his shoulder. Burke's counsel argued in court that this was insufficient evidence to bring a prosecution, but the judge, Thomas Doyle, concluded that the identity parade was 'exceptionally convincing' and Mooney was an 'exceptionally observant man' who had also noted that the bogus police car used by the gang had no garda markings.

Burke, then twenty-eight, was given a hefty twelve-year jail sentence (which he appealed against unsuccessfully in 1988).[10] He was released from Portlaoise prison in 1994 and went on to oppose the peace process. He became the national organizer of the 32 County Sovereignty Committee, a hardline organization founded by Bobby Sands's sister, Bernadette Sands-McKevitt.

Burke was the only one convicted from the gang that had abducted Tidey and brought him to Kildare, where he was handed over to the gang that took him to Leitrim.

One person was jailed in relation to the Claremorris incident. Mary McGing, twenty-six, was a member of the Sinn Féin ard comhairle and the party's candidate in the European parliamentary elections of June 1984, in which she won 4,176 votes (1.8 per cent) in the Connacht-Ulster constituency. Her trial in connection with Claremorris was held in August of that year.

McGing admitted being a front-seat passenger in a white Mercedes with the three IRA fugitives in the back when it was stopped at the garda checkpoint near Ballycroy on the night of 20 December 1983. McGing guided them to the safe house in Claremorris.

In court her defence counsel, Patrick McEntee SC, argued that McGing had no idea who the men were when she took them to the house. The only evidence against her was a statement made in garda custody, which she did not sign. Nevertheless, she was convicted of harbouring and assisting three men, knowing they had possession of firearms with intent to endanger life.[11]

As she left the courtroom, McGing raised her fist and shouted, 'Up the Provos!' She lost her job as an engineer with Mayo County Council because of her conviction. She was still in jail serving her sentence when she stood in the Westport constituency in the 1985 local elections. Clearly, the local electorate was not enamoured by her activities: she finished eighth out of nine candidates with 377 votes. In 1989 she was fined IR£1 for daubing anti-extradition signs on Claremorris garda station.

Colman O'Reilly, the twenty-six-year-old schoolteacher whose house had been occupied by McGing and the gang, also went on trial in connection with the Claremorris incident. He had built a new bungalow on the outskirts of the town and was yet to live in it. O'Reilly had been approached by McGing in the summer of 1983 and asked for the loan of the house for a couple of Sinn Féin meetings. Though he was a member of Fianna Fáil, and had once declined her offer to join Sinn Féin, he gave McGing the keys.[12]

When O'Reilly turned up at his bungalow one evening, Gerry Adams was there with others. The teacher believed it was just a political meeting.

Three days after Derrada, McGing asked again for the use of the house and he agreed. When O'Reilly called over with a Christmas tree and holly, he found three men there, two with guns. He noted that one of them was bald. O'Reilly correctly suspected that these were the men involved in the incident at the garda checkpoint in Claremorris, though he did not know they were suspects in the Tidey kidnapping too. He told them to get out. The bald man responded that O'Reilly would need to deliver a message to a woman in the Beaten Path pub in Claremorris in order to allow them to leave the house.

O'Reilly duly went to the Beaten Path, where the mystery woman told him the three men would be moving on soon. She gave O'Reilly a transistor radio to give to them, but when he returned to the house, the three had gone.

A short time afterwards O'Reilly was arrested by detectives and charged with harbouring men who were wanted for the kidnapping of Tidey. In court O'Reilly successfully argued that he did not know who the men were and had wanted nothing to do with their activities. He was acquitted on two charges of harbouring men he knew were wanted for false imprisonment and possession of firearms with intent to endanger life.

The young teacher lost both his parents around the time of the incident. He had been the unwitting host of the kidnappers in Claremorris, and almost lost his job as a result of it.

In total six people had gone on trial in relation to the events surrounding the kidnapping of Don Tidey and three were convicted. All of those involved, with the exception of Michael Burke, were peripheral figures in the Tidey kidnapping and the killing of Kelly and Sheehan. Nobody has faced trial for their murder.

While John Curnan languished in prison, his wife was left to work the farm and tend as best she could to their six traumatized children. They themselves had to cope with the distress of seeing their father being arrested, tried, convicted and jailed. They too were innocents caught up in circumstances over which they had no control but which brought down upon them a flood of pain and suffering.

Meanwhile, the local ringleaders on the ground, John Joe McGirl and Pat Rehill among them, were soon at liberty to resume normal life.

19. Frozen

Gardaí derived understandable satisfaction from thwarting the paying of a ransom for Don Tidey. And having drawn that line in the sand, they might have assumed that no such payment would ever be contemplated again by any big business, not least Associated British Foods (ABF).

Yet in February 1985 they were forced to intervene again when emergency legislation was needed to stop the payment of IR£1.75 million (€2.2 million), allegedly to the IRA, through a bank account in Navan, Co. Meath.

Gardaí were informed the money had been paid by ABF to ensure no more of its executives would be kidnapped. If true, it was a sort of illicit insurance policy. The kidnapping of Tidey had evidently spooked Galen Weston and his brother Garry, and it was claimed they attempted to pay the money through Control Risks, a London-based security firm.

The money was discovered by a stroke of good luck in America. Early in 1984 the Federal Bureau of Investigation (FBI) came across accounts associated with the IRA while they were investigating money-laundering operations by the Italian mafia in Boston.[1] On 25 May 1984 a Scotsman named David McCartney Jr went into the Bank of Ireland branch on Fifth Avenue in New York and withdrew a series of US dollar drafts equivalent to IR£1,750,866 from an account that had been opened just a fortnight previously. The account was in the name of his uncle, who shared the same name.

Five days later McCartney Jr boarded an Aer Lingus flight

to Dublin with the bank drafts in an envelope in his jacket pocket. He handed them to a businessman, Alan Clancy, in the Royal Dublin Hotel in O'Connell Street and Clancy deposited the money in the Bank of Ireland branch in Navan in the name of David McCartney Sr.

Clancy and McCartney Sr, both entrepreneurs who had made fortunes in the United States, had collaborated on several ventures, but their attempts to avoid paying tax had brought them to the attention of the authorities. McCartney Sr was involved in construction, mostly in sand-hogging, a lucrative labour-intensive form of tunnelling. He also made big profits in the Alaskan oil fields. Yet he was an illegal immigrant in the United States, and much of his money had been concealed from Internal Revenue. They were already onto him by the time the money fetched up in the account in Navan.

'Everyone else in the world would avoid paying tax if they could. It's a natural reaction,' he later explained. 'Being an illegal immigrant made life very difficult. I had over £2 million in Swiss banks. But it was doing me no good there when I wasn't happy at the prospect of not being able to spend it the way I wanted to.'

Originally from Oldcastle, Co. Meath, Clancy had made his money as a publican in New York. At one stage he had thirty bars in the city. In 1968 he financed the building of the Four Seasons Hotel outside Monaghan town (not to be confused with the international hotel chain of the same name). It was there he first met McCartney Sr, a Scot with no Irish connections but who had made Ireland his home. Clancy was noted for his rather unorthodox business methods, which included buying some pubs with cash.[2]

*

The massive transactions in Bank of Ireland's Fifth Avenue branch were red flags for the FBI. When the gardaí were tipped off about suspicious activity on the bank account in Navan, the Irish government immediately introduced emergency legislation enabling them to seize the money.

The Offences Against the State (Amendment) Act 1985 was rushed through the Dáil during a day-and-night sitting on 19 February. Only one member of the Oireachtas, Fine Gael TD and constitutional lawyer John Kelly, voted against.

During the debate justice minister Michael Noonan did not name ABF as the source of the money, instead stating it was the proceeds of 'extortion under threat of kidnap and murder'. If it were to fall into the hands of the IRA, 'the consequences for human life on this island would be grave', Noonan warned.[3] He said:

> Information has been conveyed to the garda authorities that a large sum of money which is the proceeds of criminal activity by the IRA . . . has found its way into a bank in this country and is being held to the use of, and for the purposes of, the IRA. In recent days it became apparent that the custodians of this money would find it necessary to make a move to transfer it. This necessitated urgent action by the government to prevent the money becoming available to the IRA to fund its campaign of murder and destruction. I do not need to lecture this House on the evils of the IRA. I will simply recall, because it is important in the context of this Bill, that since the IRA campaign began in 1969–70, thousands of people have been murdered and maimed on this island. In this part of the country twelve members of the security forces – Garda and Army – have been murdered in

the past fourteen years. Millions of pounds have been taken in armed robberies.

The cabinet's security committee, consisting of the taoiseach, tánaiste, ministers for foreign affairs, defence and justice plus the attorney general, then approved the seizure of the money. It was transferred from the Bank of Ireland to the High Court on 20 February.

Noonan had persuaded his colleagues to take this extreme measure, but wasn't sure he was making the right decision. Passing the emergency legislation alerted the public to the existence of the money and allowed others to claim it was theirs and not destined for the IRA. 'We wrote a provision into the Bill that anybody who wanted to claim that the money was held in the bank account legitimately could enter court and, by proving that it was held legitimately and was not funds to the benefit of the Provisional IRA, could get the money back in court,' Noonan explained some years later.[4]

In December 1985 the *Sunday Times* Insight team of investigative reporters published an extraordinary exposé on Associated British Foods in which it alleged the company had hired Control Risks to advise on paying ransoms. According to Insight, the IRA had threatened Tidey and the Weston family that their lives would be at risk if they did not co-operate. Control Risks advised Garry Weston not to pay the money or, if he decided to pay, to tell the British and Irish governments afterwards. Weston, according to the report, ignored the advice.[5]

Publicly, ABF denied having anything to do with paying a ransom to the IRA. 'It is emphasized that at no time has the company paid any money by way of ransom or extortion to any organization, nor would it do so,' Garry Weston stated, but his protestations were disbelieved by both the gardaí and MI5, who made it clear in private briefings to the press that they felt the money had indeed originated from ABF.[6] Margaret Thatcher was reported to be furious that the company had behaved in such a fashion and there were even calls in the House of Commons, not acted upon, for ABF to be prosecuted.

Clancy denied the money was destined for the IRA. 'I believe in and aspire to the unification of Ireland by peaceful means,' he said in a statement issued through his solicitor shortly after the money was sequestered. 'I condemn political violence for that or any other purpose. I have no connection with the Provisional IRA, Sinn Féin or any agent or support group of theirs, such as NORAID.'[7]

McCartney Sr also insisted he had nothing to do with the IRA. 'From what I know, I hate the IRA and anything to do with violence,' he said.[8] 'I may not have paid tax on money I have made, but the money was made legally and honestly and did not come from kidnapping. That £1.75 million was my own money, made from my own work and from shareholdings I had. It didn't come from kidnapping. That's ridiculous.'

Clancy lodged proceedings in the High Court in a bid to reclaim the money, and a protracted legal battle ensued. The seizure of the funds was 'grossly unjust' and 'tyrannical', he argued. Yet he and McCartney Sr refused to give what judges considered a satisfactory answer as to how they had acquired the money in the first place.

McCartney Sr admitted that he had been an illegal immigrant in the United States and had made a lot of money on tunnelling and pipeline construction. Because of his alien status, he had opened several Swiss bank accounts to avoid the money being discovered by immigration authorities.

Clancy claimed that revealing the origins of his share of the money would force him to reveal confidential matters about his finances. He took the case on his own, as McCartney had apparently paid back money that was owed to Clancy. The High Court dismissed his claim in 1988. Both men indicated that they would appeal the decision to the Supreme Court, but never did. They died within a year of each other in the 1990s, yet the estates of both men never made a claim on the cash. It was paid to the Irish exchequer in 2008, by which time it had accumulated with interest to €6 million.[9]

To this day, the precise evidence that prompted the Irish government to believe the IR£1.75 million was destined for the IRA has never been disclosed.

But while following the trail of subversive money remained an ongoing priority for An Garda Síochána, the price paid by colleagues at the hands of Sinn Féin/IRA was an investigative priority of a higher order.

They were never going to forgive or forget those who had killed one of their own in Derrada Wood.

PART THREE
Reckoning

20. Trial and Error

It cannot be said for certain which of the Tidey kidnappers raised their weapons, aimed them at the two uniformed men and shot them dead. But if one of them was Brendan 'Bik' McFarlane, it can be said with certainty he was capable of murder. For he had murdered before.

McFarlane's ability to put his empathy and morality on hold had been definitively demonstrated over eight years earlier. On the night of 13 August 1975, he and two accomplices murdered five people inside and outside a bar in his native Belfast. Two of the victims – Samuel Gunning (fifty-five) and his brother-in-law William Gracey (sixty-three) – were standing outside the bar when they were shot down in a hail of gunfire from an automatic weapon. At a trial the following year, evidence was given that a forensic examination of the clothes McFarlane was wearing on the night revealed residues of firearm discharge on the shoulder of his jacket.

The premises the IRA unit had targeted was the Bayardo Bar on the Shankill Road. The IRA had been on ceasefire since February 1975, but this only applied to the security forces. Protestant paramilitaries were the most prolific killers in 1975, accounting for 120 deaths, the vast majority of them Catholic civilians. Unionists suspected the British government had done a grubby deal with republicans and were willing to sell out the Union and grant a united Ireland. Loyalists hoped to provoke republicans into breaking their ceasefire.

This was a period of peak sectarian nihilism, with tit-for-tat murders carried out on a rolling timeline. On 31 July 1975 loyalists murdered three members of the Miami Showband in one of the most notorious incidents of the Troubles. The band, based in Dublin but with members from both sides of the border, was ambushed coming from a concert in Banbridge. The attack on a group of entertainers, pop musicians who were spreading fun and enjoyment in the darkest of times, caused profound shock even among a populace already weary from the conflict.

The attack on the Bayardo Bar was widely seen as a revenge mission for that massacre.[1] The bar was beside The Eagle chip shop, which was a meeting place for members of the Ulster Volunteer Force. UVF members were known to drink in the Bayardo.

On the night, McFarlane was the driver of a hijacked green Audi; his passengers were two other IRA men, Peter Christopher 'Skeet' Hamilton (twenty-two) and Seamus Joseph Clarke (nineteen). They pulled up by the pub's side door. One of them got out and opened fire on Gunning and Gracey. Another of them, identified in court as Hamilton, came through the side door, dropped a duffel bag on the floor and left.

The side door was open as ventilation for the cigarette smoke inside. The court would hear that a woman sitting close to the door saw the man enter, place the bag and walk out. She saw smoke issuing from the bag and realized it contained a bomb. The woman shouted a warning but it was already too late. The bomb exploded within seconds.

Two people died almost immediately from a multiplicity of horrific injuries. They were Hugh Harris (twenty-one), a member of the UVF, and Joanne McDowell (nineteen).

Dozens of other customers were trapped under the collapsed rubble. One of them, Linda Boyle (nineteen), was rescued but died from her injuries a week later.

A friend of Harris and Boyle was sitting alongside them when he heard the warning about a bomb. He told the court they jumped up and rushed for the exit. He shouted at Harris to 'get over the damned thing' just as it exploded. 'I just felt myself being thrown all over the place,' he testified. 'My next recollection is lying in complete darkness – and the smell of the place.'

As the terrorists drove away, one of them fired indiscriminately at a group of women and children queuing at a taxi rank. Mercifully there were no fatalities. Some ten minutes later the green Audi was stopped by an army patrol at a checkpoint. McFarlane was the only occupant. A quick survey of the vehicle was sufficient to alert the soldiers. Its rear windscreen was missing; both rear side-windows were fully rolled down; there was a bullet hole in its roof.

McFarlane was taken into custody and the car impounded. A subsequent search turned up five spent bullet cases; they matched a further four bullet cases found outside the Bayardo. The bullets that killed Gunning and Gracey had been fired from the same Armalite that was used to shoot at the people queuing beside the taxi rank.[2]

The indiscriminate nature of the bombing and the shooting was seen as an attack on the Protestant community in the Shankill and therefore a sectarian act. Yet McFarlane's good friend Gerry Adams would later tell journalist Alan Murray that McFarlane 'hasn't a single, sectarian bone in his body'.[3]

One subversive who was in Crumlin Road jail at the time said his fellow inmates were unimpressed with the atrocity – not per se because it had been committed, but because it sent out the wrong signal. The IRA was supposed to be a republican organization and therefore non-sectarian. How could they claim this after the Bayardo Bar massacre?

'The Belfast Brigade had been claiming that all the shootings of Protestants in Belfast were actually shootings of paramilitaries, but the wider IRA had become aware that the Belfast Brigade was in fact shooting innocent Protestants in sectarian attacks,' he said. When the Bayardo Bar attack happened there was supposed to be a ceasefire ... It mostly murdered Protestant civilians. We were discussing the job in Crumlin Road jail and there was a widespread feeling that sectarian attacks weren't truly republican. Some people were openly criticizing the job, and that was even before Bik landed in the prison with his comrades.'[4]

In May 1976 McFarlane, Hamilton and Clarke were each charged with five counts of murder, one of causing an explosion and one of conspiring to cause an explosion. The court heard the fingerprints of all three had been found on the green Audi; and that the car had been hijacked at gunpoint some twenty minutes before the attack.

After ten days at trial the three were jailed for life on the five counts of murder, plus an additional fourteen years concurrently for causing an explosion and seven years concurrently for conspiring to cause an explosion. McFarlane was also convicted of membership of the IRA and given a further two-year concurrent sentence. It was recommended that he serve a minimum of twenty-five years.

McFarlane, the eldest, was still only in his mid-twenties. As a teenager in Ardoyne he believed he had a religious vocation and went to train for the priesthood with the Divine Word Missionaries at St David's Catholic seminary in Wales. He had returned home to Belfast in 1969 and joined the IRA.

McFarlane did not appeal against his conviction. In June 1977 the Court of Criminal Appeal did hear appeals from Clarke and Hamilton, who claimed the fingerprints found on the getaway car arose from a previous contact, when they helped to rock it away from a kerbside as it had a flat tyre. The three-man panel of judges rejected their appeal, upholding the verdicts of the original trial judge as 'the only conclusions open on the evidence'.[5]

When the hunger strikes began at the Maze prison in 1981, McFarlane was officer commanding of the republican inmates. His involvement at the Bayardo Bar ruled him out as a candidate for hunger strike himself, according to the author and journalist David Beresford. In his 1987 book *Ten Men Dead*, Beresford described McFarlane as a 'sectarian mass murderer – or at least that would be the tag which could easily be attached to him by a hostile press. That is why he was never chosen for a hunger strike – he was potentially a one-man public relations disaster.'[6]

Clarke, Hamilton and McFarlane were among the thirty-eight escapees who broke out of the Maze on 25 September 1983. With them were three others suspected of being in the gang that imprisoned Tidey: Seamus McElwaine, Tony McAllister and Gerard McDonnell.

After Derrada Wood, McFarlane next resurfaced in January 1986 in an apartment in Amsterdam, where he and fellow Maze escapee Gerry Kelly and a third terrorist were arrested by Dutch police. In their search of the rooms, police also found false passports, bundles of cash and a weapons manual. A large quantity of firearms and explosives was discovered nearby.

McFarlane was detained for six months by the Dutch

police, during which time he gave an interview to *Magill* magazine in which he justified the IRA's campaign of violence, and said that killing people was 'messy' but necessary.

> I am affected personally. Nobody likes violence. I do it as an absolute necessity. But it is not inherent in my being, in my nature. It takes a lot to push yourself to that line – to be part of, and to witness, death. It takes a lot of consideration. The use of violence has hardened my attitude in general to those types of situations. I have learned to have a much harder outlook.

In his interview with the journalist Derek Dunne, McFarlane declined to give an account of where he went following his escape from the Maze. He claimed that to do so would entail revealing countries and dates which would in turn identify people. McFarlane claimed to be 'definitely not' involved with Derrada Wood.[7]

After a protracted legal battle through the Dutch courts, McFarlane and Kelly were extradited back to jail in Northern Ireland in December 1986. McFarlane was sentenced to a further five years in prison for his escape. He was released on parole in March 1997.

On 5 January 1998, now aged forty-seven, McFarlane was travelling from Dublin to Belfast on a bus when it was stopped by a garda checkpoint at Dromad, Co. Louth, close to the border. It was the beginning of a marathon legal saga that would play out over the next ten and a half years, finally reaching a climax at his trial in the Special Criminal Court in Dublin in June 2008.[8]

During that trial, Garda Superintendent James Sheridan said he'd arrested McFarlane on the bus following a phone call from a senior officer earlier that morning. He and several gardaí travelled to the checkpoint in Dromad, boarded the bus and identified the suspect. They brought him to Dundalk garda station. McFarlane told them he was due to get official papers that would release him from parole later that afternoon in Belfast.

Mo Mowlam, the then secretary of state for Northern Ireland, was indeed due to sign his release papers at 3 p.m. The release of paramilitary prisoners was seen as an important confidence-building measure that would soon lead to the signing of the Good Friday Agreement.

Superintendent Sheridan said in court that he wasn't aware of this at the time. McFarlane asked him to inform the Northern Ireland Office that he'd been arrested, which Sheridan did. He was then charged with falsely imprisoning Don Tidey, possession of a firearm with intent to endanger life and possession of a firearm for an unlawful purpose at Derrada Wood between 25 November and 16 December 1983.

At a hearing in Dublin eight days later, Detective Superintendent John McElligott opposed bail, arguing that the defendant was not a resident of the jurisdiction and would not turn up for trial, given the gravity of the offences and the weight of the evidence against him. This included his fingerprints on three items recovered by gardaí from the hideout at the time: an NCF (North Connacht Farmers) milk carton with a best-before date of 16/12/83, a plastic container and a cooking pot.

McFarlane was granted bail on remand with two independent bonds totalling £100,000.[9] He would remain on bail as a series of legal contests unfolded over the following decade.

At the High Court in November 1999, McFarlane was granted leave to bring an action to prevent his trial from going ahead. It was here that a solicitor for the accused revealed that the items mentioned by McElligott at the bail hearing had gone missing. They had been lost or mislaid in a garda storage depot.

A report on these proceedings in the *Irish Times* recorded solicitor James MacGuill saying that the evidence against his client primarily consisted of fingerprints on domestic items alleged to have been retrieved at the time of the incidents. As certain of these items were no longer in the custody of the gardaí, they were unavailable to McFarlane for inspection.[10]

McFarlane's trial was put on hold for the next three and a half years, pending the outcome of his High Court action. In July 2003 the High Court was told that his right to a fair trial had been prejudiced by a delay of nearly twenty years in prosecuting the charges and because of the disappearance of the items containing the fingerprint evidence. Judge Aindrias Ó Caoimh agreed and granted McFarlane the order. A stay was placed on his order to allow the state to decide whether or not to appeal to the Supreme Court.[11]

The Director of Public Prosecutions did appeal, and in March 2006 the Supreme Court upheld it.[12] Judge Adrian Hardiman addressed the issues in contention. From the affidavit of Superintendent McElligott, said Hardiman, it was clear the gardaí 'considered [McFarlane] should be sought for interview in relation to the false imprisonment of Mr Tidey and associated crimes, but that there was then [i.e. twenty years ago] insufficient evidence to commence proceedings against him'.

Instead they intended to question him, and this was why McFarlane's extradition from Northern Ireland was not sought, nor was it sought to have him prosecuted under the Criminal Law (Jurisdiction) Act 1976 while in prison there.

'Equally, he was not interviewed while serving [his] sentence in Northern Ireland because it was believed he would not co-operate in any such venture and that he would be entitled to refuse to see any Garda who sought to interview him while in prison in Northern Ireland.'[13]

Judge Hardiman pointed out that subsequent to his arrest in January 1998, McFarlane was questioned by gardaí but mostly refused to answer and simply stared at the wall:

It is alleged, however, that he made certain admissions while being questioned. Specifically, it is alleged that when asked about his involvement in Drumcroman Wood he said: 'On the advice of my solicitor I will not discuss it. I was there, you can prove that, but I will not talk about it.'

The following conversation then took place: Q: 'What do you expect will happen to you?' A: 'I am prepared for the big one. I have already talked to her [his girlfriend] about our future and house.' Q: 'Do you mean murder?' A: 'I am prepared for the worst.' These alleged statements, together with the fingerprints, constitute the case against the applicant.

On the matter of a fair trial being prejudiced by delay, Hardiman said that consideration had to be given as to what McFarlane had been up to in that period:

On 25 September 1983 he had undoubtedly escaped from lawful custody in Northern Ireland. The next uncontroversial statement that can be made about his whereabouts is that he was in the Netherlands in January of 1986 in possession of a stolen or forged Irish passport. The applicant has said nothing about his whereabouts during any part of that time and, vitally, has not asserted how he spent the time, or that he cannot recall where he was during the period of Mr Tidey's captivity in late November and up to 16 December 1983. An applicant in this position must address ... the actual specific facts of his case and this applicant has singularly failed to do so.

Addressing the absent fingerprint evidence, Hardiman was similarly unimpressed with the lack of police professionalism in this regard. He cited an affidavit from Maurice Boyle, a retired garda, which seemed to indicate the milk carton, plastic container and cooking pot had gone missing some time between 1993 and 1998.

> The affidavit of Mr Boyle, formerly a sergeant in the fingerprint section of the Garda, makes it clear these items were present in a specific room at the time of his retirement from the force in 1993. Five years later, when he was requested to come back to work for the purpose of dealing with them, the room had been changed from storeroom to library and conference room and the items were nowhere to be found.[14]

Crucially for the prosecution case, however, the items had been photographed. Drawing from a series of legal precedents with regard to the availability of material evidence, Hardiman cited a previous ruling which said 'secondary' evidence such as photos or film footage of the originals could be admitted. Then, with various caveats inserted, Judge Hardiman concluded by refusing to grant McFarlane the relief he'd sought.

Five judges had presided at the Supreme Court hearing. Three others agreed with Hardiman, thereby overturning the Ó Caoimh decision of July 2003 by a four-to-one majority.

In May 2006, McFarlane's legal team returned to the High

Court and succeeded in getting leave to bring a fresh challenge to stop the trial from going ahead.[15] The trial had been listed to start in the non-jury Special Criminal Court in October. In the eight years since he was arrested at Dromad, McFarlane had married and was now a father to three children.

His lawyer, Hugh Hartnett SC, argued that a delay of time already prejudicial to his client had been further exacerbated by the 'systemic delays' in the legal processes since his arrest. He claimed McFarlane's children were dependent on him for their day-to-day care because his wife was in full-time employment. Judge Michael Peart granted him leave to initiate another legal challenge against the state's criminal proceedings.

In December 2006 his challenge was heard in the High Court and dismissed by Judge John Quirke. It was acknowledged that McFarlane was complaining of stress, anxiety and inconvenience brought on by the delays, but the judge said that these could not outweigh the community's very considerable interest in having offences of such gravity prosecuted to a conclusion.

Quirke gave him leave to appeal, and McFarlane's legal team duly did so.[16] Another fifteen months would elapse before it was heard in the Supreme Court. In March 2008 another five-judge panel unanimously dismissed that appeal too. One of them, Nicholas Kearns, said that after a detailed analysis of the litigation in the ten years since 1998, McFarlane had not established blameworthy systemic or prosecutorial delay and, even if there was such delay, he had not demonstrated any actual resulting prejudice such as breached his right to a fair trial.[17] The road was finally clear to put McFarlane in the dock.

21. Justice Delayed

The trial of Brendan McFarlane on charges of false imprisonment, possession of a firearm with intent to endanger life and possession of a firearm for an unlawful purpose began on 11 June 2008. He pleaded not guilty to all charges. It had been twenty-four years and six months since the events at Derrada Wood. The defendant was now fifty-six years of age. Don Tidey was seventy-two. Gary Sheehan would have been forty-seven; Patrick Kelly would have been sixty.

McFarlane was accompanied to court on the first day of his trial by Martin Ferris, the convicted IRA gun runner who was by then a Sinn Féin TD for Kerry North.[1]

In the witness box, Tidey again recounted his ordeal of November–December 1983. Before his testimony concluded, he agreed that he was unable to identify any of his captors. Over the following week a succession of gardaí and soldiers also delivered eyewitness accounts of the drama that day in the woods.

In the second week of the trial, McFarlane's barrister Hugh Hartnett dissected his client's detention at Dundalk garda station in January 1998. A retired detective garda who had interviewed the suspect was challenged about the admission that McFarlane was said to have made in custody. The detective insisted that McFarlane had said: 'I was there, you can prove that, but I will not talk about it,' and that he later said, 'I am prepared for the big one.'

On 24 June Brendan McFarlane entered the witness box.

Private Patrick Kelly's widow and eldest son David watched from a seat in the public gallery. Under cross-examination from Edward Comyn SC, for the DPP, McFarlane denied that he'd ever uttered these words in Dundalk garda station. 'I did not, my Lord.' The respect he showed to the judge was noteworthy. Previous generations of republicans had refused to recognize southern courts.

McFarlane said that while the notes from each of his garda interviews in the station had been read back to him, the alleged admissions were never put to him. Comyn asked if he believed those comments were added later. McFarlane replied: 'That's precisely what I'm saying, my Lord.'

Before McFarlane took the stand, his lawyer had made an application to the three sitting judges.[2] Hartnett argued that his client had been questioned under duress by detectives at the station on 5 and 6 January 1998. He said that on three occasions McFarlane had been questioned by officers under the now outdated Section 52 of the Offences Against the State Act, which compelled suspects to respond or face being charged with committing a criminal offence.

Comyn counter-argued, saying that McFarlane had made the admissions not under duress but in response to being told by detectives that they had fingerprint evidence tying him to the scene. This was the first time McFarlane had heard about the fingerprint evidence, Comyn insisted.

McFarlane denied this, saying he'd first read about the forensic evidence in a magazine in the mid-1990s. 'It was no surprise that they put it to me they had fingerprint evidence,' he stated.

The next day, Hartnett continued to probe the disputed admissions in Dundalk garda station. He told the court that when his client applied for bail a week or so after his arrest in

January 1998, gardaí made no mention of McFarlane's supposed admissions. 'Why did Superintendent McElligott, as he was then, when asked what the strength of the evidence of the case against the accused man was, say fingerprint evidence and not mention the verbal? At no stage did he ever make the case that there was an admission.'[3]

The following day, 26 June, the court ruled that McFarlane's alleged statements in Dundalk were indeed inadmissible. Justice Paul Butler, presiding, alongside judges Alison Lindsay and Cormac Dunne, said the interviews were conducted according 'to the norms of a decade ago'. However, they were not in accordance with the statutory regulations then in existence, in that not all of McFarlane's answers were recorded and nor were all the dates of the interviews.

Taking account of McFarlane's denial that he had made the statements, and the defects in recording them, the court had a doubt, and must therefore exclude the admission. Butler pointed out that the issue would not have arisen in 2008, as interviews in garda stations were recorded by video.[4]

In response to this decision, Comyn requested some time to take instructions. After lunch Fergal Foley, the junior counsel for the prosecution, announced that the state was 'offering no further evidence'. Hartnett applied for a direction of acquittal and it was granted. McFarlane was free to go. He was entitled, said Justice Butler, to retain the presumption of innocence.

Looking back on it now, Foley says that with both the admissions in Dundalk garda station and the fingerprint evidence, the prosecution felt it had a strong case.[5] 'The late Eddie Comyn [was] an absolutely meticulous man, and if there was the slightest doubt he would have been saying, "We should pull the plug, we can't get ahead of this." He and I were both convinced that if we could get the fingerprint photographs in, and then compare them with [McFarlane's] fingerprints, we had a good case.'

Once the court ruled that the statements were inadmissible, however, the calculation changed. Foley says that in order to fly, the prosecution case needed two wings. Without the statements in Dundalk garda station, it would be like a bird trying to fly with one.

Had the trial continued and it reached the forensic evidence stage, it wouldn't have mattered, Foley contends, that the original items found in the hideout were not present in the courtroom. 'Obviously the best evidence is the actual item itself, so that it's available for examination, and if the court in this instance wanted to look through magnifying glasses and see the actual fingerprints, that could be done. But I've never seen a Special Criminal Court judge look at something through a magnifying glass. They just take the expert opinion. If necessary, or if there's a doubt, the defence will produce a counter-expert to say that this is not a proper fingerprint, or there aren't sufficient points of similarity to make an admissible fingerprint. But once you prove that items were found, that fingerprints were found on those items, that photographs were taken of the found fingerprints, and then compared with prints taken from the accused person, that's enough.'

Now accompanied by Arthur Morgan, the Sinn Féin TD for Louth, McFarlane spoke to reporters outside the Green Street courthouse afterwards. He said he was 'very, very relieved' by the outcome. 'It's been a long ten years and it's been an extremely difficult period for myself and my family. What I want to do now is put this behind me and move on, go back home and get on with life with my family.'

Asked if he had anything to say to Don Tidey or the bereaved families, he replied: 'I think I've said enough. We're glad that we're at the end of this case and it has been a very, very long period of time over the last ten years and certainly I just want to be able to get home and get on with life.'[6] Don Tidey was not in court that day.

A few days after the verdict, Caitriona Kelly and two of her sons, David and Michael, met with the journalist Ann Marie Hourihane for an interview that would appear in the *Irish Times* on 5 July 2008.

Caitriona Kelly said she had taken unpaid leave from her job as a senior care assistant in London to attend the trial. She and her sons would drive up from Moate to attend each day. 'Very disappointing,' said David Kelly when he was asked by Hourihane about the verdict. 'This is it,' he added. 'It's over. Unfortunately, it looks highly probable that no one will ever be prosecuted for the kidnappings or the killings.'[7]

But at least the story of what happened 'came out into the light', he reasoned. Furthermore, the court got to hear the testimony of some of Paddy Kelly's comrades who were in Derrada Wood on the fateful day. 'The one that stands out for me was Corporal Paddy Shine,' David said. 'He was standing next to my father when he died and was able to describe exactly what happened; to give a full, definitive account. Up to now all I've heard is snippets. My father's last moments are very important to me.'

In September 2010, following a case taken by his legal team, the European Court of Human Rights ruled that McFarlane was entitled to monetary relief from the Irish state for the delays in bringing him to trial for the kidnapping of Don

Tidey. The state's claim that McFarlane's legal challenges caused the delay was rejected by the court. It criticized the fact that it took Irish authorities some eighteen months to discover documents sought in 2000, and other delays.

'The Court finds that the Government have not provided ... any convincing explanations ... for the above-described delays attributable to the authorities in the prohibition actions, which added to the overall length of the criminal proceedings,' the Strasbourg judges ruled.[8] Brendan McFarlane was awarded a total of €15,500 in compensation and costs.

22. Memory and Loss

Gary Sheehan was into his music and he had the cool stereo system to prove it. He had the vinyl record collection to prove it too. 'Tons and tons of records,' recalls Jennifer McCann, the youngest of the four Sheehan siblings. Gary was the eldest, born on 24 September 1960. The twins, Gráinne and David, came along in 1963, and Jennifer five years later.[1]

When Gary enrolled in the Garda training college in September 1983, Jennifer was allowed to take temporary possession of her big brother's stereo system, his headphones and records. She was fifteen and the only child left in the family home. By then Gráinne had moved to Monaghan town and David was working as a chef in Navan.

Gary's collection of LPs was Jennifer's induction into the world of rock and pop. 'He introduced the rest of us to the likes of Supertramp, Joni Mitchell, Pink Floyd, Kate Bush, Rory Gallagher, Thin Lizzy and Horslips,' she says. 'He loved his music.' To this day a song might come on the radio – 'Wuthering Heights', 'Another Brick in the Wall', 'Breakfast in America' – and her mind is instantly transported to thoughts of her brother.

Gary was able to finance his vinyl purchases by doing a part-time job in a local men's draper shop during his school years. He usually managed to have a few quid in his pocket, at a time when cash was scarce. He would save up if he had a purchase in mind, such as a bicycle. 'He always had a nice bike,' his sister recalls. And he was always good to her when it came to money, always very generous.

He loved travelling, he was adventurous regarding food, and he spent summer holidays in his late teens Interrailing around Europe with his bike. 'He was a very good Irish speaker and a fairly fluent French speaker, he travelled in France, and just sort of went all over the place in the summer with his bike,' she says. 'He had a rucksack with stickers of all the countries he'd been to – Austria, Italy, Germany and Greece. He'd been to New York the summer before he was killed, with the GAA. To me it seemed like he travelled a lot for that time in Ireland.'

His GAA team was Carrickmacross Emmets and Gary was also involved in swimming, cycling, squash and soccer. He was a good golfer as well, according to his sister.

After his Leaving Cert, he took a position as a trainee manager at a clothes factory in Galway that manufactured Wrangler jeans and shirts, but the company ceased production. He then worked for the Western Health Board on a contract basis.

The Sheehans had strong Galway connections on their father's side. Jim Sheehan had been born into a large family in Carrigallen, Co. Leitrim, but they moved to Loughrea after his mother died, then to Dublin, and Tom Sheehan, Jim's father, eventually settled in Bray. Tom decided to join the new Irish police force, and left the national army on 16 December 1923 in order to do so. Sixty years later to the day, his grandson would lose his life in Derrada.[2]

At Gary's funeral Michael Noonan, the minister for justice, remarked on the continuity of service given by three generations of Sheehan gardaí, going back almost to the foundation of the state.

Gary did not necessarily join the force to uphold that family tradition. He was twenty-three, had been made redundant by the Western Health Board and was looking for a stable job in the distressed economic climate of the time. By that stage Jim Sheehan was a detective garda who had settled in Carrickmacross with his wife Margaret (née Rafferty), who was originally from Monaghan town. Jim had worked on the border his whole career; his first posting after he graduated from the training depot in 1954 was in Monaghan town, and then he went to the village of Clontibret before finally settling in Carrickmacross.

Margaret, Jennifer recalls, wasn't impressed the first time her son Gary came home from Templemore with a short back and sides. 'He joined in early September, and I remember him coming home at the end of September and the lovely curls were all gone. My mother wasn't too happy about it!'

Theirs was a happy home, one where news and current affairs were a staple of conversation. 'Our house was full of the news,' Jennifer says. 'RTÉ was always on the radio, the six o'clock news on television, the news on BBC. Daddy read the *Irish Times* daily, preferably before anyone else. And on 24 November 1983 we watched Charlie Bird report on the kidnapping of Don Tidey near his home in Rathfarnham. Little did we know how that terrible event would impact on our lives.'

On 13 December, a Tuesday, Gary phoned home from Templemore to say he and his classmates would be going up to Leitrim to help in the search for Tidey. They would be staying in a hotel in Cavan town and taken from there to Ballinamore in the morning. On Wednesday and Thursday he phoned from Cavan to say things were going well. Each day they combed the fields as part of the great dragnet of police and soldiers. In the evenings they socialized. In the bar of the Farnham Arms Hotel he'd bumped into a few teachers that he knew from Carrickmacross.

The family made plans to meet him on the Saturday evening for dinner and drinks. Jennifer and her parents would make the fifty-minute drive from Carrickmacross to Cavan for the catch-up.

On Friday afternoon Jennifer finished her classes at the St Louis Secondary School and met up with her mother to go shopping. She remembers it as a 'damp, dreary day, with a mist-like fog hanging over the town'. But there was a buzz around the streets and shops because the Christmas decorations were up and people were out buying presents.

At around 4.30 p.m., mother and daughter went into Keegan's newsagents on Main Street. A garda colleague of Jim's came in and told them to come down to the station, a short walk away. The family car was parked in front of the station, the pair got into it and waited. 'And then Daddy got into the car and he just said that Gary was dead.'

It was impossible to comprehend such news. How could it be true? They'd only been talking to him the night before. Jim drove them home, everyone in a daze, a fog of shock. Then he began making phone calls to members of the immediate family, starting with Gráinne and David, who probably did not even know their brother had been involved in the search. Next, he contacted his wife's mother. 'Gary was the first grandchild on Mum's side. Carrickmacross to Monaghan [town] is only twenty-six miles and she went home every week and brought Gary with her. He was a very treasured grandchild.'

Neighbours started calling. The evening passed in a blur.

'But I can always remember Mammy lighting the fire. That sticks in my memory for some reason. Because it was damp, dark and misty, as opposed to sunny and cold.' Tea was made for the visitors. 'The kettle never stopped for days – or weeks it seemed like.' The next day the house was packed from morning 'til night. 'People just kept coming and coming. I can remember Michael Noonan coming to the house. And I can genuinely remember waking on Saturday morning and thinking: Is this real? Was it a bad dream?'

On Sunday afternoon they went to Navan general hospital, where Gary had lain in the morgue overnight. 'It was very real then, for sure.' After prayers, the coffin was transferred to the hearse and the cortège set out for Carrickmacross. The whole town was in shock, Jennifer remembers. 'We were a small town, maybe a population of three and a half thousand or something like that. I'm not saying we knew everybody, but we knew a lot of people, and a lot of people knew us. Back then when you're a guard's child, everybody knows you, for good or for bad. "Oh, you're Guard Sheehan's daughter", that sort of thing, when you'd tell people your name.'

The funeral of Gary Sheehan, and the huge number of mourners who gathered, is still remembered in Carrickmacross as a landmark event. Life went back to normal fairly quickly afterwards. Jennifer returned to school, her siblings to work, her father resumed his role as garda detective in the station. There was no counselling or therapy. 'We all just got on with it, pretty much.'

As with the Kelly family in Moate, people reached out in their thousands with letters and Mass cards and words of consolation. This great outpouring of communal support left an abiding impression on the fifteen-year-old schoolgirl.

'It's what I remember most: the kindness of the people of Ireland, both north and south, the people of Carrickmacross and especially Daddy's colleagues.' The letters came from everywhere – 'all over Ireland and the world'. It was a lifeline of comfort and solace for the grieving family. 'People from Northern Ireland especially, people who were then in the RUC, would've written lovely things.'

Jim Sheehan never talked about his work at home, did not discuss cases he was investigating, and the same principle applied to the investigation into the murder of his son. So Jennifer never really knew what was happening, or what her father thought about the chances of a successful conviction ever being secured. 'I'm sure it was hard for him. But we didn't ask questions. Looking back, you might think "Why didn't we?" but we didn't.' She was never optimistic that someone would be held accountable in a court of law. 'I never held out any hope, not really. And nothing was going to bring him back.'

Because so much of their father's career was spent policing the border, the family was naturally well aware of the strong local support for Sinn Féin/IRA. Thomas McMahon, who in 1979 murdered Lord Mountbatten, two teenage boys and the eighty-three-year-old Lady Doreen Brabourne, was from Carrickmacross.

'It was very real where we lived,' Jennifer agrees. 'I went to school with girls who lived on the border, and who hated the British soldiers. [With] the Troubles, Daddy was part of it from the start. Holidays would be cancelled sometimes, days off would be cancelled, he was always on call. But he loved his job.'

She accepts the decision by garda management to send

recruits into the woods looking for Tidey, although experienced gardaí seemed the more logical choice. 'I mean, I would have thought that Daddy would've been going somewhere like that. So it did seem strange, but one can only presume they wouldn't have put them [the recruits] there if they thought they would be in any danger,' she reasons. 'Like, you've got to think back to where the Garda Síochána were then, you know? It wasn't *intentional* on their part. They were less prepared for what they met. He was just in the wrong place at the wrong time. It could have been any of the poor guys.'

The years passed; the everyday rhythms of life continued. The family wanted to get on with the stuff of living; they did not want to dwell in bitterness or anger. Margaret and Jim visited Gary's final resting place regularly, walking out to the cemetery, tending to his grave, saying prayers, talking to their boy. But they kept their grief private and lived discreetly.

In 1996 Jim Sheehan died at the age of sixty-three. He had retired from the force just three years earlier and was transitioning comfortably into his post-career life. 'He took sick on the Friday night and died on the Tuesday,' Jennifer recalls. It was a catastrophic aneurysm. 'Very sudden. So that was hard. He'd been in good health up to that.'

Losing her husband so suddenly at the start of their autumn years together was another dreadful blow for Margaret. 'Daddy was a very outgoing person, he was the one who was out and about, he knew everybody. They'd play golf together, and bridge. And my sister had kids at that stage. So, they were as busy and as happy as they could be.'

In May 1999, Carrickmacross Emmets opened a new stand at their pitch. It was named the Gary Sheehan Stand. Gary had started out with the club as a juvenile, winning the

Coyle Cup in 1972 as part of their under-12 side. He went on to win championship medals in both hurling and Gaelic football at under-14.

In 1978 he was a member of the minor team that won the Monaghan championship, beating Castleblayney Faughs in a memorable final. He duly progressed into the senior ranks, where the level of dedication required would have meant he didn't have a lot of spare time left over after his work. Still, in early 1983 he volunteered to take charge of the club's under-14 team.

The stand was officially opened by the GAA's president elect, their fellow Monaghan man Seán McCague. It was blessed in an ecumenical rite by both the local Catholic parish priest and a Church of Ireland clergyman. Margaret Sheehan was guest of honour, along with her children and their families.[3]

It would take another twenty-two years for Gary Sheehan's sacrifice to be commemorated at national level. On 24 September 2021, on what would have been his sixty-first birthday, he was posthumously awarded a gold Scott Medal at a ceremony hosted by Garda Commissioner Drew Harris at Dublin Castle.

The Scott Medal is the garda commissioner's award to members of the force for risks taken in the course of their duties. An Garda Síochána was in its infancy in 1923 when an American philanthropist, Walter Scott, presented it with a $1,000 gold bond for the purpose of honouring those who had distinguished themselves through an act of valour in the line of duty. Scott was an honorary commissioner of the New York City police department. The sole criterion for the awarding of a Scott Medal was 'an act of personal bravery, performed intelligently in the execution of duty at imminent risk to life of the doer, and armed with full previous knowledge of the risk involved'. In the 1940s this was amended to 'exceptional bravery and heroism involving the risk of life in the execution of duty'. The medal is in the form of a Celtic cross; it can be presented in order of merit from bronze to silver to gold.[4]

As well as Gary Sheehan, fourteen other gardaí on duty in Derrada Wood in December 1983 were honoured. It was the first time many of them were reunited in the thirty-eight years since.[5] Recipients of a bronze medal included Denis Breen and Francis Morgan, who were among the personnel taken hostage by the IRA gang in Derrada. Among those who got a silver medal was Nacie Rice, who had returned fire on the terrorists as they shot indiscriminately at soldiers and police from their speeding getaway car. Other silver medal recipients were Joe O'Connor, who was standing next to Sheehan in the wood when the gunmen opened fire; Francis Smith, the trainee who called out to the terrorists when he discovered their hide; and Eugene O'Sullivan, the detective who stood at the Ford Granada when the gang sprayed them with fire and who subsequently drove Tidey out of the danger zone. Also honoured was Noel McMahon, the detective O'Sullivan described as 'absolutely fearless' when coming under fire from the retreating gang.[6]

Absent from the ceremony, however, was Garda Sergeant Donal Kelleher. Despite being wounded in both legs in Derrada, he had not been awarded a Scott Medal. The bullet that hit him had missed a main artery by millimetres. He could not walk initially and was off work for five months. He was then the father of an infant son and a six-week-old daughter. It was a 'scary time', his wife Caroline recalls, and the young couple were beset with anxiety. His physical injuries required a long and painful rehabilitation but the psychological damage lingered for years.

By September 2021 Donal Kelleher was retired and living in Westmeath. He only found out about the medal ceremony from Don Tidey. Nearly eighteen months later, in February 2023, he died from cancer, just five weeks after diagnosis.

Caroline Kelleher says that, though Donal had never expected such honours to be awarded in the first place, he had been 'hugely upset' at being omitted from the ceremony in 2021. 'He would dearly have loved to have had the opportunity to celebrate with colleagues and friends with whom he shared the experience, to relive those memories in much happier circumstances and finally get closure on those events,' she says. 'The huge media attention surrounding the medal ceremony brought back so many memories that had been suppressed. For the first time he began to share those memories with those closest to him.'[7]

He and his family believed the decision not to include him was tantamount to blaming him for his own injuries. He wrote to garda management inquiring as to why he was excluded, but Caroline says there was never a satisfactory response.

At a ceremony in Dublin Castle in May 2023 Donal Kelleher was posthumously awarded a bronze Scott Medal. Caroline, accompanied by their children, Lesley and Daniel, accepted it on his behalf. Sadly, news that he had been awarded a medal was not conveyed to him before his death. Gardaí stressed that it was awarded following a review of the evidence and not because he had died. The citation read: 'Despite the active shooting, and in full knowledge of the potential danger, Detective Garda Kelleher provided armed

18. Caroline Kelleher is embraced by Don Tidey in May 2023 following the posthumous awarding of a Scott Medal for bravery to her late husband, Sergeant Donal Kelleher at a ceremony in Dublin Castle.

19. Don Tidey, Caroline Kelleher and her two children Lesley and Daniel at the Scott Medal ceremony.

20. Margaret Sheehan looks at the Scott Medal presented to her in memory of her son Gary at a ceremony in Dublin Castle in 2021.

21. Don Tidey speaking to Margaret Sheehan and her daughters Gráinne and Jennifer at the Scott Medal ceremony.

cover to other garda members who were escorting Mr Tidey to safety.' Although it was a 'bittersweet' day for the family, they were proud that Donal's service in the line of duty at Derrada had finally been recognized.

At the September 2021 Scott Medal presentation Margaret Sheehan accepted the gold medal on behalf of her son. She was accompanied by Jennifer and Gráinne. The guest of honour was the acting minister for justice, Heather Humphreys TD, herself a native of Monaghan. Don Tidey was also present, as were Patrick Kelly's four sons. In his speech, Commissioner Harris spoke of the 'dangers and complexity' of the rescue operation that faced the security personnel in Derrada Wood. Addressing the awardees, he said: 'You were involved in a heavy exchange of gunfire and were directly shot at. You were exposed to a terrifying situation involving very dangerous armed terrorists, and faced enormous personal risk in the execution of your duties to rescue Mr Don Tidey. The dedication to duty and the bravery you demonstrated remains an example to all of us who continue to serve.'[8]

Meeting Gary's classmates that day in Dublin Castle gave Jennifer McCann a deeper understanding of the conditions surrounding the search, the dangers they'd faced and the trauma they must have suffered from the violent death of their comrade. The Sheehan family found it fulfilling to see them being honoured all those years later. 'I mean, they had waited so long and, you know, just for us to really realize what they went through. The trauma of that. It was so hard.'

The fact that these same young men were not relieved of their duties in order to attend their classmate's funeral still baffles Jennifer. 'For them not to have been at Gary's funeral, where was the logic in that? They were in Derrada Wood [instead]. Can you imagine what it must have been like for them? I can't. The fact that they had to go back out there [searching] for another couple of days. How hard must that have been for them? They never received professional counselling from An Garda Síochána.

'I'm not blaming anyone – again, it's forty years on, and thankfully we've all moved forward. Things have improved. But it's the thought process: that it was a good idea for them to be back out at the crime scene where their colleague was killed. Maybe it was just the practical thing to do, I don't know.'

The Scott Medal ceremony was a both happy and poignant occasion. The Sheehans were happy to see the gardaí being honoured, but privately sad at the thought of what might have been. 'When I saw Gary's pals with their kids at the ceremony,' reflects Jennifer, 'I was so happy for them, but then you just think, what would he have done with his life? That's the hardest part. Everybody was so kind, but my mother found it hard. It was very difficult for her.'

Margaret Sheehan never drew attention to her loss; she chose to do her grieving in private. Still, she wasn't averse to talking about her son and sharing memories of him. 'My mum would say that it was just the wastefulness of it. Just the sense of utter waste,' her daughter says. 'The pointlessness of it all. And for what?'

Margaret is now in her mid-eighties. She is 'hardy', says Jennifer. A quiet, introverted person, she never wanted any limelight or public attention. Her grandchildren and great-grandchildren 'are great sources of happiness', but she has been a heartbroken mother for forty years. 'Just heartbroken.' A pall of sadness hung over the home and seldom went away. 'It wasn't there all the time,' says Jennifer, 'and I don't mean it in a depressing sort of a way, but there was a lot of sadness.'

As for those responsible, the family tries not to think about them. 'I'm not a religious person,' says Jennifer, 'but I think, I hope, they have a conscience and that they have [Gary's death] on their conscience. But I don't really know if people who carry out these crimes, do they have a conscience?' She wonders, too, if there are people around Ballinamore who assisted her brother's killers, and if they ever reflect on what they did. 'Or maybe they are proud of what they did, of their part, or what their silent part was, in all of that. I don't know.'

She can still remember watching the *Today Tonight* report in January 1984 with her parents, and the men outside Corraleehan Church saying 'No comment' to Brendan O'Brien, one after the other. Someone had committed the capital murder of their son and brother, and here were people refusing to condemn it. 'It was torturous for us to watch. Did they know who supplied the terrorists with food, cars, safe houses and escape routes? Did they support "the cause" or were they too scared to stand up to the supporters? It just seemed like a different world.'

For that reason, among others, she never had any desire to visit the place where her brother breathed his last. She would not visit Ballinamore either. 'I'd rather not, I think. I really don't want to see that statue to John Joe McGirl, if I'm honest. But I don't feel the people of Ballinamore are all like that. I'm sure, with education and time, people have changed their opinions. I hope so. But I don't know. Whenever the name Ballinamore came on the radio in our house, there was just silence. Nothing bad would be said. Just silence.'

The Sheehans had always taken a measure of comfort

from the fact that Tidey was saved. 'Oh, for sure. That's something that as you grow older you [realize] what his family went through as well.'

At the Scott Medal ceremony, Minister Humphreys described the actions of the gardaí in Derrada as 'truly heroic'. Does Jennifer see Gary as a hero?

She pauses to sort her thoughts before replying. 'A hero? I honestly don't think so,' she concludes. 'He had no idea. I think he was in the wrong place at the wrong time. He was unlucky. Somebody didn't get up that morning and say, "I'm going to murder Gary Sheehan and I'm going to murder Patrick Kelly." It could have been any in that group of ten [search party]. It could have been one of the other groups.

'So, I don't know. It doesn't give me any solace to say that Gary was a hero. I just know that he was a good guy. He was just an all-round good guy.'

23. The Cross

In the days and weeks after Patrick Kelly's funeral, as with the Sheehans, Mass cards, sympathy cards and letters of condolence arrived in bundles to the family home from all over Ireland. In one packet was a ceremonial silver cross, too big to be worn on a chain. David Kelly, nine or ten years old at the time, remembers this particular gift for a reason.

One afternoon his mother went upstairs to bed for a rest. 'I saw her lying down holding that cross, crying. And I was standing there and didn't know what to do. It was in the middle of the day where you'd lie down for an afternoon nap. She was completely miserable and grief-stricken, just lost to grief. It's one of those images from my childhood that stand out so much. It just captures where we were as a family: we were broken.'[1]

Caitriona Kelly woke up on the morning of 16 December 1983 as a wife and mother. That night she went to sleep as a widow with four fatherless boys to care for. David was nine, Michael was six, Patrick was four, Andrew was eleven weeks. The trauma has been reverberating inside them to this day. The hurt went too deep to be healed. It hung in the air, haunting their attempts at everyday living, defeating every effort to somehow make the family whole again.

Mrs Kelly got the older ones out to school every morning, washed and fed her children and kept one foot in front of the other as best she could. There was no bereavement counselling in 1983, no professional confidante to whom she might ration out confessions of her crippling struggle. No one had the language, or knowledge of the processes by which she might be helped. When it came to dealing with the trauma, the best she could do was to avoid the subject, almost in its entirety. Their father's absence became a taboo conversation.

'We hardly even spoke about my father,' David says. 'She was grappling with her own emotions. So I felt like I had lost her in that respect. The communication broke down between us, and that came back to haunt me, I feel, in my young adult life.'

At six years of age Michael Kelly couldn't begin to assimilate the scale of what had befallen the family unit. 'I just knew things had changed for ever,' he says. 'As time went on, there was a deep sadness in the house. The sense of your father not being around was palpable.'[2]

Andrew, a mere baby at the time, grew up with no memories of his father. There is no photograph of them together.

David and Michael have fragments of memories. Michael can remember him cooking boxty on the frying pan, and 'always fixing cars out the back'. It was how Paddy supplemented his earnings. They can picture him still with his head buried in the engine or his legs sticking out from under a car.

They can remember, too, the excitement building in the house when he was due home from a tour of duty abroad with the United Nations peacekeeping forces. He did three stints in Lebanon and one in Cyprus. He was a rifleman and a good shot, as well as a driver. He was good at writing letters home and would do so diligently. Michael remembers what was possibly his last trip home, with a big suitcase packed with 'toys, cowboys and Indians, and things like that'.

*

Paddy Kelly had joined the Irish army in December 1968. He left briefly, before rejoining in 1972, when he was assigned to the 6th Infantry Battalion in Custume Barracks, Athlone.

Born on 13 May 1947, he was the second eldest of nine surviving children raised by Michael and Mary Kelly in Ballinamuck, Co. Longford. Michael Sr was a farm labourer, his wife a homemaker. They reared their family in a labourer's cottage without running water and with an outside toilet. Paddy attended Clonback national school and, in the absence of free second-level education at the time, began working in his mid-teens for a local farmer and contractor, driving tractors and diggers. Four of his siblings emigrated to London, but ultimately Paddy never joined them.

Michael Sr had been in the FCA, the army reserve, and his three eldest sons – Jim, Paddy and Michael Joe – duly enlisted too. All three in turn joined the regular army. Jim became a company sergeant in the military police in Custume Barracks; he was serving in Lebanon when news came through that his brother had been killed. Mick Joe did six years in the army before emigrating to London.

For Paddy, the army was going to be his career. 'Oh certainly,' says David. 'I think he took it very seriously. From what I can gather, listening to his colleagues, it was his life.' With his talent for mechanics, Paddy completed an armoured personnel carrier course in 1972 and became an army driver.

It was in March 1974 that he married Caitriona Bradley from Moate, also known as Catherine. He was twenty-six, she was twenty-one. They had first met in The Well pub, a popular country & western music venue in the town. Caitriona was one of seven siblings; their father Jack worked in a local hardware store. Their mother died at the age of fifty-one in 1976. Jack Bradley died six weeks before his son-in-law was murdered.

The young couple started off married life in a flat in Moate. A year later they moved into a council house at 12 St Patrick's Terrace. One by one the boys were born. Caitriona had a number of miscarriages. Army pay was poor and money was scarce, but the children were oblivious to that, feeling secure and loved, growing up safe and content.

The area was 'teeming with children', David recalls, 'playing soccer out on the green'. They were mostly from army families as well. The men used to car-share on their way to work. 'I remember looking out a window. There was [Dad] in the driver's seat and there were three other soldiers.'

Caitriona had worked in a textiles factory in Clara before she got married. She would still clock up a few hours here and there in a local café or takeaway. As her father got older, she took care of him more and more.

After Jack Bradley died from cancer in 1983, Caitriona went to his solicitor to hand in his rent book. 'Which one of the daughters are you?' she was asked. The solicitor checked his paperwork and then told her: 'He left his home to you.'

David recalls: 'My father was waiting in the car outside. She got in and told him the good news and she said he was elated. My grandfather had bought the house from the council and willed it to her. I was told that, the weekend my father was killed, he was getting help from people with the move from one house to another.

'Her husband and father were very important in her life. Within a couple of months she lost the two men she counted on.'

Into that vacuum would come another man, himself a soldier in Custume Barracks, married with a wife and children but separated and living in a flat. The brothers remember him materializing into their lives, gradually becoming a presence in the house until he became a permanent fixture.

On the night of 16 December, people had come streaming into the living room to offer their condolences. The room had been cleared of furniture, bar one armchair, where their mother was sitting to receive the visitors. At one point David was told to join her by the armchair. 'I was standing there at her left and one of the people that came in was this man, wearing the Irish army uniform. I didn't know who he was.'

Pretty soon they would get to know who he was. He had known Paddy Kelly as a colleague in Custume Barracks. After the funeral he started to turn up regularly at their house. He taught their mother how to drive; he helped her buy her first car. 'It was a way of getting close to her,' David says, remembering that some people thought it was 'happening too quickly, that he was just turning up on the scene all the time, sort of filling my father's shoes'.

At first controlling, then domineering, the boys say he eventually became physically abusive, and was the opposite of the loving father figure they had lost.

'When I look back on everything,' says David now, 'it was coercive control. He took advantage of a grief-stricken woman. It was a classic case of this knight in shining armour; he promised he'd take care of her and us. Her own siblings warned her about him but she sort of pushed them away and became more and more reliant on this man.

'Because I was the eldest son, I felt like I had to have the role of the father, almost, you know? But I remember me and her just sitting in a room and then he came in and there's silence. This presence. He became this barrier between me and her.'

Three years after Paddy Kelly's death, his widow decided

to leave Moate and move to London with her children and new partner. David remembers the day they flew from Dublin airport – 28 November 1986 – because it was three days after his twelfth birthday. Caitriona's partner had retired from the army and planned to work on the building sites in England.

'She would never have gone to London if it wasn't for him,' says David, who feels Caitriona was aware of local hostility towards her new relationship. 'I think they felt it was the best thing, a fresh start for them – and us, I guess. Just get on the plane and leave Ireland.'

'I think she was just vulnerable,' says Michael. 'This man stepped in when she was maybe at her lowest ebb. She was a thirty-one-year-old widow with four young children. Although she had a supportive family here, there was grief and the stress of trying to deal with all this without the appropriate mental health team or counselling. What people have today just wasn't there in the early eighties.'

David remembers the flight to London. 'The plane was half-empty, and it was like, all of a sudden, the mood was very quiet. And I looked at my mother to the left of me and she was looking out the window. And then I looked across at my younger brothers and this awful feeling came over me. I said to my mother, it was like a gut instinct, I said: "I don't want to go to England." I just got a bad feeling that we weren't going for the best of reasons.'

Their first home was a flat in Cricklewood, but it was temporary accommodation. They registered with the local authority and after their short-term lease on the flat expired, the family was officially homeless. They were provided with emergency lodgings in a small hotel in West Hampstead.

From there they were transferred to a flat in Kilburn for maybe six months before finally being allocated a council house on the Grahame Park estate in the district of Colindale in north-west London. It was a vast estate with problems of crime and violence, drugs and antisocial behaviour.

Michael and Patrick were enrolled in a primary school in Cricklewood while David entered second level in St James's Catholic High School in Colindale.

'We felt completely uprooted,' says Michael. 'We'd never been outside of Moate, other than towns around here. It was a different world, going into school and sitting beside people from different countries, trying to adapt to the new environment, trying to fit in. Obviously, it was tough being Irish there in the eighties. So it was a big change for all of us.'

The boys felt that their mother's new partner became more controlling once the family moved to London. David recalls her buying groceries one day in a shop in Cricklewood and saying, 'Don't tell him how much we spent.' The Kellys and the Bradleys had relations in London, but they say he deliberately kept away from them. Unbeknownst to almost everyone, including the children, the couple got married. Being married would fast-track them up the housing list with the local council.

As a widow, Caitriona had been in receipt of an army pension since the death of her husband. She lost that after she remarried. 'It's another sign of how she became totally dependent on this man,' says David. 'Not alone had she left her home and her country, she gave up her army pension too.'

At that time the boys were not aware that a trust fund had been set up on their behalf by Quinnsworth. Caitriona kept it secret, even from her new husband. 'I overheard him say to our mother once, "If there's money there, just withdraw it."

He was suspecting there was something. But the one thing she emphasized for us was education. I think that's what she was thinking about: the trust would be there for our education. She didn't realize it was there for our welfare. A car, clothes, a family holiday, whatever it was.'

The fund was held in Allied Irish Bank and administered by trustees. To draw money from it, Caitriona could submit a request and the trustees would have to approve it. But, according to Michael, 'it wasn't touched for years'. Andrew says: 'All our relations back home believed we were well taken care of, that we were looked after. Little did they know that we were going round in squalor, in terrible clothes.'[3]

It seems that Caitriona's dream was for the boys to go to university, and the trust fund would facilitate that. It would be activated to give them the education she and Paddy never had, and which would bring her sons better opportunities in life than she had known.

According to the boys, their mother's partner graduated from coercion to violence. David remembers the first time he realized his mother was being assaulted. 'I didn't see it, but I heard it. I was in the room next door. He sort of took out his anger on her. He seemed to be, like, slapping her in the face ... What really annoyed me was just the way she took it in silence. That's what made it so particularly painful.

'I lay in bed that night, and she came in and sat on the bed and she was crying, and I was crying. She said, "I'm so sorry. It's not his fault. The army made him that way." I now know it was a case of the victim making excuses for her abuser. I fell asleep that night crying. Part of me died that night.'

The boys say there were similar incidents in the years that followed, and they often didn't feel safe in their home. David says: 'I think my saviour in those years was soccer. With all the kids in the area, it was like the UN – so many different nationalities. In our block there were Hungarians, Italians, Nigerians, and we were all out playing football on the green.

'I think it kept me going, because I loved soccer and all my energy went into it. The estate had a reputation for crime and there was a lot of drug-dealing going on, there was violence, and it got to a point that after six in the evening I wouldn't go to the shopping area. I wouldn't feel safe.'

Michael adds: 'You had to protect yourself at home, at school and in the neighbourhood. Life was just tough all round.' Of the siblings, Michael was the one who most often challenged his mother's partner. 'I did stand up to him a good bit, so maybe he took a particular dislike to me. Regularly there were confrontations between us.' It was perhaps inevitable that Michael would be the first to fly the nest. 'It was definitely easier for me just to get out of there.'

Over the years, Caitriona had done her best to nurture the boys' connection with their home town, and she had managed to fund regular trips back. In the summer of 1993 Michael left London and enrolled as a fifth-year boarder with the Carmelite College in Moate. He boarded during the week and stayed with relatives at the weekends. The trust fund took care of his school fees. Michael threw himself into his studies and eventually went to Trinity College Dublin, where he studied Business and Politics. Upon graduating he worked in a number of different jobs before joining the Revenue Commissioners in 2006. He has recently finished a degree in Applied Taxation.

Andrew was three when the family moved to London. He remembers the local kids in St Dominic's primary school in

Colindale teasing him about his Irish accent. 'They were saying, "It's not fillum, it's film," that type of thing. And I remember getting a few comments saying, "Oh, you're IRA, what are you doing over here?" Because in the late eighties the bombs were going off in London and other parts of England. I didn't really understand what was happening, but I remember kids saying that.'

It was not until he was aged ten or eleven that Andrew was told, by David, what had happened to their father. He thinks his mother postponed telling him because she didn't want to inflict the hurt on him.

In 2004 he moved back to Ireland, aged twenty. Two years later he joined the Irish army. 'Even before I was told what happened to my father, I wanted to be in the army,' he says. 'I think it was just in my blood.' Married with four children, Andrew is currently a sergeant in the military police, based in Custume Barracks.

Patrick, the second youngest, grew up with a mild intellectual disability. His mother would bring him into Athlone for speech therapy sessions. But in the state school system in London he didn't receive the specialist assistance he required. Three months after Andrew left London, Patrick also returned to Moate, where he lives to this day in the family home. He works as a delivery driver for a supermarket chain.

David did well enough in his A levels to be offered a place at Cardiff University to study Law, but says he lacked the confidence to take it on. Instead, he spent a year at a local college in London before accepting an offer from Queen's University Belfast to study Politics and History.

As with Michael at Trinity, he was able to access the trust fund to help him with fees and living expenses. He did two years before finding himself unable to continue, debilitated by the unprocessed pain stored up in his body. 'Arriving in Queen's in 1994, I was excited,' he says. 'It was a fresh start, heading off doing my own thing. Unfortunately, what tripped me up was I hadn't dealt with anything since I was nine. I hadn't dealt with any of the issues of my father's murder. My mother and I were both in grief and we just couldn't talk to each other about it. I think I internalized the whole thing. So there was anger there, and terrible sadness too.'

The psychic turbulence churning inside him eventually manifested itself physically, in a skin condition which erupted while he was in Belfast. 'Burning skin, burning out of control,' he says. 'I'm not talking about a bit of dry skin here. I'm talking about out of control, skin that was like on fire.' It affected both his studies and his attempts at relationships, and eventually the pressure became too much. 'I didn't go back for the third year. I had completed two years successfully but I couldn't go on. I'd hit that point where there was something wrong and it hadn't been dealt with.'

He returned to London in the summer of 1996, and admits he was 'a bit lost for a few years'. He worked on building sites with Irish contractors: six months on a shopping centre in Milton Keynes, six months on the HSBC Tower in Canary Wharf.

In 2000 he joined the Royal Mail as a postman and worked there for seven years. 'I could have stayed there, I'd a job for life, but I felt the pull to return to Ireland.' So, in 2007 he moved back to Moate and now works in a parcel distribution centre in Athlone.

Forty years later, he believes he is still dealing with the fall-out from the murder of his father. 'I'm trying to work through all that happened, how it affected me, affected my whole life in terms of career, relationships, everything. The amazing thing is that in our family, we never once used the word trauma.'

Their father's death affected his sons in different ways. 'I'm definitely not the person I probably should be,' Michael says. 'I internalize things, like David, maybe in a different way. But yeah it deeply affected my life in many regards.'

When Andrew was eventually told the truth, the hurt began working its way through his system and is still there. In the early years it was a struggle to even understand what he'd been told. 'You're thinking of the bombs going off at the time, you're thinking of the IRA back home in Ireland. Who are they? Who are the defence forces? It was just so confusing.

'I actually believe it affected my schooling. Going into secondary school I had this sense of anger. The hurt and sorrow that it had caused my brothers and my mother, I was angry for them. It affected me and my studies and everything else.

'I didn't go on to do my A levels in England and that prevented me from doing a commission, joining the army and becoming a commissioned officer, so I joined the enlisted ranks.'

Apart from the silent pain, there was the daily absence of a father from their lives. Something as simple, says David, as having a father who could bring him to Highbury to see Arsenal play if they'd been living together in north London. Or the reassurance of being able to get some fatherly advice during their growing-up years.

Slowly, imperceptibly at first, their mother managed to find her confidence and courage. Her sons say she was 'almost chronically shy', deeply uncomfortable with all the publicity that surrounded the funeral, and ill-at-ease with being identified subsequently as Paddy Kelly's widow.

22. Caitriona Kelly with her sons David (left), Patrick and Michael in Moate, Co. Westmeath, in June 2008.

23. Don Tidey with Caitriona Kelly at the opening of the Patrick Kelly Memorial Park in Moate in December 2008, on the twenty-fifth anniversary of Patrick's death.

While she never received counselling, Andrew believes she tried to self-educate: 'I remember her reading books on depression and stuff like that.' Her first job in London was that of teaching assistant in the primary school attended by the boys. Then she became a carer in a nursing home. The management appreciated her work ethic and promoted her to senior carer. They also encouraged her to do courses at a local college. One was on self-esteem and developing personal confidence. Gradually, she started to find her voice.

'She was pushing herself,' says Michael. 'She was doing different courses. Her employer was pushing her, even though she was in her late forties. They knew she was a really good worker, very determined. So they were really pushing her into bettering herself.'

Through this process of finding her feet, she learned to stand her ground. She eventually extricated herself from her marriage, moved out of the estate in Colindale and got her own apartment a few miles away in Hendon. Caitriona divorced in 2004; her second husband died in 2020. She didn't know it at the time, but her renewed single status meant she was entitled to claim her army widow's pension again. Andrew advised her to look into it.

With the boys living back in Ireland, her visits home became more frequent, especially when Andrew's children, her grandchildren, started coming along. She would talk about moving back for good, maybe to Galway, but she had gotten used to London life too and seemed content there.

Caitriona returned to Moate for Paddy's anniversary Mass every year. In December 2008, on the twenty-fifth anniversary of his death, she also attended the opening of the Patrick Kelly Memorial Park in Moate. Less than eighteen months later, in April 2010, she came home to be present at another event, this time the unveiling of a cenotaph in Athlone dedicated to the memory of deceased soldiers of the 4th Western Brigade. The night before the ceremony she stayed in the family home in Moate. She shared some good news: she'd received a letter saying her application for the widow's pension had been approved and she was due a considerable amount of money because it had been backdated. 'She was in good spirits and looking forward to the future,' recalls Andrew. During the night she died of a pulmonary embolism, a blood clot. She was fifty-seven.

'It was totally out of the blue,' says David. 'And I think now, fifty-seven years of age, all she went through in her life. To me she's a victim of the IRA as much as my father. There was a book, *Lost Lives*, about the victims of the Troubles. But there's no book about the people whose lives were cut short because of what happened to a loved one. Through ill-health, or whatever. They're not recognized as victims of the Troubles.'

Some weeks after the funeral a couple of the boys drove to London to collect their mother's belongings and finalize her affairs. In her mail they found an envelope with her first army widow's cheque inside. She was buried beside Paddy in Kilcurley Cemetery in Tubber, the Co. Offaly village that David says will always be close to his heart.

Kilbeggan is another midlands town that has meaning for David because it conjures up one of his happiest memories. It is a summer's morning, and the boy and his father are heading to Kilbeggan Races in the car, a Renault of some description. 'A bright fresh morning, the two of us in the car, sunbeams coming in through the windscreen, and he drives down a country lane and hitches up a horsebox in a field and next thing I know we're at Kilbeggan Races.

'I remember playing with kids, and he was with the adults; the horses and the finishing line and everyone cheering. A beautiful memory, and to me what it represented was a sign of the future. He'd done a good few years in the army, he was established in Moate as his home town, they had a house now, and things were looking good.'

Then the life they knew changed for ever. The sunlight streaming through the windscreen became a tunnel of darkness. Occasionally, Caitriona would open a door into the past, before quickly closing it again.

'Now and again, just snippets. Out of the blue she'd surprise me with a few lines. She'd go, "Oh, your dad brought me to a dance in Carrigallen when we were dating. At the end we didn't have a lift home and there was a tractor and trailer, and we sat at the end of the trailer and that brought us home from Carrigallen to Ballinamuck." It took me back to a more innocent time when they had their whole future ahead of them.'

To David Kelly, his mother was a quiet, humble hero. 'I heard someone say once that the true heroes of the peace process are the widows left behind who picked up the pieces and got on with it as best they could and tried to instil in their children not vengeance or hatred, just good values, the difference between right and wrong.'

24. 'You know the killers'

On the morning of 10 October 2011 David Kelly was pottering about the family home in Moate, enjoying a day off from work, when a local radio news bulletin stopped him in his tracks. Martin McGuinness, the reporter told listeners, would be in Athlone later that day.

The icon of the republican movement, and deputy first minister in the Northern Ireland administration, was running in the election for president of Ireland. Polling day was 27 October. McGuinness, busy on the campaign trail, would be pressing the flesh in the Golden Island shopping centre that afternoon.

A switch was tripped in Kelly's head. The prospect of McGuinness coming to Athlone canvassing for votes stirred something inside him. He spent a while ruminating on it. 'I looked at my own life, and my family's since what happened to my father in 1983, and I saw desolation: ruin of lives, of hopes and dreams.' His mother's death eighteen months earlier was still raw.

'That was the background that compelled me to confront Martin McGuinness. It was like, all those years of sadness, anger, frustration and desolation was my human story, and here he was, coming to Athlone, the town where my father went into work every day.'

It struck Kelly, too, that if McGuinness were to become president, he would also be supreme commander of the defence forces. Nobody had ever been brought to justice for his father's death, and he feared that what happened in Derrada Wood was being whitewashed from history.

'I had a thwarted career; health issues, physical and mental; ongoing trauma – even in 2011. So, I was a person living through trauma who was reacting to his candidacy, and him turning up in the local area where my father went to work every day. And I made up my mind to face him and speak my mind.'[1]

He went to the living room and picked up a framed photograph of a smiling Private Patrick Kelly in his soldier's uniform. He would bring it with him to Athlone. He wanted to humanize a man who had become just another name in the roll call of the dead. 'He wasn't just a cold statistic from the Troubles that a lot of people might have forgotten about, perhaps.'

The chosen photograph had a particular resonance for him. It showed his father 'in his prime, in uniform, as a soldier'. Kelly would look at Martin McGuinness and think: 'You want to be [the] symbolic head of the Irish defence forces. Yet here's a man in the uniform of the Irish army who was murdered by your organization.'

He drove to Athlone and waited for several hours in the shopping centre where the candidate was due to canvass customers. He was running late, but Kelly hung around, nervously whiling away the time. When McGuinness and his retinue came through the centre's sliding doors, Kelly was there to greet him. He stepped forward, holding the photograph of his father chest-high. The candidate was forced to stop and face him. This man, he told Martin McGuinness, was his father, Private Patrick Kelly, murdered by the IRA in 1983.

24. David, Michael and Andrew Kelly at their parents' grave in Co. Offaly. (*Their mother also used the spelling Katherina for her first name.*)

25. Andrew Kelly (left) and David Kelly, who accepted the Military Star and citation on behalf of their father, Private Patrick Kelly, with Don Tidey at a ceremony at Custume Barracks, Athlone in 2012.

RACE FOR THE ARAS

FACE TO FACE: 'My soldier dad was killed by IRA and he knows who did it'

DEMANDING ANSWERS: David Kelly confronts Martin McGuinness and (inset) his father, Patrick Kelly

Valiant ... moment a hero's son took on IRA godfather

By Niall O'Connor

IT WAS the moment IRA godfather Martin McGuinness finally came face to face with the truth.

The encounter was so powerful that even RTE, which many say is so soft on Sinn Fein, was forced to lead its news bulletins with footage.

And David Kelly used the words "liar" to describe McGuinness when he denied any knowledge of the incident in which the IRA man's unit gunned down David's dad.

David, son of Private Paddy Kelly, confronted the Sinn Fein politician during his canvass in Athlone – and demanded that he name his father's killers.

David was just nine years old in 1983 when his father died in a hail of bullets during a bloody battle in Co Leitrim.

The 35-year-old – the first soldier killed in active service in the Republic since the Civil War – was murdered alongside 25-year-old Garda Gary Sheehan as they were searching for kidnapped supermarket boss Don Tidey.

The dead soldier's son yesterday stood squarely in front of the former IRA boss and asked him who killed his father.

"Martin McGuinness, hello – I'd like to ask you a question. My father, Private Patrick Kelly, was killed in Derrada wood, Ballinamore, Co Leitrim, in 1983 by the Provisional IRA.

"No one has ever been prosecuted for his murder, and that of Garda Gary Sheehan, two brave servants of this State.

"I want justice for my father. I believe that you know the names of the killers of my father. I want you to tell me who to tell me who they are."

McGuinness today tried to play down the encounter. "I think its very important that we are sympathetic to people like Private Kelly's son David Kelly and the family because they are obviously still hurting," Mr McGuinness said.

"And I have many friends that are hurting so I know what it's like when people hurt," he added.

During the encounter, Mr McGuinness alleged to Mr Kelly he did not know who killed his father. However, Mr Kelly dismissed this.

Private Kelly and Garda Sheehan were gunned down during a shoot-out with a gang of IRA kidnappers who were holding Don Tidey captive in a wooded area in Ballinamore.

Belfast man Brendan 'Bik' McFarlane was tried for falsely

imprisoning Mr Tidey but his trial later collapsed.

Speaking after his encounter with Mr McGuinness, Mr Kelly vowed to wage a campaign against the Sinn Fein man until he reveals his father's killers.

"His words were hollow. He could have the role of Supreme Commander of the Defence Forces and he won't say who killed a member of that same army," said Mr Kelly.

The families of murder victims Jean McConville and Frank Hegarty have also demanded answers from Mr McGuinness.

hnews@herald.ie

STOP TREATING US LIKE FOOLS AND REVEAL THE TRUTH

ANDREW LYNCH

alynch@herald.ie

DAVID KELLY has achieved what some of the mostly highly-paid broadcasters in Ireland could not.

He has stared into Martin McGuinness' eyes, called him a liar and forced him to confront the human suffering caused by the IRA for 25 bloody years. By doing so, he has created the most powerful television moment of this presidential election so far – and while it may not scupper Mr McGuinness' campaign, it does mean that anybody who saw it and still votes for the Sinn Fein man can have absolutely no excuse.

MURDEROUS

As a military man, Mr McGuinness might even have a professional admiration for the way he was ambushed while campaigning in Athlone yesterday. With the cameras rolling, he had no choice but to stop and look at the framed photograph of Private Patrick Kelly, murdered by the IRA along with a garda recruit

during a kidnapping raid in 1983. He then stood there and issued a series of wooden denials as the dead man's son asked him the most basic question of all: "Who killed my father?"

Nobody should be surprised that Mr McGuinness was not actually reduced to a gibbering wreck. If you can survive hours of interrogation by British security forces, you can bluff your way through an awkward encounter in a shopping centre.

Even so, he was sufficiently rattled by the meeting to address it at a rally later that evening, where he claimed that he would never stand over attacks on the Irish police or defence forces (so presumably it was only okay to kill Brits or unionists).

Mr Kelly's direct challenge to Mr McGuinness was also a useful lesson for Gary Mitchell and his Fine Gael colleagues. When you make vague allegations about US multinationals pulling out of Ireland because of a Sinn Fein president, you only make yourself look paranoid.

When you force a Shinner to stare into the eyes of a man who grew up without a father because of their murderous actions, you might just get the message across.

Patrick Kelly was a 35-year-old Irish soldier who had represented his country on peacekeeping missions in Lebanon and Cyprus. In 1983 he was part of a search party looking for Don Tidey, a wealthy businessman who had been kid-

napped by the IRA as he was driving his 13-year-old daughter to school.

When Private Kelly and 25-year-old Garda Gary Sheehan came upon the gang's hideaway, they did not even get a chance to negotiate. The IRA fugitives threw a grenade and opened fire without warning, killing the two men instantly. The gang then scattered like the cowards they were and nobody has ever been convicted of the crimes.

WARPED

Of course, cutting down Irish soldiers was not actually part of the IRA's gameplan. As far as they were concerned, however, Pte Kelly and Gda Sheehan were just collateral damage in the overall context of pursuing a united Ireland.

Even now Sinn Fein will not actually condemn the killers, because of what would be a betrayal of their former comrades according to the Provos' warped moral code.

As even some of his celebrity supporters admit, Mr McGuinness was a key IRA leader throughout the Troubles. It is completely absurd to suggest that he does not know the names of the men who kidnapped Don Tidey and then murdered Pte Kelly and Gda Sheehan.

By presenting himself as an innocent bystander, he is again treating the Irish people like fools – it would be nice to think that sooner or later, we might show the same contempt.

David Kelly says that anybody who canvasses for Martin McGuinness is spitting on his father's grave. The same should go for anybody who wants to vote him into Aras an Uachtarain.

This election is now a real test of Ireland's moral character – and for the sake of Pte Kelly and all the IRA's other innocent victims, we must not flunk it.

See Terry Prone page 14

26. David Kelly's confrontation with Sinn Féin candidate Martin McGuinness made headlines during the 2011 presidential election.

RTÉ's then midlands correspondent Ciarán Mullooly, together with a camera crew, had been shadowing the Sinn Féin contender on his walkabout in the town. McGuinness, buoyed by the warm reception he'd received earlier when crossing the Shannon bridge on foot, had bounded into the shopping centre. The smile froze on his face as he realized this was not a well-wisher but a victim of the organization of which he once had been a leader.

The confrontation was captured by the camera crew, reported by Mullooly and broadcast on the main RTÉ news bulletins at 6 p.m. and 9 p.m. A growing crowd of onlookers gathered around the protagonists as the exchanges continued.

DAVID KELLY: I want justice for my father.

MARTIN MCGUINNESS: Absolutely.

DK: I believe you know the names of the killers of my father.

MMCG: No, I don't.

DK: And I want you to tell me who they are.

MMCG: I don't know their names.

DK: You were on the Army Council of the IRA.

MMCG: That's not true.

DK: Yes, you were.

MMCG: No – well, how do you know that?

[The next part of the exchange is edited out of the news report before continuing.]

DK: You're a liar.

MMCG: No, I'm not a liar.

DK: You are a liar, yeah.

MMCG: I'm not a liar, I'm not a liar.

DK: I want justice for my father. I want you to get your

comrades who committed this crime to hand themselves in to the gardaí.

MMCG: This is in the past. You are heartbroken on account of it. My sympathy is one hundred per cent with you and with your family. Absolutely.

DK: I'd just like to say to you that before there can be any reconciliation in this country, there has to be truth.

MMCG: Absolutely, and we have proposed that there should be an international, independent commission on truth.

DK: I want truth now. Today.

MMCG: OK, I appreciate . . .

DK (*interjecting*): Murder is murder. [*A section of the crowd breaks into applause.*] Murder is murder.[2]

They were nearly eyeball to eyeball by the time it ended. Over a decade later, Kelly still remembers the change in McGuinness's facial expression and body language, from the smiling, glad-handing politician to a defensive, narrow-eyed demeanour.

'I noticed there was a turn in him. I'd heard he was very charismatic, but that's when everything's going his way. It's a classic sign of a bully, you know? When things aren't going his way, you see the other side and he could be quite menacing. I did get a sense of that menace. But I was coming from a powerful position, as a son of a murdered soldier.'

As far as Kelly was concerned, McGuinness was a director and leader of a powerful terrorist organization, not just somebody on the ground taking orders. 'A ruthless individual, I would say. I got a sense of that ruthlessness, but it didn't stop me, because where I'm coming from was powerful too. All I had to do, if I felt I needed to maintain my strength, was think of my father in those woods, and nothing was going to stop me.'

Kelly had no idea that RTÉ would have a reporter and camera crew on hand to record the incident. 'And I was lucky too because I noticed in other towns he was surrounded by heavies,' he recalls. '[In Athlone] it was more local support-ers; a local councillor as well, I think. So yeah, RTÉ, it was the top story that day.'

When he got back to Moate that evening, Kelly found he had a lightness about him that he hadn't felt in a long time. 'I actually felt an awful weight off my shoulders, I felt relieved. I was carrying all that weight of what happened to my father and my family. I felt I'd done right by my father, to do what I did. And I did it for my mother as well. That's where I was coming from: my father *and* my mother.'

McGuinness's past haunted him throughout that presidential campaign. When Sinn Féin announced his candidacy, Gerry Moriarty, northern editor of the *Irish Times*, had presciently observed that there was unfinished business as far as victims of the Troubles in the Republic were concerned. McGuin-ness had dealt with his past in a northern context, but now 'southerners will be asked to look back on the Troubles in a manner most of them previously shied away from'.[3]

While campaigning, McGuinness spoke of being a presi-dent for the whole of Ireland. Yet his constitutional role would be as first citizen of the Republic, and for many people that was problematic, given the long-standing republican ambivalence towards the twenty-six-county polity and, during the Troubles, the downright hostility towards it.

Sinn Féin had hoped the Irish public would embrace McGuinness the international statesman and peacemaker, and forget the erstwhile terrorist godfather, yet his campaign was dogged from the start by questions about his paramilitary past. Early in the campaign he dismissed those highlighting his past as 'West Brit elements, in and around Dublin – some of them are attached to some sections of the media, others are attached to political parties and were formerly involved in political parties'.[4]

McGuinness would later distance himself from this unpresidential sounding comment, saying it had been 'off the cuff', but it was indicative of the beleaguered mentality that would characterize his campaign.[5]

He had stood down as deputy first minister at Stormont to run in the presidential election. In an interview with Moriarty published on 19 September, just before he departed from his office in Stormont, McGuinness claimed he had left the IRA in 1974.[6] The Sinn Féin candidate evidently hoped that this assertion would clean the slate with voters in the South. But there weren't many buyers for this proposition on either side of the border.

In a live debate on the independent station TV3, the veteran journalist Vincent Browne vigorously challenged McGuinness's assertion. Browne brandished eight books in front of McGuinness, each written by reputable chroniclers of the Troubles, all stating he had remained an IRA commander after 1974. Browne himself had been a reporter in the North and his IRA contacts had told him McGuinness had been involved long after he claimed to have left the organization.

'How come we are all wrong?' Browne asked rhetorically.[7]

Another veteran chronicler of the Troubles, the British journalist Peter Taylor, identified McGuinness as head of the

IRA's northern command. Moreover, McGuinness allegedly knew in advance about the notorious Enniskillen bomb of 1987, a claim McGuinness dismissed as a 'securocrat fantasy'. Twelve people were killed by the bomb, dozens maimed, hundreds traumatized.[8] McGuinness was also confronted by issues that resonated closer to home with a southern electorate. The murder of Detective Garda Jerry McCabe in 1996 had shocked Ireland deeply and was still vivid in the public consciousness.[9] Jerry McCabe's name and memory were precious in Irish life, his widow Ann much admired for her dignity and courage. McCabe had been savagely killed by a PIRA gang during a botched raid on a post office van in Adare, Co. Limerick, on 7 June of that year. A colleague, Detective Garda Ben O'Sullivan, was almost mortally injured, sustaining eleven bullet wounds and lasting psychological trauma. He died in 2022.

Pearse McAuley, Jeremiah Sheehy, Michael O'Neill and Kevin Walsh were all convicted in 1999 of the manslaughter of Jerry McCabe. The nation's disgust at the IRA attack was compounded by Sinn Féin's reaction to the convictions. No sooner were the gang jailed than party spokespeople started demanding their early release under the terms of the Good Friday Agreement.

In 2003 McCauley's then wife, the future Sinn Féin TD Pauline Tully, read out letters sent from prison by the killers at the party's ard fheis. The Sinn Féin delegates responded with a standing ovation. Tully would later describe her husband as a 'political prisoner'.

The four men were eventually released in 2009 and generated fresh outrage when they were picked up outside Castlerea prison and driven away by the Sinn Féin TD Martin Ferris.

Two years later, the Sinn Féin candidate was challenged

about all this during the presidential election campaign. McGuinness said he 'unreservedly condemned' the killing, which had 'brought no credit on Irish republicanism whatsoever'.[10] But his organization's track record left many citizens of the Republic sceptical about his sudden contrition: were his words sincere, or a matter of expediency, given the office he was seeking?

Other skeletons came back to haunt him on the hustings. Mary Conaghan was a teenager getting ready for school one morning in September 1974 when she heard a knock on the door. The IRA shot dead her father, Rory Conaghan, a judge, in the hallway of his own home in Belfast. Mr Conaghan was a northern Catholic, one of the few in the North's judicial system, and was noted for his moderate judgments. He was one of 337 Catholics killed by the Provisional IRA in the Troubles, thirty-five more than the combined total of the British security forces. Mary Conaghan was following the 2011 presidential campaign through the media. She became angered at suggestions by McGuinness and supporters that the media was guilty of 'stirring up' the feelings of victims to damage his bid for the presidency. She told Róisín Ingle in the *Irish Times*:

> The victim's feelings are there all the time. It may all be in the past for the perpetrators, but this is our present. Our feelings never go away. I want to speak for my father, to honour his memory. He was a good man. A man who lived for the rule of law and for justice, and a man who could have contributed so much more to Northern Ireland had his life not been cut short at the age of 54. I suppose I'd like the perspective to be aired that the war was not just waged by the IRA on the British and Protestants but on Catholics or anyone who got in the way of their project.[11]

Other relatives to speak up included the mother of Frank Hegarty, the IRA man turned informer who was found with a bullet in his head on the side of the road in May 1986. Rose Hegarty claimed that McGuinness had promised her on bended knee that it would be safe for Frank to return to Derry from his hiding place in London. Hegarty was abducted from Buncrana and shot dead after he was lured home. Edward Daly, the Bishop of Derry, privately told the Department of Foreign Affairs that McGuinness personally set up the rendezvous at which Hegarty was snatched.

One of the most notorious deaths of the Troubles was that of Patsy Gillespie, who was forced to drive a lorryload of explosives into a checkpoint in Derry in 1990, blowing up himself and five British soldiers. Daly described it as 'the work of Satan'. Gillespie's widow Kathleen blamed the atrocity squarely on McGuinness, who subsequently described her husband as a 'legitimate target of war' because he was working as a civilian cook at a British army base.

McGuinness was also widely believed to have sanctioned the murder of Joanne Mathers, the twenty-nine-year-old mother of an infant boy, gunned down in Derry in 1981 while collecting census forms door to door.

These questions about a litany of deaths stalled Martin McGuinness's momentum in what should have been a strong campaign. The country was going through the turmoil of a great recession, the collapse of the 'Celtic Tiger' and the ignominy of an IMF bailout in 2010. Fianna Fáil had received such a battering in the general election of February 2011 that it did not even field a candidate for president. Sinn Féin had won just 9.9 per cent in that election and McGuinness would have to poll a multiple of that number to have any chance of winning the presidency. However, he was the most high-profile of the seven runners and when he first declared his candidacy he was on 16 per cent support, just five percentage points behind the then frontrunner, Senator David Norris.[12]

David Kelly's confrontation with him in the Athlone shopping centre forcibly reminded the nation that a man who had led an organization that shot dead an Irish soldier was now seeking to become titular head of the Irish defence forces. That juxtaposition jarred. Many people were disinclined to believe McGuinness when he told Kelly he did not know who the killers of his father were.

The voters' scepticism was shared by many historians and reporters of the Troubles, including Ed Moloney, author of the authoritative 2002 book *A Secret History of the IRA*. Moloney believes it is inconceivable that McGuinness did not know who was involved at Derrada Wood. 'Not for a moment would he not know,' he says. 'Confrontations with southern security forces were something to be avoided because of the negative political consequences. I don't know this for sure but I would expect there to have been an inquiry ordered by the Army Council. McGuinness was on that Army Council, so would have been intimately aware of crucial detail such as who was involved. The Army Council would have had to approve the operation in the first place because of the political sensitivities of an operation in the South that could result in conflict with the gardaí/Irish army.'[13]

The confrontation between McGuinness and Kelly emboldened other victims of IRA violence in the Republic. Ann McCabe released a statement that led to McGuinness cancelling a walkabout in Limerick city. 'We can't move on if Mr McGuinness assumes he can aspire to the symbolic status of first citizen without first discharging the most basic responsibility of any citizen,' she said. 'If Martin McGuinness cannot or will not assist the authorities with its investigations into the murders of police officers, soldiers and prison officers how can we expect the rule of law to prevail under his presidency?'[14]

Michael Hand, brother of Detective Garda Frank Hand, who was murdered by the IRA in a post office raid in Meath in 1984, described the prospect of McGuinness becoming supreme commander of the defence forces as 'an abhorrence', adding: 'As far as I'm concerned, he has my family's blood on his hands.'[15]

In an interview with Bryan Dobson on RTÉ News, McGuinness again said he 'unreservedly condemned' any attack on gardaí or members of the defence forces, but Dobson produced another reminder of McGuinness's past – an interview he gave to the journalist Michael O'Higgins in *Hot Press* magazine in 1985. O'Higgins, now a senior counsel, had asked McGuinness to state categorically that gardaí patrolling the border were in no danger of attack. McGuinness had responded: 'Except in circumstances, like in Ballinamore, where IRA volunteers felt they were going to be shot dead and were defending themselves against armed gardaí and soldiers.'[16] McGuinness now said he could not recall the interview.

In the end McGuinness finished third, winning just 13 per cent of the popular vote. His candidature got barely any electoral endorsement beyond Sinn Féin's core supporters. Quoted afterwards in the *Guardian*, Ed Moloney believed McGuinness had fundamentally misjudged how southern society viewed the Troubles. 'In the north there is a tendency in the media not to put the actors in the peace process under too much scrutiny because the process couldn't withstand it,' he said. 'They forgot that in the South, the peace process marked the end of the need to indulge the North, so the media had no misgivings about putting McGuinness's very questionable account of his own life under scrutiny, and they found his cupboard as full of skeletons as is Gerry Adams's.'[17]

In 2013 Adams apologized in the Dáil to the families of members of the Irish state's forces killed by republicans during the Troubles. The apology was prompted by the murder of a garda in his own Louth constituency. Detective Garda Adrian Donohoe was shot dead while he and Detective Garda Joe Ryan were driving an unmarked police car on a routine cash escort to Lordship credit union in Bellurgan, a few miles from the border. A car approached and blocked the entrance to the credit union. Four men emerged from behind a wall and one of them, Aaron Brady, shot Donohoe in the face with a shotgun.

It was not officially a republican murder of a garda, but its proximity to the border, the fact his killer was from south Armagh, and the ruthlessness of the attack, brought flashbacks of IRA atrocities committed against gardaí. The parallels were unavoidable. Adams could not reasonably condemn the murder of Donohoe without also condemning other murders carried out by republicans during the Troubles.

Adams's successor Mary Lou McDonald apologized to the Kelly family in August 2020. The Sinn Féin leader told the *Westmeath Independent* that, if she could, she would rewrite that family's history. 'I can't do that. But I can assure them of my utmost respect, my absolute sympathy,' she said. McDonald recognized that there should be a process by which families like the Kellys got comfort and succour, and so feel less alone with their grief. 'This is about getting answers for families. And I have no difficulty committing myself to that, irrespective of who the family is, irrespective of the circumstances.'[18]

David Kelly responded by stating that he would judge Sinn Féin by its deeds not its words in relation to the murder of his father.

On the following St Patrick's Day in 2021, when much of the world was still in lockdown as a result of the Covid-19 pandemic, Sinn Féin staged an online concert bookended by contributions from McDonald and her northern counterpart Michelle O'Neill. There was 'no better man', O'Neill said, to end the online concert than Bik McFarlane.[19]

The appearance of the chief suspect in relation to the events at Derrada Wood prompted a letter from David Kelly to the *News Letter*:

> The acquittal of Brendan McFarlane on one charge of false imprisoment and two firearms charges in June of 2008 in the kidnapping of Don Tidey does not take away from the fact that he has never given an adequate explanation to a key matter. He has not explained why his fingerprints were found to be present at the scene in Derrada Woods, Co. Leitrim, where two members of the security forces were murdered on 16 December 1983. No one has ever faced prosecution for the murders up to the present time. Therefore, you can appreciate how distraught I personally felt to see Mr McFarlane topping the bill of an online Sinn Féin St Patrick's Day Concert in recent days when my father has missed out on so many life celebrations, including St Patrick's Day, these past thirty-seven years . . . I would like to invite Mr McFarlane to publicly explain how his fingerprints

were found to be present at the scene of my father's murder and that of Garda Gary Sheehan's. I would also invite his party president, Mary Lou McDonald, who also participated in the concert, to persuade him to come forward with any information he may have about the events of that terrible day.[20]

Kelly put the same challenge to McFarlane via an interview with the *Irish Times* in January 2022. McFarlane has not responded to either request.[21] He remains a feted individual in republican circles because of his status as the officer commanding during the H-Blocks protest and also his role in the Maze prison breakout. He has appeared in a number of television documentaries in relation to both events, but has been silent about Derrada Wood, and about his role in the Bayardo Bar atrocity.

He continues to maintain his public profile by playing music in republican bars around Belfast.[22]

25. On the Run

While Brendan McFarlane entertains republicans in bars around Belfast, the other Derrada Wood suspects have kept a much lower profile.

Gerard 'Blute' McDonnell was arrested a year after the 1983 ambush during the hunt for the Brighton bomber Patrick Magee. The device at the Grand Hotel, planted with the intention of murdering Margaret Thatcher, killed five people and injured dozens more during the Conservative Party conference on 12 October 1984. The IRA attack prompted one of Britain's biggest manhunts, and Magee was eventually tracked down to a safe house in Govanhill, Glasgow, an area where many Irish republican sympathizers were based.

On 22 June 1985, Scottish police surrounded a block of flats in Langside Road. Unsure exactly where the IRA gang was holed up, they knocked on the door of each flat pretending to be pizza-delivery men. Magee himself opened one of the doors and was arrested without a struggle. With him were McDonnell and three others: Peter Sherry, Ella O'Dwyer and Martina Anderson, who would go on to become a Sinn Féin MLA and MEP.

The five were taken completely by surprise and had no time to destroy incriminating evidence. McDonnell had a fake Irish birth certificate, a loaded Browning pistol and almost £5,500 sterling in cash. He was also found with what Scottish police called a 'bombing campaign calendar'.[1] A folded note in a money belt strapped around McDonnell's waist referred to time-delayed bombs primed to go off in English holiday resorts over the months of June, July and August.

There were sixteen bombs in all, four in London and twelve in seaside resorts, one for each of the days between 19 July and 5 August 1985. The device at the Rubens Hotel in Buckingham Palace Road, central London, was already primed and ready to explode on 29 July, at a time when many dignitaries and celebrities would be attending a Buckingham Palace garden party.[2]

The bombs were designed to cause maximum damage during the height of the holiday season and to spread terror to all areas of Britain. In their hunt for the Brighton bomber, British police had stumbled across what was intended to be the biggest bombing campaign in Britain since the Second World War. McDonnell and his co-conspirators were all given life sentences for conspiring to cause explosions. The trial judge, Leslie Boreham, told McDonnell he was 'cynical, cruel and cowardly' and a danger to society.[3] He would have liked to have jailed him for longer, the judge said, but was constrained by the law. McDonnell was eventually released under the terms of the Good Friday Agreement in 1999.

Seamus McElwaine lived by the gun and died by the gun. He joined the IRA in 1974 at the age of fourteen and spent the rest of his short life either on 'active service' or in jail.

As officer commanding in south Fermanagh, he was responsible for terrorizing the Protestant population in that district. Arlene Foster, the former DUP leader and former Northern Ireland first minister, has stated many times that she believes McElwaine was one of two men who shot her father John Kelly in the head at their family home near Roslea in Co. Fermanagh in 1979.[4]

A year later McElwaine shot dead an off-duty UDR man, Aubrey Abercrombie, and later killed an off-duty RUC reserve constable, Ernest Johnston. He was jailed in 1981 for thirty years.

After his escape from the Maze prison, McElwaine went on the run and ended up in Leitrim. On the morning of 26 April 1986 he and another IRA man, Seán Lynch, who went on to become a Sinn Féin MLA from 2011 to 2021, were preparing a landmine to ambush British soldiers travelling between Lisnaskea and Roslea. They ran into an SAS patrol and McElwaine died in a hail of bullets.

According to Lynch, who survived the attack, an injured McElwaine was questioned on the ground by SAS officers before they shot him dead. The incident occurred at a time when the British security forces were allegedly conducting a policy of 'shoot to kill'. An inquest jury found he had been unlawfully killed as the soldiers opened fire without giving him a chance to surrender.

In 2021, the thirty-fifth anniversary of his death was marked by an online video in which Matt Carthy, the Sinn Féin TD, described him as 'by all accounts an intelligent, humorous, engaging young man', albeit that Carthy never personally knew McElwaine.[5]

Oliver McKiernan was picked up at a house in Aghacashel, Co. Leitrim, almost three years to the day after Derrada Wood. He had been living under an assumed name locally for many years, but his past had finally caught up with him.

At dawn on 15 December 1986, gardaí armed with Uzi sub-machine guns turned up with a search warrant to a local house. They discovered a mobile home on site and demanded the keys, at which point a man emerged and inquired what the rumpus was about.[6] A garda spotted that a window in the mobile home had been opened, as if someone had just escaped. McKiernan vaulted a nearby fence and ran down the side of a field. Gardaí pursued him and eventually caught up. As they grappled with him, McKiernan punched Detective Sergeant Michael Barrett in the face.

In custody, McKiernan was questioned about events in Derrada Wood. David Kelly heard from detectives that he 'stared at the wall' and told them nothing. McKiernan was never charged in relation to Derrada Wood, but he was returned to the Special Criminal Court to face charges arising out of an incident while he was on the run from Portlaoise prison. In January 1976 he was alleged to have pulled a gun on two gardaí who were searching outhouses at a farm in Smithboro, Co. Monaghan, and told them to turn around and keep walking. He then fired two shots at the men as they made a run for it over an earthen bank.

At his trial McKiernan denied being involved at Smithboro, but Justice Liam Hamilton gave him a total of nine years for the offences of possessing an illegal firearm, resisting arrest with a firearm and assaulting a garda. Hamilton suspended the sentences because of the lapse of time since the first two offences had been committed. McKiernan walked free from court with only a gentle admonition from the judge to stay out of trouble. He seems to have done so, and now lives quietly in Cavan.

Tony McAllister is the only Maze escapee unaccounted for; he seemed to have completely disappeared post 1983. His name surfaced in 2002 in a report relating to IRA prisoners still 'on the run' and it was believed he had gone into exile.[7] According to Gerry Kelly, the Sinn Féin MLA, he went to live abroad and 'passed away through natural causes under an assumed name. He had carved out a new life with a loving wife and children.' Gardaí, who had wanted to speak to him in connection with the incident in Claremorris, also believe he is now dead.[8]

The murders at Derrada Wood are still being investigated by An Garda Síochána's Serious Crime Review Team. The investigation was reopened at the request of the Kelly family in 2019 to deal once and for all with rumours, which had circulated since December 1983, that Private Patrick Kelly had been killed by friendly fire. The allegation, circulated by republicans, was the subject of a thematic review in October 2019 which concentrated exclusively on ballistic evidence from the scene.

Detective Sergeant Patrick Ennis, who in December 1983 spent eight days examining the scene, gave evidence at the Brendan McFarlane trial in 2008. He said he had carried out an examination of the body of Private Kelly and determined that he was shot from in front. Ennis had calculated that the weapons were fired from between the makeshift tent used by the kidnap gang and where the bodies were located, and in their direction. A friendly fire shot would have been from behind.

By examining the bullets and spent cartridges taken from the scene, Ennis determined that three weapons were fired, all by the IRA, and that the security forces had not fired at all.

Assistant Commissioner John O'Driscoll was in charge of the review until his retirement from the force in 2022. 'There was no discharge of weapons by An Garda Síochána or the Irish army. There was never a shoot-out at the hide. All you have is the shots that are discharged by the terrorists,' he said.[9]

'All the shots discharged by the gardaí and soldiers were around the periphery. There is only one [garda weapon] fired in [the centre of] Derrada Wood afterwards and that is by a garda after the shooting dead of Kelly and Sheehan. He fires shots into the air to contain them [the gang] and keep them within the woods until assistance arrived. Patrick Ennis specifically said that the bullets discharged were not from state weapons. Bear in mind this is a number of years before weapons are found in Northern Ireland that are believed to be the weapons that were used.'

The weapons fired by the IRA at Derrada Wood were a 7.62mm x 39mm calibre AK variety automatic rifle and a 7.62mm calibre G3 Heckler & Koch automatic rifle, both models in common use by the IRA at the time. Detective Sergeant Donal Kelleher was shot in the legs by a .45 Colt revolver.

The Heckler & Koch rifle was found abandoned in a graveyard at St Mary's Church, Newtownbutler, on 7 August 1986. It was linked to a shoot-out between the RUC and the IRA on 2 August 1982 at Claret Rock, Co. Armagh, and later at Lisnaskea, Co. Fermanagh, in May 1984. The Colt .45 was also recovered from the graveyard. A third weapon linked to Derrada was recovered from Lettergreen in Co. Fermanagh on 19 December 1985.

Gardaí have examined hundreds of items taken from the three crime locales in 1983 – Derrada Wood, Claremorris and the original kidnap scene at Woodtown – to see if any of them might yield useful DNA, a technology not available at the time. None of the items involved have yielded further evidence, but fingerprints found in Claremorris match those of Gerard McDonnell and Tony McAllister.

It is considered doubtful at this stage that any prosecutions will ever be brought.

Nonetheless, O'Driscoll hoped the ballistic evidence would provide some comfort to the Kelly family. 'There is a huge importance on outcomes other than prosecution for victims and victims' families,' he says. 'Being realistic with the Kelly family, we set out from the beginning to tell them that the chances of additional prosecutions are slim, but we could potentially prove conclusively their father did not die as a result of friendly fire, and that is of huge significance to the family.

Reflecting on the tragedy now, John O'Driscoll says, 'It was a bad day in the history of the IRA. One would have to assume within their own ranks it was not good that they had killed a member of the defence forces and of An Garda Síochána. Members of the defence forces being held hostage by an alternative army is unique in the history of the Troubles. The IRA's capacity to overrun the institutions of the state was quite a concern. The fact [is] that nobody will ever be charged [with the murders of Kelly and Sheehan]. So be it, but let's have the truth.'

26. Kidnapped

Except for that short press conference the day after his release and the evidence he gave in two court cases, Don Tidey always declined to give his account of the circumstances he confronted from the moment he was taken until his release twenty-three days later. Almost forty years on, he agreed to talk to the authors of this book about the kidnapping and the severe challenges he faced.

One of those suspected of having been involved in the planning was Kevin Mallon. Tidey had unknowingly witnessed Mallon in action almost exactly ten years earlier. Quinnsworth was the anchor tenant in the Phibsboro shopping centre, on Dublin's northside, at the time. The campus was dominated by a grey concrete office block known as Phibsboro Tower. Tidey had his boardroom on the top floor. From this vantage point he had a clear view of both the adjoining Dalymount Park football ground and the nearby Mountjoy jail.

Tidey was in his boardroom on 31 October 1973 when he saw a helicopter hovering over the jail before descending and then lifting off again. Later news reports revealed that three terrorist prisoners were inside it – and one of them was Kevin Mallon.

He shrugs his shoulders about that quirk of circumstance back then – it was just one of those things that happened in Ireland at the time.

It is now known that the IRA had been monitoring Tidey's

comings and goings in the winter of 1983. During the Troubles, he had crossed the border every week, visiting premises that were bombed out, and comforting traumatized staff. 'I was fourteen years looking after my own security,' he says. 'I had travelled for a decade in the most dangerous circumstances, that very few businessmen experienced. I was constantly aware of my personal vulnerabilities and safety from 1969 onwards to 1983 when the kidnapping happened. Many of my staff had been the victims of violence.'

While he was accustomed to varying his routes and habits, a practical problem was that Woodtown, where his house was located, was a cul-de-sac. There was no other way out if someone was trying to do him harm.

His physical fitness, Tidey believes, would have been noted by the IRA, which no doubt was anticipating a pro-longed stand-off over the payment of a ransom. They needed a hostage who could endure the rigours of outdoor exposure in the depths of an Irish winter. Here was a forty-eight-year-old man who 'looked to be as fit as a fiddle. They probably knew me to be a disciplined individual. They needed a person who was going to be able to withstand the undetermined length of time that he was going to be in captivity.'

Tidey's durability was put to the test immediately after he was abducted. The unnerving deprivation of his sight and hearing began as soon as he was bundled into the car outside his home. The compressed rib cage, which he suffered when he was thrown across the transmission of the getaway car, was a source of continuous pain and caused him further aggravation when moving.

In the dark of the first night he was put into a hollow in

the ground. The rain was falling in sheets, a winter wind was drumming up spooky noises in the trees. Lying in the hollow, he realized it had some sort of polythene cover serving as a makeshift tent. Tidey actually never saw his hide during the whole of his confinement. He could only gauge its dimensions by reaching out and touching the sides, which was difficult to do with his wrists in chains. He estimates it was no more than two metres square and that his bed was most likely a natural depression in the ground rather than a man-made hole. At most it could hold two people. He recalls that the tree he was chained to and the water he used for ablutions and latrine duties were sufficiently far away to ensure that the hide was well maintained.

'When it rained, the outer cover filled.' He would be lying on the ground with the plastic sagging down into his face: 'I could feel the polythene with the rain almost resting on my nose.'

For the first seven days it seemed to rain non-stop. Later came snow and ground frost. To protect their asset, the kidnappers had ordered Tidey out of his business suit, shirt and shoes, and replaced them with a thick flannel shirt, a combat-style jacket and wellingtons stuffed with straw. For sustenance he was given tea and bread, occasionally with jam, and once or twice a segment of fruit. He was sometimes given soup. Milk was taken from cartons produced by the North Connacht Farmers Co-Op in Sligo, a brand sold widely in the region, including Ballinamore.

One of the cartons with its distinctive green and orange NCF lettering was subsequently found by gardaí at the camp and taken away for forensic examination. It had a best-before date of 16/12/83 – the day he was liberated.[1] 'Thankfully, the food was nutritious enough to keep somebody like me reasonably fit and well under very demanding conditions, and to protect me against illness and infection. I needed to have the energy to move if they needed me to move.'

In subsequent court testimony, Tidey filled out more detail about his daily rituals as a hostage. 'There was no question of shaving. I did on occasions have [access to] what I believe was a communal toothbrush and toothpaste, which we used sparingly,' he recalled.

After a couple of days he was allowed to remove the headgear to wash his face properly, always under the close watch of his captors. 'I needed to exaggerate the fact that, for the brief time I was washing my head, my eyes were tightly closed.' There were visits to a latrine area every morning and evening. His legs were unchained for those visits, but a halter rope was placed around his knees and held by a captor.

Sleep was possible but intermittent in the twenty-four-hour cycle. Tidey could shuffle himself into the sleeping bag provided, but his chains and padlocks diminished his physical comfort. 'The question of needing to relieve oneself during the course of the very long hours became a serious and tedious business,' he recalled. 'This was due to my confinement in the sleeping bag ... which made movement within an area of which I had no understanding exceedingly difficult.'

The handcuffs on his wrists were 'antiquated' and too small and caused considerable discomfort. His ears were permanently wrapped in a tight bandage; his blindfold was removed only for ablutions.

With the constant shackling and surveillance, in a place that was utterly alien to him, he knew his chances of making an escape were slim. 'There was no way that I could have broken out of that situation.'

One of the few moments that the kidnappers engaged with him came when his captors suddenly pulled off Tidey's blindfold one day. They sat him down in a chair and handed him a cup of tea and a copy of the *Evening Herald* dated 28 November 1983, four days after he was seized. The story was, once again, on the front page. They ordered him to hold it for a photograph, and to 'look cheerful and alive'.[2]

'I knew my family would derive some encouragement from the fact that I was still alive. The picture was proof that I was seemingly uninjured.' The plan for the photo never came to anything.

Throughout his captivity Tidey kept preparing himself for what he calls *le moment critique* – an opportunity to escape that might somehow materialize. With manacles on his wrists and ankles, he was severely limited in what he could physically do. So he drew on his military training, doing a form of exercise that involves the static contraction of muscles without any visible movement. Tidey would brace his arms, shoulders and torso, tensing all the muscles while holding his breath for as long as he could. Then he would release them, thereby accelerating the flow of oxygen through his body. He did the same with his legs, bracing them against each other, holding fast and then releasing.

He quietly practised these exercises over and over. 'I kept myself for an unknown period of time as fit as I could under extremely restrictive conditions. The body is a remarkable machine. It meant that it was strengthened and maintained as if I was actually moving.'

Psychologically, he switched into survival mode early on. Tidey was mentally tough enough not to allow himself to ruminate too deeply on his plight. It didn't help to dwell on the emotional implications of his situation. It was all about concentrating on his immediate environment and staying present in the moment. This management of his mind made a difference, he would later reveal. 'I think that what you learn under the circumstances is not to anticipate the future. Looking forward makes you feel the very real physical constraint that is on you.'

Then a medical complication arose. Tidey had suffered periodically from ear infections brought about by air travel, which he used almost weekly. He had been prescribed antibiotic ear drops by his doctor. He warned the kidnappers that, without his medication, he would become susceptible to bad ear infections and acute pain. The problem duly developed. 'It was a very worrying moment during my confinement because if that ear infection had developed as it normally did, it would have presented a problem not just to me but to my kidnappers too.' His captors finally became alarmed enough to source antibiotic ear drops from one of their local helpers three days before the end of the kidnapping. 'One of the fortunate things to happen is that I was rescued before my ear infection got really bad.'

Communication between captors and captive was otherwise kept to a bare minimum. Nor did Tidey attempt to reach out to them. 'It was a deliberate policy for me not to engage. I just wanted to keep my counsel – and they clearly were going to keep theirs. There was no small talk.'

His disciplined behaviour in the hide was matched by his kidnappers, who ensured he could never make a positive identification. Tidey sat through the trial of Brendan McFarlane in 2008, but the man in the dock was a stranger. 'Whether he was [in Derrada] or wasn't, I don't know.'

The question of who these people were was not relevant;

the priority was to remain alert in case circumstances changed. He knew there would have been an enormous manhunt going on with a nationwide media campaign behind it.

Towards the end of the saga, Pope John Paul II was approached to intervene. The impetus for this initiative came from an unusual source. The directors of Quinnsworth contacted Revd Horace McKinley and asked him to help. The board had been impressed by the ecumenical nature of the gatherings at Revd McKinley's church every evening, where people continued to pray for Tidey's safe return. This had led to a joint day of prayer in Dublin churches called for by the Catholic and Anglican archbishops of Dublin, Dermot Ryan and Henry McAdoo, which occurred on Sunday 10 December.

Revd McKinley contacted Archbishop McAdoo, seeking permission to approach the papal secretary in Rome, Fr John Magee from Newry, about the Tidey kidnapping. The coming of the Christmas season injected a fresh energy into everyone's efforts. Archbishop McAdoo gave his approval. Revd McKinley says it was fortunate that the papal secretary was Irish and therefore well acquainted with the story.

'All this was completely new territory for me. I found Fr Magee to be a good listener and reasonable. I had stressed that Mr Tidey was a man of deeply rooted Christian faith. Clearly that discussion resulted in a positive Vatican response. Archbishop McAdoo was co-chair of the Anglican-Roman Catholic International Commission (ARCIC), which was involved in discussions to heal the historic differences between Anglicanism and Rome. I think all that must have had a positive impact on the Vatican's decision to agree to this visit.'[3]

The Pope had come to Ireland four years earlier, in September 1979. In Drogheda, as close as he could get to the border without venturing into the North, he'd made a heart-felt plea for peace to those republicans who claimed to be Catholics.

'On my knees I beg you to turn away from the paths of violence and to return to the way of peace,' John Paul II had pleaded. Predictably, the Provisional IRA ignored his entreaties, as they had done many others, but this did not deter Church leaders from trying four years later to recruit his enormous authority to their cause.

Those involved agreed it should be Tidey's two sons, Andrew and Alistair, who would meet the Pope. On 16 December the brothers left Dublin to fly via London to Rome for the meeting. In London that day they stopped off at the head office of Associated British Foods to meet Garry Weston. While there, word came through that their father had been found and freed. They immediately headed to the airport to catch a flight back to Dublin. 'Instead of meeting the Pope, they met me,' says Tidey with a smile.

In the weeks and months afterwards he was gratified to discover that his kidnapping had brought so many people together to work and pray for his release. 'It has been good for me to reflect on that over the years ever since. Whitechurch under the mountains, where we worshipped for twenty-odd years, was an ecumenical church. There were people in my own staff who had never before been within a Church of Ireland or Protestant church. Out of it all there is another story to be told – in the sense that people were genuinely moved, whether they were Jewish, Catholic, Protestant, or nonconformist. That was in the South. A similar situation pertained in the North.'

All of this he would find out later. But in captivity he was comforted by the thought that many people would be moving heaven and earth to save him. So, there was always hope. And to avail himself of it he needed to keep on top of his emotions, including fear. For strategic reasons he remained consciously deferential to his kidnappers. 'All the time I had to make certain that I was sufficiently in control of my own emotions not to jeopardize the situation by some careless or irrational act born out of frustration.'

On the twenty-second day of his captivity – though he himself did not know what day it was – Tidey realized that his kidnappers were keeping him especially confined, not allowing him to move at all. The kidnappers knew, but he did not, that a search party had been through the woods the previous day, but missed the hide.

'But the following morning things started to change because I was stood up and – this would've been mid-morning I suppose – my chains were removed, my head-dress was removed and a balaclava put on.' The eye and mouth holes in the balaclava were twisted to the back of his head, meaning he still could not see.

'I was in a situation where I was calculating, what's going to confront me next? And I proved to myself that I was sufficiently in control of myself to take advantage of what happened.'

The gang formed into single file, he believes, with him behind the leader and being pushed from behind by the next man. His head and shoulders were forced down so that he was crouching, his forehead almost touching the lower back of the man in front.

'The leader was going to make a break, presumably. I had no other intention but to stay with them. I had to stay alive. We started to move and then I heard "*Bing!*"' He recognized the sound from his army days: a pin had been pulled from a hand grenade. 'I've thrown hand grenades and I've had them thrown at me,' he explains. It exploded nearby and then automatic gunfire broke out.

So now the climax, *le moment critique*, had arrived. 'There was a lot of firing about, and I was neither frightened, nor petrified, nor anything. All my faculties came into play. My next conscious movement was to hit the ground and do a military roll, and in that moment in time I found cover under low-hanging branches and bracken, which meant I had cover from all that was going on around me with the security forces and the IRA. As I lay there, I raised my head to find that I was looking at the barrel-end of a rifle pointed right at my head. I looked along the barrel to see a soldier lying on the ground. This was Private Patrick McLaughlin I later learned.

'I also learned some months later from the chief of staff of the army that the soldier was on first pressure on his trigger, which meant at the slightest movement I could have been shot in the head,' he says. 'However, while looking at him, I had a brief moment to make a movement with the right hand, to point at myself and say, "I'm Don Tidey. I'm the hostage." The soldier involved thought the movement I was making was [for] a weapon. By the look of me, I looked like a terrorist and was dressed as one. In that second I believe it was ordained that he would not fire.'

Francis Smith, the garda recruit, made him take off his wellington boots and run across a 'big Leitrim field'. They encountered Inspector Bill Somers, the man in charge of the Security Task Force at Derrada Wood. As Tidey remembers it, Somers put a revolver to his head and said, 'Identify yourself.' He replied: 'I'm Don Tidey, don't you know my accent?'

He recalls diving onto the road surface as the IRA gang drove down the road in their getaway car, firing as they went.

'I felt a very intense sharp pain in my arm and felt that I had been hit. I quickly got to my feet and ran to the open gate in the field to a deep Leitrim ditch and jumped in.' He found himself up to his ankles in freezing ditch water. For the first time in twenty-three days, he was now on his own, albeit just for a moment. He looked down at his elbow. 'To my great relief, the sharp pain and numbness in my arm was improving. I had only hit that sensitive nerve that is in the elbow. The next thing, I heard somebody calling my name, and Bill Somers looked over the top of the ditch at me, and I was taken back to the road and the greater security of an enlarged group of gardaí.'

Twenty-three days after being thrown into the back of a car by strangers, Tidey was now being bundled into another one by strangers too. But these were friendly and they were driving him away to safety. In those moments he had his first and last glimpse of the hostile wilderness that had been his al fresco prison since the night of 24 November. He left it behind him without so much as a backward glance. He could not wait to get the hell out of there.

In Ballyconnell garda station he met Chief Superintendent J. J. McNally, the garda in overall charge of the search. McNally produced a map and showed it to Tidey. The map was laid out like a grid, with sections marked off according to the alphabet. He told him search teams had been through Derrada Wood the day before. McNally did not say why, but he'd ordered another search of Derrada Wood. This one found Tidey. 'It was an extraordinary coincidence. If he had picked another grid area, I might never have been found,' Tidey believes. McNally gave Tidey the map as a keepsake. He has it to this day.

An Irish army doctor pronounced him to be in good

shape, all things considered. The doctor was soon called away. Some of those who had been searching for Tidey were in a worse state and needed attention, he says.

A few hours later he was on his way home. As the car moved through towns and villages on the way back to Dublin, he watched the Christmas lights twinkling in the December darkness. They seemed unusually bright and vivid, he recalled, maybe because his eyes had seen so little light in the previous three weeks. And he noticed the people going about their Christmas shopping, immersed in their own urgencies, utterly oblivious to the bearded man in the car savouring the sweet taste of freedom. 'It was unreal,' he says.

When he was deposited by the gardaí back home, Susan was the first to wrap her arms around her father. His sons had yet to make it back from London. Visitors to Woodtown included Garret FitzGerald, Michael Noonan and Larry Wren.

Revd Horace McKinley was already there. He recalls that Tidey was barely able to raise his voice above the level of a whisper but was still able to provide a compelling account of the events of that extraordinary day to his distinguished guests. It was, the rector says, 'a memorable performance'.

27. Fade to Black

John Joe McGirl died from cancer in December 1988. He was sixty-seven. Thousands lined the streets of Ballinamore for his funeral. The eulogy was given by an old friend, the author Fr Dan Gallogly, who depicted McGirl almost as a Christ-like figure: 'misunderstood, misrepresented, rejected at the polls, the victim of condemnations and denunciations'.[1]

The old Latin adage *De mortuis nil nisi bonum* applied, he said. Of the dead, nothing but good is to be said. Amidst the many obsequies and diplomatic euphemisms, nobody cared to mention that John Joe McGirl had espoused a violent ideology that was rejected by the majority of his fellow countrymen and women.

The funeral oration was given by Gerry Adams, who exhorted local republicans to carry on the fight against British rule in Ireland. Adams had a particular reason to be grateful to McGirl. At a rambunctious Sinn Féin ard fheis two years previously, the party's policy of abstentionism from Dáil Éireann, an article of faith for generations of Irish republicans including McGirl, was dropped.

By 1986, the northern leadership of Sinn Féin believed abstentionism had become an obstacle to its declared intention of building an electoral platform on both sides of the border. Though most Sinn Féin members had come to the realization that the policy had outlived any usefulness it ever had, getting the required support of a two-thirds majority at an ard fheis was not certain.

Adams needed somebody who had credibility throughout the republican movement to speak in favour of the motion. Moreover, he needed a southerner, given that most of the opposition to dropping abstentionism was coming from party members in the Republic. John Joe McGirl was that man. He seconded the motion and, dressed nattily in a suit and waistcoat and wearing professorial spectacles, he gave a memorable speech in which he explained that many young unemployed people wanted him to represent them, but were not satisfied with him refusing to take a Dáil seat if elected a TD.

When McGirl spoke at that 1986 ard fheis he had been a local councillor for twelve successive years, and for twenty years in total. He'd been the chairman of Leitrim County Council for one year and had sat on myriad committees. He knew from personal experience that ordinary Irish people cared not a jot for the philosophical arguments in favour of abstentionism.

Moreover, McGirl said, having consulted with other veteran republicans such as former chief of staff Joe Cahill, they agreed it would be 'necessary to make [a] change if we are not going to hand on this struggle to another generation'.[2] Implicit in that statement was an acknowledgement that Sinn Féin/IRA now needed an alternative to violence, which had failed to dislodge the British from the North. The vote was carried, Adams's strategy won the day. In the twilight of his life, McGirl's last significant contribution to the republican movement was to help nudge it towards electoral politics.

On Remembrance Sunday a year later, 8 November 1987, the Provisional IRA detonated a bomb in Enniskillen, killing twelve people who were there to mourn the dead of both world wars. Dozens more people were maimed in the atrocity. The bomb was intended to go off as members of the Ulster Defence Regiment were marching past. Instead, all who died were civilians sheltering from the rain outside the local library. Eleven people died at the scene; a twelfth victim died after thirteen years in a coma.

Among the eleven dead was a twenty-year-old nurse, Marie Wilson. She was the daughter of Leitrim man Gordon Wilson, who was also buried beneath the rubble beside his daughter, but survived. The eighteen-kilogram Semtex bomb was made in an IRA safe house near Ballinamore, which is just twenty-five miles from Enniskillen, and was smuggled across the border in relays.[3]

The Enniskillen bomb was an outrage that left the people of Ireland and further afield stunned. At the following meeting of Leitrim County Council, when a minute's silence was observed for the victims, McGirl joined in. According to a report in the *Leitrim Observer*, he looked 'visibly unsettled when he stood up to express his sympathy'.[4]

As the undisputed boss of Sinn Féin/IRA in his region, did he know about the construction of the bomb in the safe house outside of Ballinamore? Did he facilitate those who made it and transported it to Enniskillen?

On 14 March 1995 his nephew Francis McGirl, who had been acquitted of the murder of Lord Mountbatten and three others at Mullaghmore, was making his way home from Ballinamore on his tractor late at night when it overturned, killing him instantly. He was thirty-nine. His funeral was a republican affair. A lone piper played and his coffin was draped in the tricolour. Many members of the Sinn Féin ard comhairle attended. In the following week's *Leitrim Observer*, the former Sinn Féin MP Owen Carron said that it had been

Francis McGirl who helped two of the Tidey kidnappers to escape. Carron wrote:

> During the 80s, he ended up on the run for a period follow-ing the Tidey kidnap episode. With major troop searches in Leitrim, Francis helped make good the escape of several wanted men, including Long Kesh escapees. Despite the Ballinamore area being saturated with Free State troops and gardaí, Francis led his party around Sliabh an Iarainn through Arigna into South Sligo and all the way to Mayo. Here, they were confronted by armed detectives but again escaped. Such was the character of Francis.

In 1990, less than two years after his death, a John Joe McGirl Memorial Committee was set up by the members of the Leitrim comhairle ceanntair of Sinn Féin. Their aim was to erect a memorial not just to McGirl but to the 'whole repub-lican struggle to which his entire life was devoted' – which meant the Provisional IRA.[5] Many of those on the organiz-ing committee, including Pat Rehill, knew that McGirl had helped the kidnappers of Don Tidey, and the murderers of Private Kelly and Garda Sheehan.

Planning permission for a memorial, beside the bridge overlooking the waterway that runs through Ballinamore, was lodged with Leitrim County Council on 10 May 1990 and a notice published in the *Leitrim Observer* that month. It was a single paragraph lodged between sundry planning notices for septic tanks and house extensions. 'Planning per-mission is being sought from Leitrim County Council to erect a memorial to Sean Seosamh McFeargail at Aughadark, Ballinamore, Co. Leitrim,' it said. The application was signed by the John Joe McGirl Memorial Committee.[6]

27. A memorial to one of the founders of the Provisional IRA, John Joe McGirl, in Ballinamore was unveiled by Gerry Adams and Martin McGuinness in 1994. McGirl is believed to have had a central role in the kidnapping of Don Tidey.

Locals were never asked if they wanted a memorial to a founder member of the Provisional IRA in their town, and their views were moot anyway. The McGirl family claimed the site belonged to them, even though it was beside a path and a road used by the public every day, from schoolchildren to joggers to shoppers. Waterways Ireland asked the council if they owned the site, and were told they did not, but were given no further details as to who did.

Gerry Reynolds, then a Fine Gael TD, met with Paddy Doyle, the Leitrim county manager, to object privately to the memorial. He recalls saying: 'Paddy, that planning application is on the council land, it's not on the McGirls' land, and you should refuse it.'[7] Planning permission was granted anyway, just seven weeks later. Like many others in Ballinamore, Reynolds now regrets not doing more to stop the memorial being built. 'A lot of people were intimidated, and still are,' he says. 'But when it doesn't impact on them personally in any great way, nobody wants to take it on.'

The organizing committee set about raising IR£20,000 (about €25,400) for the memorial. Much of the money came from the republican diaspora. Ken Livingstone, then a Labour Party MP and later the Mayor of London, attended a fundraising event in the city.[8] 'I am proud,' he said, 'to pay tribute to a great man who stood by and contributed to the strategy of the republican movement which has so successfully isolated Britain in world opinion.'

The memorial was designed by the artist Robert Ballagh, using black marble with a surrounding phalanx wall of Arigna stone, into which are sculpted the symbols of the four provinces of Ireland. It was unveiled by Adams and Martin McGuinness in May 1994, three months before the first IRA ceasefire. It is now in a prominent place beside the cross-border Shannon–Erne Waterway, formerly the Ballinamore–Ballyconnell Canal, which was opened shortly afterwards as one of the early dividends of the peace process. The memorial states that McGirl was an 'unbroken and unbreakable Fenian'. In other republican encomia he is described as 'the gentle soldier'. Beside the monument is a message board remembering the ten hunger strikers who died in 1981.

A casual visitor to Ballinamore might conclude that McGirl was a universally admired figure there, and that the terrorism he enabled was condoned by its people. The electoral record suggests otherwise. In the 1985 local elections, for example, McGirl got just one vote in five in the town.

The memorial has become a focal point every August for speeches by a who's who of senior figures in the republican movement, Michelle O'Neill and Adams among them. Adams gave an address in 2018 to mark the thirtieth anniversary of McGirl's death. He told those present who had sheltered the Maze escapees back in 1983 to give themselves a 'bualadh bos', a round of applause. 'Gerry Kelly often tells that when he and others arrived in Leitrim, it was John Joe who dispersed them in safe houses around Ballinamore. So don't let on if you took in any of those prisoners,' Adams quipped to the crowd.[9]

Unsurprisingly, he made no reference to the role of these Maze escapees in the kidnapping of Don Tidey and the murder of a recruit garda and Irish soldier at Derrada. To this day, the silent majority in the town keep their opinions on the memorial, and the man it honours, to themselves.

In 2003 the local Sinn Féin cumann erected another republican memorial. It stands outside Corraleehan Church, within a mile of where the garda and soldier were killed. The memorial is to Philip Meehan, a tenant farmer who was shot dead by his landlord in 1880 and is now known as the first martyr of the Land War. Also mentioned is another local man, John Joe Martin, Meehan's grandnephew, an IRA veteran of the England campaign of 1939–40 and of the border campaign.

Today Derrada Wood is merely a tuft of trees on the top of a hill, indistinguishable from other patches of pine trees in the area. One member of the extended Kelly family who visited in recent years left flowers at the wrong spot. It is easily done. For there is no monument anywhere in Derrada, or Ballinamore, in memory of Garda Gary Sheehan and Private Patrick Kelly.

28. By the Grace of God

As he began to recover during that first weekend of freedom, Don Tidey learned of the deaths of Paddy Kelly and Gary Sheehan. The news that a soldier and a young garda had lost their lives in the rescue mission weighed heavily upon him. He wanted to attend both funerals but was strongly advised against it by senior security personnel.

On 16 December 2008, the twenty-fifth anniversary of the tragedy at Derrada, Tidey attended the official opening of the Patrick Kelly Memorial Park in Moate. He placed a wreath at the memorial. Then the septuagenarian, who in boyhood had saluted passing soldiers while holding his wooden rifle, re-enacted the solemn gesture once more. 'It afforded me the opportunity,' he explains, 'to stand to attention and render a military salute in his honour. I was privileged to be part of that ceremony.

'It was me totally expressing my deep appreciation for the life Private Kelly had given in my rescue. The ceremony was a remarkable tribute to him.' Separately, he attended the awarding of the Military Star to Private Kelly in 2012 at Custume Barracks.

'I was also pleased to be at the Scott Medal ceremony for Gary Sheehan in 2021 in Dublin Castle. It was important for me to be at those events.' In February 2023, following the death of Donal Kelleher from cancer, he found himself again saluting another of his rescuers. Kelleher was the twenty-nine-year-old detective wounded in both legs at Derrada. Tidey had remained in touch with him.

'Every year on 16 December, the day of my release, Donal and I exchanged greetings and good wishes,' Tidey says. 'I was in Lanzarote [when he died], but I said to his family I would stand at attention at eleven o'clock [on the morning of his funeral] and salute the memory of Donal Kelleher. He was right next to me when he was shot in the leg. And Bill Somers was right next to me when he was shot, and he had bullet holes in his flak jacket. I hit the ground in my military way and thought I'd been shot too.'

When Donal Kelleher was posthumously – and belatedly – awarded a Scott Medal in June 2023, it was a bittersweet day for his family, and for Don Tidey too. Tidey attended the ceremony with his second wife Barbara. Kelleher had phoned him on Christmas Eve in 2022 to wish him a happy Christmas and to express the hope that their families could meet up in 2023. 'It would have been a wonderful moment to have been present as he received his medal, as I was by his side in Derrada.'

Tidey met the Kelly family in private some weeks after the funeral in 1983. He particularly remembers David Kelly, the eldest brother, from that meeting, and being impressed by his bravery. 'I've great respect for David, in the way he confronted [Martin] McGuinness,' Tidey says.

In July 2022 Tidey was invited to Collins Barracks for the defence forces' annual National Day of Commemoration for those who have died in the line of duty. There he was introduced to some of the soldiers who had been in the search party that found him. 'It was a great privilege to meet them and to say thank you to them as a military group.

Private McLaughlin, the rifleman, wasn't there but I'd have liked to have shaken his hand and thanked him too.'

After the trauma of Tidey's abduction, he and his family did their best to resume a normal life, despite living with a constant security presence for almost two decades afterwards.

The teachers at Alexandra College had been particularly attentive to Susan during her father's ordeal. Her talent for art was nurtured by a teacher, Barbara Dunne, who was head of that department. On several occasions while Tidey was missing, Barbara, who was also a housemistress at the school, had accompanied the boarders up to Whitechurch for the evening vigil to pray for the safe return of their classmate's father. She and Tidey met professionally to discuss Susan's progress and a personal relationship began.

'Chance encounters have always affected my life,' he says, 'but none was more important than meeting Barbara.'

Eighteen months later they married, but not in Ireland,

28. Barbara and Don Tidey at an event in Dublin's Convention Centre for the state visit of Queen Elizabeth to Ireland in 2011.

where they were warned it would be too high-profile an event for the capacity of a place like Whitechurch. Instead, the Anglican Bishop in Europe, John Satterthwaite, gave them permission to marry in the Anglican Cathedral of the Holy Trinity in Gibraltar, not far from where Barbara's parents had retired to live in Spain. They were married by Reverend Horace McKinley, with forty guests in attendance.

It has been a happy thirty-seven years of marriage since. 'It's been wonderful,' says Tidey. 'Barbara has been so strongly and lovingly supportive in all this time, a rock amidst the shifting sands of life.'

Susan went on to study arts in UCD; Alistair and Andrew pursued their respective business careers. In 1993 Don and Barbara had a daughter, Saskia, who became a double Olympian in sailing, competing for Ireland at the 2016 Games in Rio de Janeiro, and – with the approval of the Irish Olympic Committee and the Irish Sailing Association – for Great Britain at Tokyo in 2021. (Her transfer to Team GB was simply because her partner in the Irish boat retired after Rio and there wasn't another Irish partner of comparable experience available.)

Saskia's Olympic exploits brought great joy to her parents. But, as ever, in the midst of blessings came sorrow. In 2015 Andrew died from cancer at the age of fifty-three, leaving behind a wife and young family.

On the professional front, Associated British Foods sold its supermarket businesses – Quinnsworth, Crazy Prices and Stewarts – to Tesco in 1997 for an estimated £640m (about €726m). This was Tidey's cue to retire and conclude twenty-eight eventful years as an employee and ultimately as a main board director of Associated British Foods. 'I took the view that I would enjoy the years I was given and the wonderful gift of a second daughter and grandchildren.'

Tidey remained on the board of a quite different organization until 2022. More than thirty years earlier he had been approached by the Salvation Army in Dublin for help with a new homeless accommodation project in the north inner city. Through his parents, he'd been steeped in the values of the Salvation Army from childhood and he was happy to help. The Granby Centre near the Rotunda hospital in central Dublin currently provides residential and medical services for 101 men and women.

Don Tidey's belief in the divine leaves him open to the idea that it played a part in his delivery from captivity. 'I firmly believe, notwithstanding all the things that happened to other people – other people were to lose their lives and have dreadful outcomes from that whole kidnapping event – for some reason my outcome was different. I think I had, and continue to have, the presence of God in what I do. I had it in captivity and, if anything, it [my belief] was strengthened during that time because I felt [His] presence. It was destined that the man with first pressure on that rifle didn't panic when I said, "I'm the hostage". Garda Sheehan and Private Kelly were killed in front of me. And I was so close to it I heard the pin taken out of the grenade. And I emerged unscathed, too, from the indiscriminate gunfire that wounded Donal Kelleher beside me. The fact of the matter is that I survived in some miraculous way.'

In captivity Don Tidey would reflect on a prayer, originally attributed to the sixteenth-century Spanish nun St Teresa of Ávila, which he knew by heart.

> Let nothing disturb thee;
> Let nothing affright thee:

All things are passing;
God never changeth.
Patience, endurance
attaineth to all things.
Who God possesseth,
In nothing is wanting
Alone God suffices.

Revd McKinley had been a pillar of support for the Tidey family through all their trials. As a token of his gratitude, Don later presented the rector with a framed copy of the prayer.

In 1997 Don, Barbara and Saskia moved from Woodtown. In a further gesture of his esteem for Revd McKinley, and for his fellow parishioners, Tidey commissioned a stained-glass window for Whitechurch as a parting gift. It would be designed by the artist Willie Earley.

He and Revd McKinley debated an appropriate theme for the window. They landed on the Book of Tobit, a source that is not well known except to those who have made a deep study of the Bible. Tobit is a holy man who is captured by the Assyrians and taken from Israel to Nineveh in what is modern-day Iraq. There he is kept for many years. Eventually, he returns home to his wife and son, Tobias, who has since grown up. Tobit has been blinded and suffers great misfortune, but never loses his faith in God. His son sets out on a journey to recover some money that Tobit had lent a friend. A mysterious man accompanies Tobias. Along the way a fish jumps out of the Tigris river and on to the bank. The mysterious man advises Tobias to keep the gall bladder, noted in biblical times for its healing powers. Tobias returns home and rubs the fish gall on his father's eyes, curing his blindness. The mysterious man reveals himself to be the archangel Raphael sent by God to reward Tobit for his faith in adversity.

The scene in Whitechurch depicts Tobit and his son along with the fish and Raphael, the angel of healing who also guards pilgrims on their journeys.[1] For Tidey the story of Tobit, a man taken away from everything he loves and forced into exile, has a parallel with the story of his own incarceration and safe deliverance.

The words in the window are taken from Psalms 91, verse 11: 'For he shall give his angels charge over thee'. The full verse continues: 'To keep thee in all thy ways'. It is taken to mean that God will send his angels to protect and guide. This psalm was recited every night at the vigils in Whitechurch when people prayed for Tidey's safe return. It was also chosen as a prayer of hope that the Kelly and Sheehan families will find consolation in their great loss.

The window was dedicated in a ceremony in September 1998 by Walton Empey, the then Church of Ireland Archbishop of Dublin. A plaque beneath it reads: 'This window was given by the Tidey family to thank God for His protective and healing presence, through His holy angels, during the years 1979–1997. The family lived in this parish and worshipped in this church.'

In 2023 Don Tidey remains a grateful survivor. The physical fitness and psychological fortitude that carried him through his ordeal forty years ago are still evident in his bearing. Age seems not to have wearied his natural authority and commanding presence. Nor does it seem to have softened him into sentiment and nostalgia. When he speaks, he does so

29. Don Tidey, May 2023, Dublin.

with clarity and conviction. In Derrada Wood he was subjected to the orders of self-appointed soldiers, but in reality
they were dealing with an officer and a gentleman of the old
school. His courage and forbearance were never compro-
mised, even in those most harrowing of circumstances.

He could have left Ireland after Derrada Wood but chose
to stay, 'much to everybody's surprise. I had too great a
responsibility not only to the business owners, but to all the
people we employed. I wanted to see those I worked with
pursue successful careers and to grow successful businesses.
I was more in touch with the thirty-one counties of the
country at that stage than most native people were.' The reference to 'thirty-one counties' is a quip which he first used as
his closing comments at a business lunch in the Shelbourne

Hotel shortly before he retired. The thirty-second county is Leitrim.

Tidey hadn't been to Leitrim before 1983 and hasn't been there since. As far as he is concerned, he didn't visit Leitrim in 1983 either. He quite literally did not see it during those twenty-three days, except for those few minutes it took to drive him away from Derrada and then over the county boundary into Cavan. So, no, in his mind he has never visited the county. He has though, he stresses, become friendly with some people from Ballinamore that he met through personal connections in the years since.

He is proud of the Irish citizenship that was bestowed on him by the government at a private ceremony in Fitzwilliam Square in 2018, and of his honorary membership of the Royal Dublin Society. He is a Fellow of the Irish Management Institute, and was a council member of the Dublin Chamber of Commerce and the Confederation of Irish Industries.

On his journey through life, Tidey believes he has acquired a richness of perspective about people, society and faith. 'My beliefs have been strengthened, not weakened, as a result of living,' he asserts. Still, like all persons of faith, he wrestles with the moral conundrum as to why bad things happen to good people, such as the Sheehans and the Kellys.

'I can see that people who have led lives rather similarly, with faith, have by and large not been prevented from disaster and the greater sadnesses. My goodness, even today I could probably tell you half a dozen stories of things happening to people who've lived a total life of goodness and faith where they've been afflicted in a way that you wouldn't believe.'

He has had his own share of 'the greater sadnesses',

alongside many blessings. Now in his late eighties, he still enjoys robust good health, impressive mental faculties and the love of his wife and family. He cannot ask for anything more and would not want to. 'I have had a lot of highs and lows. By the grace of God, I am where I am.'

Acknowledgements

As natives of Co. Leitrim, the authors believe it is important to break the forty-year silence in relation to the terrible events of Derrada Wood and to confront the awkward questions not just about what happened, but how it has been remembered or, more precisely, forgotten.

Many people contributed generously to this book. We are particularly grateful to the families of the late Private Patrick Kelly and Recruit Garda Gary Sheehan. In seeking their help and co-operation, we were reopening old and painful wounds. But they were willing to take us on that journey. We thank especially David Kelly and his siblings, and Jennifer McCann, sister of Gary Sheehan, for their valour and their support.

30. Tommy Conlon, Don Tidey and Ronan McGreevy, May 2023, Dublin.

In sharing his memories, Don Tidey gave us an insight into the resilience and courage that enabled him to endure his twenty-three days in captivity. We thank him most sincerely for his generosity too, and for the rigour and thoroughness which he brought to the process of telling his story. We thank also Don's wife Barbara and the staff at the Royal Irish Yacht Club, Dun Laoghaire, especially club secretary Sarah Breen, for their hospitality and for facilitating our meetings. We are also most grateful to Reverend Horace McKinley for his many judicious intercessions and observations.

Various gardaí and Irish soldiers who helped in the search and its aftermath made important contributions to our narrative. We are indebted to Eugene O'Sullivan, Joe Feely, P. J. Higgins, Kieran Dalton, Liam Wall, Paul Gillen, John O'Driscoll, Walter 'Nacie' Rice and Jim Wall for their recollections and reflections. A special mention too for Caroline Kelleher, wife of the late Donal Kelleher.

The authors would like to express their appreciation of Gerard Reynolds, Ita Reynolds Flynn and Gabriel Toolan for speaking candidly about a difficult time in the life of a small Irish town. In doing so they have set an example that will hopefully inspire others.

Many other people, too numerous to mention individually, made valuable contributions to the overall tapestry of the story, some in the pages herewith, some by way of research and background information. Every thread was much appreciated.

The extensive research on this project was supported by a wide bibliography and a range of contemporary news archives.

Gerard Lovett's 2022 book, *Ireland's Special Branch: Defending the State 1922–1947*, was a timely account of the Irish state's early confrontations with the IRA. Gerard was also generous with his wider support.

Gearóid Ó Faoleán's two-volume history, *A Broad Church: The Provisional IRA in the Republic of Ireland*, was very helpful for contextualizing the events of 1983. Brian Hanley's *The Impact of the Troubles on the Republic of Ireland 1968–1979: Boiling Volcano?* also provided important context.

Cormac Ó Súilleabháin's in-depth work of local history, *Leitrim's Republican Story (1900–2000)*, was also a valuable source.

We would like to acknowledge some outstanding journalistic work from the time, including, among others, the reportage of Peter Murtagh (*Irish Times*), Don Lavery (*Irish Independent*), Tommie Gorman (*Magill* magazine/RTÉ), and the authors' former journalism tutor at NUIG, Cormac MacConnell (*Irish Press*). The archives of *Magill*, which have been digitized, also helped shape the narrative. Lynda O'Keeffe in the *Irish Times* provided access to the newspaper's extensive photo archive. Frank McNally was also helpful and his 'Irishman's Diaries' in the *Irish Times* about his visit to Derrada Wood and his friend Gary Sheehan are worth re-reading.

Brendan O'Brien's television investigation for RTÉ's *Today Tonight* has stood the test of time. We would like to thank Brendan, and Don Lavery, for their additional contributions to this book. Some of RTÉ's contemporary coverage can be viewed on YouTube. Also available online is the station's 2021 documentary on the episode, *The Case I Can't Forget*, and Virgin Media's *Ireland's Most Shocking Crimes: Don Tidey* (2018).

Leitrim County Library in Ballinamore has an extensive archive on the subject, including a copy of the *Today Tonight* programme broadcast in January 1984, and Philip McGovern's follow-up film. The library staff were most helpful with all our inquiries.

ACKNOWLEDGEMENTS

Our publishers Penguin Sandycove have nurtured and guided this project from the beginning. We are indebted to Michael McLoughlin and Patricia Deevy for seeing the promise in the story from its first chapter. The authors thank Patricia sincerely for her commitment and expertise. Thanks also to editor John Burns, copy-editor Trevor Horwood and proofreaders Kit Shepherd and Pat Rush. And to Flora Moreau, Ellie Smith and Charlotte Faber for helping to steer the manuscript through the editorial process.

Tommy Conlon in addition would like to acknowledge his *Sunday Independent* editors John Greene and Alan English for their continued support over many years. He would also like to give a shout-out to Ballinamore Seán O'Heslin's GAA club, and to its people past and present, for a lifetime of good memories.

Ronan McGreevy would like to thank his agent Faith O'Grady from the Lisa Richards Agency for taking on this project on our behalf and for her helpful advice throughout.

Reader feedback is welcomed at rmcgreevy1301@gmail. com.

Picture Credits

Irish Times: 1, 2, 3, 4, 7 and 8 (Pat Langan); 9 and 10 (Peter Thursfield); 20 and 21 (Alan Betson); 22 (Cyril Byrne); 23 (Brenda Fitzsimons); 25 (Eric Luke); 28 (Dara Mac Donaill)

Mediahuis Ireland: 11 (Tom Burke) and 26

Alamy Stock Photos: 12 and 13

Kelly family: 15

Sheehan family: 16

Ronan McGreevy: 5, 6, 17, 18, 19, 24, 27, 29 and 30

Notes

Chapter 1: 'I'm Don Tidey; I'm the hostage'

1 *Irish Times,* 14 June 2008.
2 Interview with the authors.
3 *Irish Farmers Journal,* 7 January 1984.
4 *Magill* magazine, 31 December 1983.
5 *Irish Examiner,* 12 June 2008.
6 *Cork Examiner,* 7 April 1984. The hide had been prepared in advance of the kidnapping, according to John Curnan at his trial.
7 *Irish Examiner,* 12 June 2008.
8 *Irish Independent,* 14 June 2008.
9 Interview with the authors.
10 Ibid.
11 *Irish Independent,* 5 December 2021. See also RTÉ, *The Case I Can't Forget,* www.rte.ie/player/series/the-case-i-can-t-forget/SI000008064?epguid=IP000067303, accessed April 2023.
12 *Leitrim Observer,* 17 March 1984.
13 *Irish Independent,* 18 June 2008.
14 *Sunday Independent,* 15 June 2008.
15 Interview with the authors.
16 *Irish Times,* 12 June 2008.
17 Ibid.
18 John Courtney, *It Was Murder!* (Dublin: Blackwater Press, 1996), pp. 92–3.
19 Interview with the authors.

20 *Irish Independent*, 13 June 2008.

21 *Irish Independent*, 14 June 2008.

22 *Irish Times*, 14 June 2008.

23 Interview with the authors.

24 Ibid.

25 *Magill* magazine, 31 December 1983.

26 Interview with the authors.

27 *Irish Independent*, 18 June 2008.

28 *Irish Times*, 14 June 2008.

29 *Leitrim Observer*, 17 March 1984.

30 Interview with the authors.

Chapter 2: Getting Away with Murder

1 RTÉ, *The Case I Can't Forget*.

2 RTÉ, *Today Tonight*, 14 January 1984.

3 *Irish Times*, 21 December 1983.

4 Interview with the authors.

5 Interview with the authors.

6 RTÉ, *Today Tonight*, 14 January 1984.

7 RTÉ, *Garda ar Lár*, 16 February 2009.

8 Cormac Ó Súilleabháin, *Leitrim's Republican Story* (Ballinamore: Cumann Cabhrach Liatroma, 2014), p. 373.

9 See *Magill* magazine, 31 December 1983, and RTÉ, *Today Tonight*, 14 January 1984.

10 Interview with the authors.

11 Ibid.

12 Ó Súilleabháin, *Leitrim's Republican Story*, p. 373.

13 *Cork Examiner*, 2 November 1984.

14 RTÉ, *Today Tonight*, 14 January 1984.

Chapter 3: Enemies of the State

1 Tim Pat Coogan, *The IRA* (London: HarperCollins, 1993), p. 545. As quoted in Cain online, https://cain.ulster.ac.uk/oth elem/organ/docs/coogan/coogan93.htm, accessed April 2023.

2 Dáil Debates, vol. T., no. 15, 7 January 1922, Debate on Treaty.

3 The provenance of this phrase is disputed, but the first public use of it was in the Dáil on 19 December 1921 by Seán Mac-Swiney TD. Dáil Debates, vol. T., no. 6.

4 Lynch's famous phrase was included in a letter to his brother Tom Lynch in November 1917.

5 Ronan McGreevy, *Great Hatred: The Assassination of Field Marshal Sir Henry Wilson MP* (London: Faber & Faber, 2022), p. 294.

6 Gearóid Ó Faoleán, *A Broad Church: The Provisional IRA in the Republic of Ireland* (Newbridge: Irish Academic Press, 2019), p. 30.

7 Coogan, *The IRA*, p. 221.

8 McGreevy, *Great Hatred*, p. 119.

9 *Saturday Herald*, 30 March 1935.

10 Brian Hanley, 'Frank Ryan', *Dictionary of Irish Biography*, www.dib.ie/biography/ryan-francis-richard-frank-a7865, accessed May 2023.

11 David McCullagh, *De Valera: Rule (1932–1975)* (Dublin: Gill Books, 2018), p. 140.

Chapter 4: A Disastrous Campaign

1 Patrick Bishop and Eamonn Mallie, *The Provisional IRA* (London: Corgi, 1987), p. 41.

2 *Irish Times*, 20 November 2009.

3 Edward Longwill, "No Longer Stand[ing Idly] By?" Irish army contingency plans, 1969–70', *History Ireland*, vol. 17, no. 4 (July–August 2009), www.historyireland.com/no-longer-standing-idly-by-irish-army-contingency-plans-1969-70/, accessed June 2023.

4 Brian Hanley, '"I Ran Away"? The IRA and 1969: The Evolution of a Myth', *Irish Historical Studies*, vol. 38, no. 152 (November 2013), pp. 671–87.

5 Matt Treacy, *The IRA, 1956–69: Rethinking the Republic* (Manchester: Manchester University Press, 2014), p. 13.

6 'Where Sinn Féin Stands', statement issued by Caretaker Executive of Provisional Sinn Féin, 17 January 1970, https://cain.ulster.ac.uk/issues/abstentionism/obrien99.htm, accessed April 2023.

7 *Irish Times*, 10 July 1972.

8 *Irish Times*, 17 December 1971.

9 Barry Desmond, *Finally and in Conclusion: A Political Memoir* (Dublin: New Island Press, 2000), p. 62.

10 2.1 Article 38(3) of the Irish Constitution provides for the establishment by law of Special Courts for the trial of offences in cases where it may be determined, according to law, that the ordinary courts are 'inadequate to secure the effective administration of justice and the preservation of public peace and order'. University of Minnesota Human Rights Library, http://hrlibrary.umn.edu/undocs/819-1998.html, accessed April 2023.

11 Section 31 of the Broadcasting Act was introduced by the minister for posts and telegraphs Gerard Collins in September 1971, www.rte.ie/brainstorm/2021/0507/1217560-section-31-broadcasting-ban-censorship-troubles/, accessed April 2023.

Chapter 5: Dispensing Death and Destruction

1 Brian Hanley, *Boiling Volcano: The Impact of the Troubles on the Republic of Ireland, 1968–1979* (Manchester: Manchester University Press, 2018), pp. 53–6.

2 *Irish Times*, 4 April 2015.

3 Sean O'Driscoll, *Heiress, Rebel, Vigilante, Bomber: The Extraordinary Life of Rose Dugdale* (Dublin: Sandycove, 2022), p. 117.

4 'The IRA: Finance and Weapons', Ulster University Cain Project, https://cain.ulster.ac.uk/proni/1987/proni_NIO-12-525A_1983-05-26h.pdf, accessed April 2023.

5 *Magill* magazine, 31 August 1980.

6 See David Blake Knox, *The Killing of Thomas Niedermayer* (Dublin: New Island Books, 2019).

7 Paul Howard, *Hostage: Notorious Irish Kidnappings* (Dublin: O'Brien Press, 2014), pp. 75–116.

8 Ibid., pp. 184–214.

9 Howard, *Hostage*, p. 193.

10 Ibid., pp. 184–214.

11 RTÉ Radio 1, *Sunday with Miriam*, 4 May 2014, www.rte.ie/radio/radio1/clips/20573062/, accessed April 2023.

12 An Sionnach Fionn, https://ansionnachfionn.com/2016/12/13/gerry-adams-the-conservative-press-and-the-brian-stack-controversy/, accessed April 2023.

13 Desmond, *Finally and in Conclusion*, p. 252.

14 *Sunday Independent*, 11 September 2022.

15 *Kerryman*, 22 October 1976.

16 *Irish Independent*, 29 December 2006.

17 *Sunday Independent*, 9 October 2011.

18 *Sunday Independent*, 2 March 2014.

19 *London Review of Books*, 2 February 1989.

Chapter 6: Banana Republic

1 *Hot Press*, 27 November 2019.
2 Ibid.
3 Charles Haughey, 'Living Way Beyond Our Means', *Irish Times*, 4 August 2018.
4 *Irish Times*, 11 January 1983.
5 Population at the 1986 census was 3.54 million; in 1991 it was 3.525 million.
6 *Sunday World*, 1 January 1984.
7 New Ireland Forum, 'The Cost of Violence Arising from the Northern Ireland Crisis Since 1969', Ulster University Cain project, https://cain.ulster.ac.uk/issues/politics/docs/nif/nif83 cost.pdf, accessed April 2023.

Chapter 7: It Was All About the Money

1 PBS, Frontline, The IRA and Sinn Féin, www.pbs.org/wgbh/ pages/frontline/shows/ira/readings/america.html, accessed April 2023.
2 Channel Four, *Who Kidnapped Shergar?* (2004), www.youtube. com/watch?v=RK0KG7z28bw, accessed April 2023.
3 Interview with the authors.
4 Gearóid Ó Faoleán, *A Broad Church, The Provisional IRA in the Republic of Ireland*, vol. 2: *1980–1989* (Dublin: Merrion Press, 2023), pp. 102–3.
5 Jonathan Trigg, *Death in the Fields: The IRA and East Tyrone* (Dublin: Merrion Press, 2023), p. 37.
6 *Irish Press*, 16 April 1975.
7 *Irish Independent*, 24 October 1974.

8 *Irish Independent*, 9 January 1975.

9 *Evening Echo*, 8 January 1975.

10 Kieran Conway, *Southside Provisional: From Freedom Fighter to the Four Courts* (Dublin: Orpen Press, 2014), p. 97.

11 Channel Four, *Who Kidnapped Shergar?*

12 Howard, *Hostage*, pp. 11–74.

13 *Irish Times*, 4 June 2018.

14 *Irish Press*, 16 February 1983.

15 Channel Four, *Who Kidnapped Shergar?*

16 BBC, *Searching for Shergar*, 7 June 2018, www.bbc.co.uk/programmes/bob623r9, accessed May 2023.

17 *Irish Independent*, 11 April 1983.

18 Interview with the authors.

19 Interview with the authors.

20 *Irish Press*, 8 August 1983.

21 *Evening Press*, 4 November 1983.

22 *Irish Press*, 30 April 1983.

23 *Irish Central*, 25 September 2022, www.irishcentral.com/roots/history/ira-maze-prison, accessed April 2023.

24 Gerry Kelly, *The Escape: The Inside Story of the 1983 Escape from Long Kesh* (Belfast: M&G Publications, 2015), pp. 300–310.

Chapter 8: Ballinamore

1 Father Dan Gallogly, *Sliabh an Iarainn Slopes: History of the Town and Parish of Ballinamore*, Co. Leitrim (Ballinamore: self-published, 1991).

2 *Roscommon Herald*, 29 January 1920.

3 Elections Ireland, 'Patrick T. Reynolds', www.electionsireland.org/candidate.cfm?ID=1722, accessed May 2023.

4 Interview with the authors.

5 Marie Coleman, 'Patrick Reynolds', *Dictionary of Irish Biography*, www.dib.ie/biography/reynolds-patrick-a7649, accessed May 2023.

6 Gallogly, *Sliabh an Iarainn Slopes*, p. 233.

7 *Sunday Independent*, 4 January 2023.

8 Elections Ireland, 'John Joe McGirl', https://electionsireland. org/candidate.cfm?ID=2623, accessed May 2023.

9 *Sunday Independent*, 18 December 1983.

10 *Irish Press*, 25 May 1981.

11 Gallogly, *Sliabh an Iarainn Slopes*, p. 81.

12 Interview with the authors.

13 *Roscommon Herald*, 13 May 1939.

14 *Sligo Champion*, 19 February 1982.

15 *Longford Leader*, 25 November 1961.

16 Interview with the authors.

17 Ó Súilleabháin, *Leitrim's Republican Story*, pp. 296–7.

Chapter 9: The Man Before the Storm

1 This chapter is based on various interviews by the authors with Don Tidey.

Chapter 10: With the Life of a Man at Stake

1 *Evening Echo*, 24 November 1983.

2 Ibid. All quotations relating to Tidey's immediate kidnap and incarceration on the first day are from a garda statement used by John Courtney in *It Was Murder!*

3 Interview with the authors.

4 Gemma Hussey, *At the Cutting Edge: Cabinet Diaries, 1982–1987* (Dublin: Gill & Macmillan, 1990), p. 71.

5 *RTÉ News*, 1 December 1983.

6 *Irish Examiner*, 2 December 1983.

7 *Evening Press*, 30 November 1983.

8 *Irish Times*, 2 December 1983.

9 Margaret Thatcher Foundation, 'Northern Ireland: Taoiseach FitzGerald message to MT (kidnapping of Don Tidey by IRA) [need to prevent Associated British Foods from paying ransom] [released 2013]', www.margaretthatcher.org/document/132084, accessed April 2023.

10 Éire Kidnapping: Police Action, Hansard, House of Lords Debates, vol. 445, 1 December 1983.

11 Dáil Debates, vol. 346, no. 5, 1 December 1983.

12 *Irish Times*, 3 December 1983.

13 *Irish Times*, 9 December 1983.

14 Ibid.

Chapter 11: Closing in on Leitrim

1 *Irish Times*, 11 October 1984.

2 Seán O'Callaghan, *The Informer* (London: Corgi, 1999), p. 165.

3 Courtney, *It Was Murder!*, p. 93.

4 *Irish Times*, 3 December 1983.

5 *Irish Independent*, 18 December 2005.

6 Greg Harkin and Martin Ingram, *Stakeknife: Britain's Secret Agents in Ireland* (Dublin: O'Brien Press, 2012), p. 145.

7 RTÉ, *Today Tonight*, 14 January 1984.

8 Interview with the authors.

9 Liz Walsh, *The Final Beat: The Gardaí Who Died in the Line of Duty* (Dublin: Gill & Macmillan, 2001), p. 138.

10 Interview with the authors.
11 Interview with the authors.
12 RTÉ, *Today Tonight*, 15 December 1983.

Chapter 12: 'If you get it wrong, you're dead'

1 Garda Service records courtesy of the Garda Museum.
2 Interview with the authors.
3 Interview with the authors.
4 Ó Súilleabháin, *Leitrim's Republican Story*, pp. 403–5.
5 Interview with the authors.
6 Interview with the authors.

Chapter 13: Harrods

1 *Irish Times*, 19 December 1983.
2 Ibid.
3 Ibid.
4 *An Phoblacht*, 5 January 1984.
5 'Don Tidey Rescued, 1983', RTÉ Archives, Don Tidey, 1983, www.rte.ie/archives/2013/1216/493118-don-tidey-free-after-23-days/, accessed April 2023.
6 *Fortnight* magazine, December 1987.

Chapter 14: Meeting Fire with Fire

1 *Sunday Tribune*, 27 November 1983.
2 *Evening Press*, 23 December 1983.
3 Ibid.

4 *Irish Times*, 16 August 1984.

5 *Irish Independent*, 22 January 1985.

6 *Irish Independent*, 19 March 1984.

7 In December 1984 McGlinchey was given a life sentence for the murder of Hester McMullan, but he won an appeal in October 1985 at Belfast appeal court. Immediately re-extradited to the South, he was sentenced to ten years by the Special Criminal Court in February 1986 for arms offences relating to his arrest in Clare.

8 Ed Moloney, *A Secret History of the IRA* (New York: W. W. Norton, 2002), p. 242.

9 Interview with the authors.

10 *Evening Press*, 20 December 1983.

11 Interview with the authors.

12 *Irish Press*, 19 December 1983.

13 *Irish Press*, 29 December 1983.

Chapter 15: In the Line of Duty

1 *Irish Independent*, 20 December 1983.

2 *Westmeath Examiner*, 24 December 1983.

3 *Irish Times*, 20 December 1983.

4 Ibid.

5 *Irish Press*, 20 December 1983.

6 Interview with the authors.

7 Interview with the authors.

8 *Northern Standard*, 22 December 1983.

9 *Irish Press*, 20 December 1983.

10 RTÉ, *Today Tonight*, 20 December 1983, www.youtube.com/watch?v=iKY-BM3MG6U, accessed April 2023.

11 Ibid.

12 Interview with the authors.
13 Interview with the authors.
14 *Irish Independent*, 10 February 1984.
15 *Leitrim Observer*, 17 March 1984.
16 Interview with the authors.
17 Interview with the authors.

Chapter 16: No Com-mint

1 Interview with the authors.
2 Interview with the authors.
3 *An Phoblacht*, 4 January 1984.
4 Taken from Seamus Heaney, *North* (London: Faber & Faber, 1975).
5 Interview with the authors.
6 *Leitrim Observer*, 24 December 1983.
7 Ibid.
8 Interview with the authors.

Chapter 17: Seething with Sedition

1 *Evening Press*, 11 January 1984.
2 Philip McGovern, *December 16, 1983*. A copy of the film is in Leitrim County Library in Ballinamore.
3 Ibid.
4 *Irish Farmers Journal*, 4 January 1984.
5 McGovern, *December 16, 1983*.
6 *Leitrim Observer*, 29 June 1985. In the June 1985 local election in the Ballinamore electoral area, John Joe McGirl received 190 out of the 895 votes in the four Ballinamore town voting

booths, according to tallies. He was outpolled two-to-one by future Fine Gael TD and senator Gerry Reynolds in the town. McGirl's main support lay in the rural districts of Augh-nasheelin and Clogher. In Aughnasheelin, his home parish, he got 110 out of the 332 votes, 33.1 per cent of the poll.

7 *Leitrim Observer*, 14 January 1984.

8 Ibid.

9 'The Ballad of Ballinamore' was the B side to Moore's single 'Hey Ronnie Reagan', which was released before the US president's visit to Ireland in 1984.

Chapter 18: Locking the Stable Door

1 *Irish Press*, 12 April 1984.

2 Ibid.

3 *Cork Examiner*, 7 April 1984.

4 Ibid.

5 *Irish Press*, 6 April 1984.

6 *Roscommon Herald*, 13 July 1984.

7 *The Kerryman*, 12 October 1984.

8 *Cork Examiner*, 22 June 1985.

9 *Cork Examiner*, 20 June 1985.

10 *Cork Examiner*, 25 March 1988.

11 *Cork Examiner*, 2 November 1984.

12 *Connaught Telegraph*, 16 May 1984.

Chapter 19: Frozen

1 'Alan Clancy and the IRA Money', *Magill* magazine, 21 March 1985.

2 Ibid.

3 Dáil Debates, vol. 356, no. 1, 19 February 1985.

4 *Irish Times*, 5 May 1988.

5 *Sunday Times*, 1 December 1985.

6 *Irish Times*, 21 February 1985.

7 AP News, 26 February 1985, https://apnews.com/article/ d43955c44692749da8a11671625ea05f, accessed April 2023.

8 *Sunday Independent*, 20 July 1986.

9 *Sunday Times*, 29 June 2008.

Chapter 20: Trial and Error

1 Peter Taylor, *Brits: The War Against the IRA* (London: Bloomsbury, 2001), p. 182.

2 *Belfast News Letter*, 4 May 1976.

3 *Belfast Telegraph*, 10 March 2011.

4 Interview with the authors.

5 *Belfast Telegraph*, 18 June 1977.

6 David Beresford, *Ten Men Dead: The Story of the 1981 Irish Hunger Strike* (London: Grafton, 1987, and HarperCollins, 1994), p. 66.

7 *Magill* magazine, 1 April 1986.

8 *Irish Independent*, 19 June 2008.

9 *Irish Examiner*, 14 January 1998.

10 *Irish Times*, 2 November 1999.

11 *Irish Independent*, 19 July 2003.

12 *Irish Times*, 8 March 2006.

13 Ibid.

14 Ibid.

15 *Irish Times*, 16 May 2006.

16 *Irish Times*, 9 December 2006.

17 *Irish Times*, 6 March 2008.

Chapter 21: Justice Delayed

1 *Irish Times*, 13 June 2008.
2 *Irish Times*, 27 June 2008.
3 *Irish Examiner*, 25 June 2008.
4 *Irish Times*, 27 June 2008.
5 Interview with the authors.
6 *Irish Times*, 27 June 2008.
7 *Irish Times*, 5 July 2008.
8 https://hudoc.echr.coe.int/?i=001-100413, para. 154.

Chapter 22: Memory and Loss

1 Interview with the authors.
2 Tom Sheehan's service records were supplied by the Garda Museum.
3 *Dundalk Democrat*, 22 May 1999.
4 An Garda Siochána, 'The Scott Medal', www.garda.ie/en/about-us/our-history/the-scott-medal, accessed May 2023.
5 *Irish Times*, 25 September 2021.
6 Ibid.
7 Interview with the authors.
8 Garda Press Office, 'An Garda Síochána –' Scott Medal Ceremony, 24 September 2021, https://www.youtube.com/watch?v=mmGDWj59ZKo, accessed May 2023.

Chapter 23: The Cross

1 Interview with the authors.
2 Interview with the authors.
3 Interview with the authors.

Chapter 24: 'You know the killers'

1 Interview with the authors.
2 *RTÉ News*, 10 October 2011, www.youtube.com/watch?v= JkcWV9n_uCg, accessed April 2023.
3 *Irish Times*, 17 September 2011.
4 *The Journal*, 20 September 2011.
5 *Irish Examiner*, 23 September 2011.
6 *Irish Times*, 19 September 2011.
7 TV3 presidential debate, www.youtube.com/watch?v=u CnH2v1h_dw, accessed May 2023.
8 *Irish Times*, 22 April 2008.
9 Slugger O'Toole, https://sluggerotoole.com/2015/12/07/ sinn-fein-walks-an-excruciating-line-between-mcauley-the-hero-and-mcauley-the-villain/, accessed May 2003.
10 *Irish Times*, 21 September 2011.
11 *Irish Times*, 22 October 2011.
12 *RTÉ News*, 24 September 2011.
13 Interview with the authors.
14 *Independent*, 20 October 2011.
15 *Guardian*, 12 October 2011.
16 *The Journal*, 21 October 2011.
17 *Guardian*, 23 October 2011.
18 *Westmeath Independent*, 30 May 2020.

19 Sinn Féin St Patrick's Day online concert 2021, www.youtube.com/watch?v=_axduTPkVzE, accessed May 2023.

20 *News Letter*, 26 March 2021.

21 *Irish Times*, 2 January 2022.

22 McFarlane plays regularly at the Rock Bar in Belfast.

Chapter 25: On the Run

1 *Cork Examiner*, 10 June 1986.

2 BBC News, http://news.bbc.co.uk/onthisday/hi/dates/stories/june/25/newsid_2519000/2519673.stm, accessed May 2023.

3 *Irish Times*, 24 June 1986.

4 *Irish Independent*, 26 April 2021.

5 *Irish Times*, 26 April 2021.

6 *Leitrim Observer*, 28 February 1987.

7 *Belfast Telegraph*, 14 March 2002.

8 Kelly, *The Escape*, p. 294.

9 Interview with the authors.

Chapter 26: Kidnapped

1 Information from Ret'd Assistant Commissioner John O'Driscoll.

2 Courtney, *It Was Murder!*, p. 199.

3 Interview with the authors.

Chapter 27: Fade to Black

1 The sermon is printed in a booklet, 'John Joe McGirl, 1921–1988: The Gentle Soldier', published in 1990.

2 Sinn Féin 1986 ard fheis debate, www.youtube.com/watch?v=
ZGMTezoebrA, accessed May 2023; McGirl's speech is from
23:12 to 31:15.

3 *Irish Times*, 28 October 1997.

4 *Leitrim Observer*, 14 November 1987.

5 *Leitrim Observer*, 16 May 1990.

6 The file relating to the application for the John Joe McGirl
memorial is in the offices of Leitrim County Council.

7 Interview with the authors.

8 *Leitrim Observer*, 2 May 1990.

9 'John Joe McGirl, an Unbreakable Fenian – a Tribute by Gerry
Adams', www.youtube.com/watch?v=nthfRmhjuDM&t=
1301s, accessed May 2023.

Chapter 28: By the Grace of God

1 'Archangel Raphael', *Encyclopaedia Britannica*, www.britannica.
com/topic/Raphael-archangel, accessed May 2023.

Index

Page references in *italics* indicate images.